Jens Andermann is Professor of Latin American and Luso-Brazilian Studies at Birkbeck College, University of London and an editor of the *Journal of Latin American Cultural Studies*. He has published widely on Latin American visual, literary and material culture, including the books *The Optic of the State: Visuality and Power in Argentina and Brazil* and *Mapas de poder: Una arqueología literaria del espacio argentino*.

TAURIS WORLD CINEMA SERIES

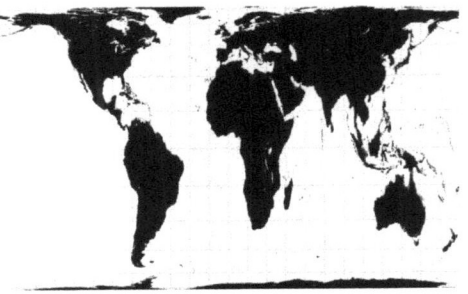

Series Editor: Lúcia Nagib, Professor of World Cinemas, University of Leeds
Advisory Board: Laura Mulvey (UK), Donald Richie (Japan), Robert Stam (USA), Ismail Xavier (Brazil)

The **Tauris World Cinema Series** aims to reveal and celebrate the richness and complexity of film art across the globe, exploring a wide variety of cinemas set within their own cultures and as they interconnect in a global context.

The books in the series will represent innovative scholarship, in tune with the multicultural character of contemporary audiences. They will also draw upon an international authorship, comprising academics, film writers and journalists.

Published and forthcoming in the World Cinema series:

Brazil on Screen: Cinema Novo, New Cinema, Utopia
By Lúcia Nagib

Contemporary New Zealand Cinema
Edited by Ian Conrich and Stuart Murray

East Asian Cinemas: Exploring Transnational Connections on Film
Edited by Leon Hunt and Leung Wing-Fai

Lebanese Cinema: Imagining the Civil War and Beyond
By Lina Khatib

New Argentine Cinema
By Jens Andermann

New Directions in German Cinema
Edited by Paul Cooke and Chris Homewood

New Turkish Cinema: Belonging, Identity and Memory
By Asuman Suner

On Cinema
Glauber Rocha
Edited by Ismail Xavier

Performing Authorship: Self-inscription and Corporeality in the Cinema
By Cecilia Sayad

Theorizing World Cinema
Edited by Lúcia Nagib, Chris Perriam and Rajinder Dudrah

Viewing Film
By Donald Richie

Queries, ideas and submissions to:
Series Editor, Professor Lúcia Nagib – l.nagib@leeds.ac.uk
Cinema Editor at I.B.Tauris, Philippa Brewster – philippabrewster@gmail.com

New Argentine Cinema

Jens Andermann

LONDON · NEW YORK

Published in 2012 by I.B.Tauris & Co Ltd
6 Salem Road, London W2 4BU
175 Fifth Avenue, New York NY 10010
www.ibtauris.com

Copyright © 2012 Jens Andermann

The right of Jens Andermann to be identified as the author of this work has been asserted by him in accordance with the Copyright, Designs and Patent Act 1988.

All rights reserved. Except for brief quotations in a review, this book, or any part thereof, may not be reproduced, stored in or introduced into a retrieval system, or transmitted, in any form or by any means, electronic, mechanical, photocopying, recording or otherwise, without the prior written permission of the publisher.

ISBN: 978 1 84885 462 8 (HB)
       978 1 84885 463 5 (PB)

A full CIP record for this book is available from the British Library
A full CIP record is available from the Library of Congress

Library of Congress Catalog Card Number: available

Designed and typeset by 4word Ltd, Bristol

Contents

	List of Illustrations	vii
	Acknowledgements	ix
	Introduction	xi
Chapter One	Transitions: How Argentine Film Survived the 1990s	1
Chapter Two	Locating Crisis: Compositions of the Urban	27
Chapter Three	Margins of Realism: Exploring the Contemporary Landscape	61
Chapter Four	Perforated Presence: The Documentary Between the Self and the Scene	93
Chapter Five	Embodiments: Genre and Performance	129
Chapter Six	Accidents and Miracles: Film and the Experience of History	155
	Endnotes	175
	Filmography	189
	Index	201

Illustrations

Figures 1 and 2	Violeta Naón in Raúl Perrone's *Labios de churrasco* (1994). Ezequiel Cavia in Martín Rejtman's *Rapado* (1991)	20
Figures 3 and 4	The margins of the city in the opening shots of Israel Adrián Caetano's and Bruno Stagnaro's *Pizza, birra, faso* (1997)	32
Figure 5	Gonzalo Heredia in Edgardo Cozarinsky's *Ronda nocturna* (2005)	48
Figure 6	Natasha Dimytriuk and her son in Eva Poncet, Marcelo Burd and Diego Gachassin's *Habitación disponible* (2005)	53
Figure 7	A Bolivian dance training session in Buenos Aires observed by Martín Rejtman in *Copacabana* (2006)	56
Figure 8	A close-up shot of Rosa (Rosa Sánchez) at work in the restaurant in Israel Adrián Caetano's *Bolivia* (2001)	59
Figure 9	Machines in the landscape in Pablo Trapero's *Mundo grúa* (1999)	68
Figure 10	The city of San Juan from the unfinished government building in Marcelo Donoso's *Opus* (2005)	74
Figure 11	Peppers, woodlands and mountains in the opening shots of Lucrecia Martel's *La ciénaga* (2001)	79
Figure 12	Jorge Román in Santiago Otheguy's *La León* (2006)	84
Figure 13	Argentino Vargas in Lisandro Alonso's *Los muertos* (2004)	89
Figure 14	Assembling a 'typical' shantytown in real time in Federico León and Marcos Martínez's *Estrellas* (2007)	105
Figure 15	An interview shot in David Blaustein's *Cazadores de utopías* (1996)	112

Figures 16 and 17	Family photographs spread out across a table in María Inés Roqué's *Papá Iván* (2000), as the director reads her father's farewell letter to his children. Nicolás Prividera's shot of himself next to a portrait of his mother projected on a screen in *M* (2007)	117
Figure 18	Playmobil animation sequence from Albertina Carri's *Los rubios* (2003)	118
Figure 19	A photograph of Ada Falcón in Sergio Wolf and Lorena Muñoz's *Yo no sé qué me han hecho tus ojos* (2002)	127
Figure 20	Julio Chávez in Rodrigo Moreno's *El custodio* (2005)	136
Figure 21	Valeria Bertuccelli and Julio Chávez in Santiago Loza's *Extraño* (2003)	139
Figure 22	Julio Chávez in the shootout scene from Israel Adrián Caetano's *Un oso rojo* (2002)	146
Figure 23	Jorge Román in Pablo Trapero's *El bonaerense* (2002)	151
Figure 24	María Alché and Carlos Belloso in Lucrecia Martel's *La niña santa* (2004)	157
Figure 25	María Onetto in Lucrecia Martel's *La mujer sin cabeza* (2008)	160
Figure 26	The panoramic shot of San Nicolás at the end of Enrique Bellande's *Ciudad de María* (2001)	166

Acknowledgements

This book is in many ways but an attempt to critically engage with the work of film-makers, critics and intellectuals whose brilliant, passionate arguments about film have challenged me to think in more complex ways about cinema and its particular place in the cultural landscape of a new millennium. Although I sometimes dissent with their opinions (what could be more boring in a conversation about film than complete agreement?) their writing and conversation have shaped the way I watch, and think about, cinema – and their generosity in sharing DVDs and bibliography has been absolutely vital for this project. I would especially like to thank Gonzalo Aguilar, Ana Amado, Emilio Bernini, Mario Cámara, Alejandro Kaufman, Mariano Mestman, David Oubiña, Martín Rejtman, Sílvia Schwarzböck, Javier Trímboli and Sergio Wolf in Argentina, John Kraniauskas, Claire Lindsay, Laura Mulvey and Joanna Page in the UK, and Christian Gundermann, Laura Martins and Isis Sadek in the USA, for conversations, support and intellectual stimulation over the years. I would also like to thank Lúcia Nagib, the series editor at I.B.Tauris, for her confidence in this project. My co-organisers of an international research network on the poetics of the real in contemporary Argentine and Brazilian cinema, Álvaro Fernández Bravo, Maurício Lissovsky, Denilson Lopes and Gabriela Nouzeilles, have become a kind of intellectual family over the last years, in an ongoing conversation that has opened up new, and sometimes surprising, avenues of thought for me. Apart from the support of the AHRC's international networks and workshops scheme, funding for the research on cinematic landscapes was provided by a British Academy Research Development Award. I would also like to thank all the film-makers who have generously agreed to let me reproduce images from their work in this book. Finally, a big thanks – yet again – to Ana Alvarez for her encouragement, critique and suggestions on previous drafts. And to Maja and Oliverio, our kids, for their incredible patience when I was once again occupying the telly.

Introduction

Two sequences from Argentine films made just before the millennium, and just prior to the unprecedented financial and social crisis leading up to the popular insurgency of 2001, caught the attention of critics in their prescient, premonitory anticipation of scenes that had yet to reach the TV screen. The raid and torching of a neighbourhood supermarket by desperate mobs of urban poor in Jorge Gaggero's short *Ojos de fuego* (Eyes of Fire, 1996)[1] – part of Buenos Aires' Universidad del Cine's first compilation of graduate work, *Historias breves* (Short Stories, 1995) – and the lock-out of angry customers from a bank in Fabián Bielinsky's *Nueve reinas* (*Nine Queens*, 2000), after the board of directors has run off with their deposits, seemed proof of a cinema uniquely in step with its time and place. In fact, so well attuned was its social diagnostics that cinema could even foresee the imminent catastrophe when the news media were still deluding themselves and their viewers about monetary stability and the free-market reforms imposed by subsequent neo-liberal governments. If cinema could predict what was coming, the most current reading went, this was because it was itself exposed to the social and economic firestorm it took as its main subject. According to Quintín, a leading film critic and former head of the Buenos Aires Independent Film Festival (BAFICI), in contemporary Argentine cinema 'poverty is not an offscreen horror nor a touristy postcard of the shantytown but the very material from which these films are made'.[2] Quoting Quintín approvingly, British film scholar Joanna Page adds that, by making 'virtue out of economic necessity' and turning the scarcity of means into an aesthetic choice of formal austerity, the new Argentine cinema also reconnected 'with cinematic productions of the 1960s in Latin America, which [...] turned poverty into a "signifier" in their representation of underdevelopment and inequality'.[3]

As a 'testimonial space' where 'the traces of the present took shape',[4] cultural critic and film historian Gonzalo Aguilar suggests, Argentine cinema in the second half of the 1990s and the first years after the millennium changed from being a producer of allegorical narratives of the nation's plight – as it had during the period following the end of the military dictatorship in 1983 – into a collector of indexical marks, a means of observing and investigating the social worlds of the present. Thus, veteran director Edgardo Cozarinsky adds, 'certain images and forms of behaviour' have surfaced 'that evoke a whole country and its people as if they were being filmed for the first time'.[5] Even while they caution us against misreading 'New Argentine Cinema' as a fully-fledged programmatic movement, all these critics focus their attention on a crop of young, 'independent' film-makers identified, to varying degrees, by their shared preoccupation with the national present as a time of crisis, often encountered through neo-realist chronicles of the social and geographical margins.[6] At the same time, they contend, this new generation of directors has resolutely parted with previous models of film funding and production, exploring both out of necessity and of aesthetic and political choice the possibilities of a more open, fragmented and improvisational process of film-making closer to the pulse of time than the more polished and self-contained film-narratives of an older generation. Rather than to survey recent Argentine film production at large, these and other critics have been focusing on a particular – and, they claim, uniquely innovative – phenomenon within it: a 'New Argentine Cinema' with capital letters, characterised by its both heroic and dialectically astute response to the crisis of the nation it both chronicles and incorporates into film form itself. In many ways, this seemed like a cinephile's dream come true: a genuine 'New Wave' of neo-neo-realists, transplanted from *Cinecittá* and the Rive Gauche to the shores of the River Plate, as well as reconnecting, in marked contrast with the glitzy-gritty, transnationally produced poverty-cum-action movies emerging out of Mexico or Brazil, with the central tenets of Latin America's leftist film avant-garde of the 1960s and 1970s.

However, if this critical narrative has had its part in paving the way for new Argentine film on the international festival stage and has helped establish several of the young directors with national and international funding bodies – thus also being instrumental in getting more films made – after the cusp of social and political emergency in Argentina had passed and the initial excitement had worn off, critics could predictably do little but detect the 'exhaustion' of the very movement they had conjured up. The reserved if not openly hostile reception of Lucrecia Martel's *La mujer sin cabeza* (*The Headless Woman*, 2007) at the 2008 Cannes Film Festival – despite arguably being her finest, most complex and politically devastating film – was only the most obvious symptom of this recent sea change in Argentine cinema's critical fortunes.[7] Even though it is undoubtedly true that Martel's and her contemporaries' first films revolutionised film practice in Argentina in the late 1990s, the time has perhaps arrived for looking at new Argentine cinema without the capital letters. That is, perhaps it makes sense today to look beyond the uncertain boundaries of an 'independent' generational project, which has in many ways been but a critical fiction – albeit certainly a productive and stimulating one. Yet what this critical narrative missed was the wider, more contradictory and multilayered landscape of film-making in Argentina, including for example the recent resurgence of a middlebrow entertainment cinema or the boom of political documentary and of activist film and video, not to speak of ongoing work by film-makers established well before the 1990s such as Héctor Olivera, Fernando Solanas or Leonardo Favio. Apart from setting the younger directors' work in the wider context of Argentine film practice, such a move from a normative and partisan to a descriptive approach will also allow us here to assess their most recent films on their own merits and regardless of apocalyptic murmurings about the end of an era.

The sole advantage this book can claim over its predecessors and over the bulk of articles and reviews published over the last decade and a half, then, is that of hindsight. Whereas, until a few years ago, critical readings of new Argentine cinema were very much put together, just as the films themselves, on the heels of the social and political moment – constructing their own exploration of the contemporary in a game of call and response between the film text and its critical exegesis – a book published some 14 years after the release of Israel Adrián Caetano's and Bruno Stagnaro's *Pizza, birra, faso* (*Pizza, Beer and Cigarettes*, 1997) and almost 20 after Martín Rejtman made *Rapado* (Skinhead, 1991) must of necessity adopt a different, more 'anthological' stance. That does not mean that this book is 'more complete' than others in its overview of film production in the country – on the contrary, the fact that many of the film-makers starting to work in the late 1990s now have four or more films to their name also entails the need for a more rigorous selection of examples in order to come up with an approximately representative corpus.

What the longer view allows to see more clearly than in the years just after the crisis of 2001, however, is the degree to which Argentine cinema's fortunes have *not* run parallel to those of the nation at large. As I will discuss in more detail in chapter 1, by the time the speculative consumption boom of the nineties imploded, sustained through the artificial and costly pegging of the national currency to the US dollar, cinema had already recovered from its near-extinction earlier in the decade and was well on course for a sustained annual increase in the number of releases despite national funding freezes before and after 2001, thanks to a reconfiguration of film distribution and access to new funding sources abroad. More importantly, cinema also lacked the immediacy with which television, the internet and video-activism constructed and transmitted images of the social process in real time and as part of the event's very unfolding. By contrast, because of the limitations inscribed in its own mediality and process, film had to construct a *different* image of the present, detached from, and discontinuous with, the political events as they occurred. Constructing this differential vantage point included ways of incorporating this non-immediacy into reflexive, film-specific forms of narrative and staging. Yet it was perhaps also this very *difference* of the filmic image, which endowed cinema with a uniquely critical and reflexive perspective, compared to those of the other media. Rather than, as the critical mainstream has agreed, to distinguish between an observational, 'realist strand' in new Argentine cinema and an experimental, 'non-realist' one true to cinematic modernism's critique of the image, here I suggest that 'reality' is never directly and naively 'encountered' in recent Argentine films, but that different strategies of refraction and staging are at work in order to acknowledge the filmic image's difference and deferral with respect to contemporary reality.

I will return to the relation between cinema and the unfolding of history in contemporary Argentina in the final chapter of this book. In order to understand this relation as one of critical distance rather than merely in terms of representational content, I have organised this study in different sections, some of which focus more on the conditions of film production, others on formal traits such as actoral performance, the incorporation of genre elements in the construction of narrative, or the manifestations of subjectivity in documentary storytelling. The two largest chapters chart the critical transformations of the nation's social geography under the impact of crisis and its effects on cinematic tropes, settings and landscapes. In taking a tropological and formal approach, I have also attempted to move away from the 'auteurial' discourse, which predominates in many critical assessments of new Argentine cinema – in order, precisely, to portray it as a movement of young film-artists tenaciously defending their autonomy and aesthetic sovereignty against the impositions and temptations of the market. Although I have reserved sections of chapters to discuss the work of directors I consider of particular relevance – Raúl Perrone, Martín Rejtman, Pablo Trapero, Lisandro Alonso, Lucrecia Martel, among others – on the whole I consider this notion of the director-auteur somewhat misleading. To begin with, in Argentina there is no industrial studio system – or, for that matter, an internal market capable of sustaining a national film *industry* – an independent, auteurial cinema could be pinned against. Moreover, the notion of the auteur also tends to obfuscate the multiple other agents intervening in the actual making of a film – an objection frequently made against auteur theory, but which becomes especially pressing in relation to recent Argentine films, I think, whose very success has been very much to the credit of a crop of exceptionally capable editors such as Alejo Moguillansky, Nicolás Goldbart or Alejandra Almirón, cinematographers such as Guillermo Nieto, Bárbara Alvarez and Lucio Bonelli, and sound engineers such as Catriel Vildasola, Jésica Suárez, Fernando Soldevila and Rufino Basavilbaso, apart from a new generation of actors alternating between film, theatre and television. To think of film exclusively as the mind-work of the all-powerful director-auteur would, I think, substantially impoverish our understanding of these other film professionals' work, not to mention the contingencies of film shooting as an intensely intersubjective process.

In order to maximise the number of films discussed across the various chapters, I have generally used different examples in order to analyse particular aspects of film form, production models or actoral performance. Many of these films could, and should indeed, have been studied under several of these aspects. However, in the interest of keeping this survey as inclusive and widespread as possible, I have opted instead for extending the number of examples. The selection of films may thus sometimes come as a surprise, as it occasionally spurns more well known in favour of more obscure ones in order to demonstrate particular points in my argument. Indeed, just as I have generally sought to avoid constructing a pantheon of directors, there is no attempt here at proposing a canon of most relevant, must-see films. While I have made a point of discussing films I have personally found interesting and stimulating, some of these I nonetheless consider to be aesthetically flawed or politically misguided, whereas other films that are among my personal favourites – say, Luis Ortega's *Monobloc* (2004), Gustavo Postiglione's *Días de Mayo* (*Days of May*, 2009) or Jorge Gaggero's *Cama adentro* (*Live-in Maid*, 2004) – could not be discussed at any length for reasons of argumentative and thematic order. Wherever relevant, I have sought to make my own value judgements explicit and indicate alternative assessments, as a way of giving each film a fair hearing. Those films I have not personally been able to watch have been altogether left out of the discussion. I have done my best to make use of film-theoretical concepts and of socio-political background information in such a way that their meaning remains clear, at least as far as the film under discussion is concerned, even for readers unfamiliar with either of these. Although with some hesitation, I have opted against including a chapter on Argentine politics between the neo-liberal devastation of the Menem and De la Rúa presidencies and the post-2001 progressive turn under the administrations of Néstor Kirchner and Cristina Fernández, as this would have interrupted the flow of the text without being able to give more than the sketchiest of overviews. A readable account of economic developments can be found in Patrice M. Franko's *The Puzzle of Latin American Economic Development* (Lanham, MA: Rowman & Littlefield, 2007); for a rather more tangible and committed analysis of their social and political impact, readers are referred to Javier Auyero's *Routine Politics and Violence in Argentina: The Gray Zone of State Power* (Cambridge, New York: Cambridge University Press, 2007).

I start my itinerary with an overview of the changes in film funding, production and distribution in the 1980s and 1990s, which laid out the framework for the phenomenon under discussion here. From the early 1990s, I argue, and with increased vigour after a change of film legislation in 1994 resolved some of the problems of access to state funds and screen time, a change occurred in the way films were being made in Argentina. This also had a profound impact on their formal appearance, their appeal to national and international audiences and their relation to national politics and history. I especially focus on the work of Raúl Perrone and Martín Rejtman as early examples of innovation in the cinematic field, in many ways still unsurpassed in their radicalism. In chapter 2, I focus on the city as the principal location in which social crisis is being staged. After briefly discussing the December 2001 uprising as a cinematic-urbanistic intervention, I move on to consider four aspects of, or itineraries through, the contemporary city as a location of crisis: the nomadic space of the social margins, the threatened domestic interior of middle-class society, the nocturnal, coded spaces of sexual diversity, and the alternative, unhomely city inhabited by migrants and exiles. All of these itineraries, I argue, can be understood as attempts to construct a displaced, distanced perspective in order to account for the estrangement that all inhabitants of Buenos Aires experience as a result of urban crisis. Chapter 3 moves on to the cinematic explorations of the rural interior. In Pablo Trapero's and others' work, we see a resurgence of the road movie, at the same time as subverting its promise of spatial pleasures by questioning the capacity of the gaze to access and render places transparent. I move on to discuss the 'dark ruralities' portrayed in neo-naturalist films such as Lucrecia Martel's *La ciénaga* (*The Swamp*, 2001) and Albertina Carri's *La rabia* (*Anger*, 2008), which construct stark counter-images to the traditional association of the countryside with ideas of childhood, innocence, and unburdened, tender and 'free' sexuality. The chapter closes with an analysis of Lisandro Alonso's pulsation-images of a radically violent and excluding 'nature'.

Having completed this provisional social geography of contemporary Argentine cinema, I move on to analyse some of its formal and generic characteristics. In chapter 4, I assess new developments in the field of documentary, in particular the way in which the narrative subject itself is being foregrounded as a target of epistemological curiosity and of ethical and political reflexivity. In particular, I focus on the impact of subjectivity and performance in the exploration of the social margins, the remembrance of the dictatorship and of leftist revolutionary struggle in the 1960s and 1970s on behalf of survivors and of second-generation witnesses such as the children of the 'disappeared'. Finally, I analyse a number of documentaries dealing with cinema itself as an archive and monument of modernity, associated with the both irretrievable and irrepressible, truncated promise of the national-popular – or Peronist – state. In chapter 5, I move on to the analysis of actoral performances and of the incorporation of genre elements into film narrative. Rather than solely in the use of 'real people' over professional actors, I see instead the principal innovation of recent Argentine films in the work of actors, often with a background in theatre, whose 'performances of seeing' create a space of ambiguity and suspension, 'held' by their embodied look, which encourages active spectatorial participation. Focusing in particular on performances by

Julio Chávez and Valeria Bertuccelli and on the ensemble improvisations of Gustavo Postiglione's films, I argue that we are enabled to appreciate the presence onscreen of non-actors and real locations through 'performances of showing and seeing', which organise the screen as a space for attentive observation. Meanwhile, elements of film genres such as the western, the grifter thriller, or film noir, have been used as a form of political commentary on the national present. For some critics, they are therefore being employed in a soothing, ideological fashion that runs counter to the realist and observational exposure of the contemporary in non-genre fictions. Discussing films such as Adrián Caetano's *Un oso rojo* (*Red Bear*, 2002), Pablo Trapero's *El bonaerense* (2002), and Fabián Bielinsky's *Nueve reinas* (2000), I argue that this antagonism fails genre cinema for something it never claimed to deliver in the first place. Rather, we need to assess genre narratives by their success in crafting figurative expressions for particular forms of historical experience, something that all three films deliver for the way national crisis is understood and processed from different class perspectives. In chapter 6, I close this discussion of the politics of film by focusing on the narrative tropes of accident and miracle in the work of Lucrecia Martel and in Enrique Bellande's documentary *Ciudad de María* (*Mary's City*, 2001), in all of which, I argue, these two also function as formal incorporations of a mode of historical experience proper to the age of global capitalism: a time when subjects have been stripped of control over their own lives.

This sense of self-alienation is of course one that could be extended to Argentine cinema itself (as well as most other 'national cinemas') which, as quantitative analyses of film distribution and consumption have long established, even at home is really occupying a minoritarian niche-market, only holding its own against the overwhelming dominance of Hollywood imports thanks to more or less well-policed screen quota, subsidies and festivals.[8] Thus, the idea of national cinema as a self-sufficient discursive and visual space, which can be studied 'on its own terms' and without considering this wider context of global film culture and economy and their local intersections, is as much a critical fiction as the literary tradition of national philologies from which it takes its cues. Although in chapter 1 I briefly discuss the financial and political constraints under which contemporary Argentine cinema operates (returning to the issue in chapter 5 with regard to its peculiar incorporation of global film genres), on the whole I have chosen to bracket the discussion about national cinema and its oppositional potential to or alignment with, Hollywood, which has overshadowed many debates in Latin American and world cinema studies. As Lúcia Nagib has pointed out, such debates run the risk of effectively confirming Hollywood's dominance as the sole centre and point of reference on which even dissident cinemas remain focused.[9] Therefore, instead of taking it merely as a case study for the 'nationalist' or 'transnationalist' argument in debates on world cinema, I have rather sought to take stock of cinematic production in Argentina and its critical reception over the last 15–20 years, its political stances and aesthetic affiliations, so as to produce the archival evidence on which such arguments could and should be based.

Nevertheless, even if pursuing the aim of a comprehensive survey rather than of arguing a specific case, some methodological and conceptual underpinnings are necessary in order to organise the archive, or to map out the territory – especially if one wants to study a national filmography without losing sight of its global intersections. Fredric Jameson's concept of 'cognitive mapping' (a concept he extrapolates from urban geographer Kevin Lynch to refer to 'that mental map of the social and global totality we all carry around in our heads in variously garbled forms'[10]) has been a useful starting point for bringing to light through formal analysis the modes of cinematic self-reflection: the way in which films think about their own place and intervention in both the national and 'global distribution of cultural power'.[11] Jameson's notion of cognitive mapping convolutes the spatial dimension of Lynch's mental image of the city, to which local inhabitants have recourse in order to negotiate their way through the contingencies of urban space, with Althusser's idea of ideology as the imaginary representation of subjects' relationships to their real conditions of existence. Likewise, for Jameson, films and other cultural artifacts construct on the level of form – rather than on that of representational 'content'— models of their relation to the social totality (which is now irredeemably global in scale due to the internationalisation of capital), including a conceptualisation of their own medium and its place and function within that totality.[12]

In spite of its abstract and complex nature, Jameson's concept is useful for the way in which it allows to develop critical insights on films' engagements with local as well as global constellations, without seeking these exclusively on the level of 'content' and of a more or less truthful representation of reality. But neither does cognitive mapping fall completely into the realm of production models as determining filmic output, demanding instead a critical movement back and forth from the economic and cultural conditions of enunciation under which a film is being made and the transformative intervention it performs into these conditions. At the same time, I also follow Dudley Andrew's suggestion of taking literally Jameson's terminology, in order to 'examine the film [itself] as map – cognitive map – while placing the film *on* the map'. Films, Andrew suggests, in the way they engage with the natural and man-made landscape, including its gestural and linguistics habits, literally map out a territory and the ways in which it is subject to historical change, for both locals and foreign viewers: 'Films make palpable collective habits and a collective sensibility. In their inclusions and exclusions, in their scope and style, films project cognitive maps by which citizens understand both their bordered world and the world at large.'[13]

Films, then, enact our belonging to place as well as contesting it: they offer us a different angle on the locations we inhabit, thus putting them in relation to their universal context. Cinema's cognitive mapping of place and space can respond to a narcissistic longing for self-confirmation, yet it can also trigger a curiosity for the strange and unsuspected that is shown to inhabit the familiar and the everyday. Both tendencies, I argue in this book, are present in recent Argentine cinema: the first, in the attempts to re-ignite a national blockbuster production through the affective conduits of action, melodrama and the star system, by offering onscreen references of identification and escape to an audience in the throes of socio-economic crisis. Meanwhile, the observational, naturalist aesthetics of many non-mainstream films finds in this same crisis an opportunity for de-familiarising the everyday and its routines, forcing out the strange and unseen from a change in the perspective and duration of the image. In teasing out the political and cultural meanings of these different poetics of the image, and of narrative and actoral performance, I seek the specific, local modulations of universal trends in contemporary cinema as well as the ways in which they are being deployed in terms of continuity or rupture with earlier moments in Argentine cinema itself. That is, I attempt to *locate* the critical engagement with the cinematic present, not in some timeless essence of national identity but, following Wimal Dissanayake's suggestion, in taking the national as a 'sit[e] of discursive contestations, or representational spac[e], in which changing social and cultural meanings are generated and fought over'.[14]

Thus, even though film critics such as Stephen Hart, Ann Marie Stock and Julianne Burton-Carvajal, among many others, are right in pointing us to the ways in which, through co-productions as well as the internationalisation of viewing audiences, 'globalization increasingly impacts that body of work known as Latin American Cinema',[15] the conclusion that therefore only 'a postnational critical practice' can adequately account for 'present-day and future film production and distribution practices related to Latin America'[16] rather overstates the case. On the one hand, as Joanna Page rightly insists (and as will be discussed further in chapter 1), state funding of film production and screening venues in most Latin American countries including Argentina remains crucial to the very survival of a 'national' cinema, however multiple now in its funding sources and aesthetic affiliations.[17] At the same time, Paul Willemen's point still strikes me as fundamentally true that the question of 'the national' in film is not merely one of hermeneutics – in which film theory has all too often been at fault for deploying 'the paradigms of Euro-American film and aesthetic theories'[18] upon non-European cinemas without considering the culture-specific modulations and meanings ascribed to film's apparently universal formal arsenal – but that it is also about the way in which market imperatives determine the possibility of making and watching films. As Willemen argues, there are fundamental differences between countries with relatively large internal markets, where an industrial logic often results in formally homogenising effects on cinematic output, and those who need to cater to multiple audiences for lack of sufficient demand at home to recover production costs. As Ivana Bentes has suggested in a polemical essay on recent Brazilian cinema, the former case can result in 'a "popular" and "globalized" film industry, dealing with local, historic and traditional subjects wrapped in an "international" aesthetics',[19] while the latter often implies, in Willemen's expression, the need 'to engage with the questions of national specificity from a critical, non- or counter-hegemonic position', in order to find spectators among national and foreign arthouse audiences. Rather than in absolute terms, Willemen is quick to add, we need to think of this opposition as a relational one, where one end of the spectrum sustains the other, albeit in constellations that differ between one country and the next: 'a cinema positively yet critically seeking to engage with the multi-layeredness of specific socio-cultural formations is necessarily a marginal and a dependent cinema: a cinema dependent for its existence on the very dominant export and multinational-oriented cinema it seeks to criticise and displace.'[20] This both 'national' and 'transnational' relation between production models, viewing publics, and the contested images that emerge from it of a particular time and place referred to as Argentina, will be the objects of these pages: a way of thinking about film as a particular, situated cognitive mapping of the present.

Chapter One

Transitions
How Argentine Film Survived the 1990s

While it may be difficult to pin down a single 'starting point' for new Argentine cinema, to date the demise of the previous cycle, which ensued on the country's return to democracy in 1983 after seven years of the bloodiest military dictatorship in its history, is relatively straightforward. Production figures reached an all-time low in the first half of the 1990s, with only ten feature-length films produced in 1992 and a mere five in 1994 – the lowest number since the coming of sound film in 1930 – their share of screen time representing an almost negligible 2 per cent of the overall national total. In 1984, the respective figures had been 23 feature-length productions, with a share of 18 per cent of screen time – a ratio maintained, or even improved on, throughout the decade of the 1980s.[21] For the most part, this near-death of national cinema a few years later was the effect of Argentina's monetary crisis, which had peaked during the galloping hyper-inflation of 1989, rendering state subsidies almost worthless by the time approved projects went into production.

Paradoxically, it was during the regime of financial austerity imposed under Carlos Menem's terms in government (1989–99), the devastating social consequences of which would become one of the new cinema's central topics, that film production returned from the abyss, first, as a result of the introduction of 'economic convertibility' legislation in 1991 pegging the national currency to the dollar and, more importantly, the passing of a 'new law for film development' in 1994, a cross-party project introducing a taxation scheme not just on cinema entries but also on video rentals and TV exhibition of films. Although the currency reforms more than tripled production costs, the price of cinema entries also increased fivefold between 1989 and 1991, taxation income from screenings, video rentals and broadcasting subsequently allowing the National Film Institute to raise the annual total of credits available for new productions from 50 to 300 million pesos.[22] Meanwhile, the new film law succeeded in making cinema commercially viable again, by acknowledging the diversification of film outlets beyond the cinema showroom, and channelling part of the income from broadcasting and video rentals back to producers and the institute (now called the National Institute for Film and the Audiovisual Arts [INCAA]) as well as subsidising TV screenings of national produce.[23] Through a system combining seed funding to incentivise new projects with post-exhibition payouts based on box office success and TV broadcasts, the new subsidising system especially attracted the private media conglomerates, which had emerged over the 1990s following Menem's privatisation of state television, into the production of blockbusters intended for cinema and subsequent TV exhibition – action and animation movies such as the children's TV spin-off *Dibu, la película* (Dibu – the Movie, 1997), which attracted over a million spectators, being particularly successful. Overall production figures have steadily risen since 1994, effectively breaking through the ceiling of 100 feature films per year in 1997 (now putting Argentina just below France in terms of quantity of cinematographic output).[24]

Critics of the new law have argued, however, that despite this overall surge in numbers, the system of state film financing introduced in 1994 may have hindered rather than supported the consolidation of a national cinema combining artistic quality with audience appeal. According to Octavio Getino, for example, its combination of small subsidies for aesthetically inventive works and performance-based post-release payouts has produced the abnormal effect of, on the one hand, fuelling the production of low-cost arthouse movies directed towards a small cinephile elite and exhibited almost exclusively on the international festival circuit, and, on the other, of channelling the lion's share of state subsidies towards blockbusters which are in fact transnational ventures. Indeed, the main blockbuster-producing companies such as Patagonik and Pol-Ka are controlled largely by US and European capital: Walt Disney Productions owns a 30 per cent share of Patagonik, with another 30 per cent, respectively, owned by Telefónica de España and Grupo Clarín, Argentina's largest media conglomerate that is itself part-owned by the Spanish El País group and also controls a 30 per cent share of Pol-Ka.[25] Losing out to this unholy alliance of avant-garde and commercial cinema in the reaping of federal subsidies, Getino argues, is the kind of middlebrow cinema which up until 1994 had combined artistic quality and socio-political critique with considerable audience appeal. As I shall argue here, to blame the crisis of certain aesthetic protocols and models of film production so exclusively on state policy probably overestimates the latter's importance and does not take into account the change of film audiences and modes of exhibition that have occurred since the mid-1990s. Nonetheless, such a critique has at least the merit of alerting us to a situation that is more complex and ambivalent than superficial accounts pinning an 'independent' against an 'industrial' cinema would have it, urging us to think instead of the ways in which both respond to, and are bound up with, the changing fortunes of neo-liberal specularisation and transnationalisation of the Argentine economy. In this chapter, I give a brief overview of the crisis of the post-1983 'cinema of transition' and the ways in which it created an opening for new – initially marginal – aesthetics and modes of film-making to emerge. As examples of these, after laying out the general socio-economic context of film production and reception during the period, I focus particularly on the work of Raúl Perrone and Martín Rejtman.

The crisis of transition

Cinema was one of Argentine culture's central pedestals in the years immediately following the downfall of the military dictatorship in 1983, a period in which, according to one critic, 'the Argentine public seemed primed to use the darkened movie house like a confessional'.[26] In the words of Manuel Antín, the director of the National Film Institute from 1983 to 1989, the way in which a large number of films released during these years focused on dictatorial repression – 16 out of 26 films made in 1984 alone dealing with the problematic – made cinema-going akin to a collective experience of self-purging, a kind of 'psychoanalytic session on film'.[27] As well as installing the renowned arthouse director Antín at the helm of the Institute, the government of Raúl Alfonsín dissolved the Cinematographic Classification Authority (the film censorship body created by the military regime) and, as a way of forging democratic consensus, actively incentivised through state subsidies a cinema that returned to the darkest aspects of the dictatorial past: the abduction, torture and assassination of tens of thousands of citizens. The two most successful films of the decade – Luis Puenzo's Oscar-winning *La historia oficial* (*The Official Story*, 1985) and María Luisa Bemberg's *Camila* (1984), the latter attracting over 2 million viewers in Argentina alone – also stand for the dominant approaches to the past in this period. In the former strand of films, dictatorial violence was being called up and denounced through a figure which, as Norma Aleandro's middle-class housewife in Puenzo's film who gradually finds out about her adopted daughter's 'missing' parents, simultaneously absolved Argentine society from all complicity with terror, as yet another unknowing victim. In the latter, the roots of authoritarianism were being revisited through historical allegory – as in Bemberg's account of the state's assassination of a young woman and her Jesuit lover under the regime of nineteenth-century dictator Juan Manuel de Rosas, with the complicity of the Catholic church – or genre-specific metaphor as in Fernando Solanas' tango melodramas *El exilio de Gardel* (*Tangos, the Exile of Gardel*, 1985) or *Sur* (*The South*, 1988).

Albeit to different degrees, these films approach politics from the viewpoint of an economy of affect closer to television melodrama rather than to the political cinema of the 1970s, many of whose principal protagonists had themselves been victimised by dictatorial terror – a re-accommodation of aesthetic protocols film critic B. Ruby Rich has called 'a shift from the "revolutionary" to the "revelatory"'.[28] Combining cinematic suspense with a gradual, didactic revelation of political truth, the recent past appears in the cinema of the 1980s in the form of a mystery, the 'resolution' of which is entrusted to an intradiegetic stand-in for the audience, a 'social detective' figure – using Fredric Jameson's expression[29] – endowed with pedagogical or redemptive qualities: the medical doctor in Alejandro Doria's *Darse cuenta* (*Taking Notice*, 1984), the rural teacher in Miguel Pereira's *La deuda interna* (*The Internal Debt*, 1988), the journalist in Emilio Alfaro's and Rafael Filipelli's *Hay unos tipos abajo* (*There's Some Guys Downstairs*, 1985). As Gustavo Aprea concludes, for the great majority of films made over the decade, 'politics occupy the place of a complot invisible to the citizen collective, that is, to the audience watching the film [...] If the attempt was to reach a mass audience, this was not the moment for adopting the viewpoint of the victims or the perpetrators but rather that of a society ignoring the very existence of the drama it had been involved in.'[30]

Cinema thus performed a key role during the 'transition' government of Raúl Alfonsín, using a rather conventional formal language in order to forge an equally nebulous social consensus around core values associated with democracy and human rights, but without identifying or discussing the political identities and logics of either victims or perpetrators of state terror. While this vagueness played well for some time not just with national but international audiences, too, prompting a number of co-productions such as Jeanine Meerapfel's German-funded *La amiga* (*The Girlfriend*, 1989) and Carlos Lemos' Swedish-Argentine *Los dueños del silencio* (The Lords of Silence, 1987) – both of them dealing with themes of violence and exile – it also failed to address the complicity of governments and corporations in Europe and the USA with the military regime, leaving overseas viewers unchallenged in their well-meaning distance.

Alongside the 'quality cinema' identified with political issues and predominantly catering to middle-class and international viewing publics, a more popular, domestic entertainment cinema also persisted throughout the 1980s, representing roughly 35 per cent of the production total as compared to arthouse's 65 per cent.[31] While 'quality cinema' drew on the melodramatic aspects of TV aesthetics, film entertainment was often no more than a feature-length spin-off from popular television comedies, including stars such as comic duo Alberto Olmedo and Jorge Porcel, and incorporating among its attractions elements prohibited on state TV such as female nudity, political satire, offensive or openly sexual jokes. The privatisation of TV channels and the arrival via satellite of US serial fare for the 'Latino' market, as well as the rapid spread of VHS and subsequently DVD since the end of the eighties, spelled the end of this relatively artisanal entertainment cinema, which had until then maintained production companies such as Aries and Argentina Sono Film – the remains of a once glorious national studio system – in business. Argentine film entertainment would only recover towards the end of the following decade, with the entry of private TV production companies into the market – now, however, not with relatively low-budget comedy but sophisticated animation and action fare, in an attempt to challenge Hollywood at the national box office. Jorge Nisco's *Comodines* (*Cops*, 1997) – a star vehicle for TV actor Adrián Suar produced by Pol-Ka and a spin-off from the popular TV action series *Poliladrón* – with its sophisticated special effects and slick action sequences, complete with *rock nacional* soundtrack and an unashamed use of product placement advertising, set a new benchmark in production standards, grossing a total only marginally lower than Steven Spielberg's *Jurassic Park*, released in Argentina that same year. Together with other national blockbusters such as Juan Bautista Stagnaro's *La furia* (*The Fury*) and Marcelo Piñeyro's *Cenizas del paraíso* (*Paradise Ashes*), Argentine cinema in 1997 for the first time in years effectively outperformed US and other imports at the box office by almost 3 million dollars (26 compared to 23 million).[32]

Traditional entertainment cinema may have been the principal casualty of hyperinflation and the neo-liberal adjustment policies introduced under the Menem government, but mainstream arthouse itself was soon to follow suit. Over the second half of the 1980s, an estimated 40 per cent of cinemas in Argentina closed down under pressure from rapidly declining ticket sales: of the 900 existing showrooms in 1984, only 427 remained in 1989, with neighbourhood and smalltown cinemas in the provinces being particularly hard-hit. Numbers reached rock bottom in 1992, with a mere 280 screens still in business. In subsequent years, these figures would gradually recover due to the arrival of multiplex companies such as Hoyts General, Village and Cinemark and the spread of cinemas in shopping centres – almost all of them now confined, however, to the commercial districts of the big cities. By 1999, the levels of the early 1980s had been reached once again, with 920 screens operating throughout the country, further growth effectively breaking through the 1,000 screen barrier in subsequent years.[33]

There is, then, a remarkably parallel rhythm of decline and recovery between film output, screening facilities and visitors' numbers, all of which, moreover, do not exactly match the pattern of national macro-economic trends. If the decline of film in the late 1980s and early 1990s was clearly related to the hyperinflation crisis over the same period, the financial default of 2001 provoked nothing so much as a blip in the ascending curve of film production and attendance figures. The concentration of film audiences in large cities and in such middle-class refuges as shopping centres, with ten or more screens playing at the same time, as well as the increased availability of international film fare through private television channels, VHS and DVD, kept raising the pressure on a vernacular 'quality cinema' aimed at a more or less homogeneous nationwide audience and the national box office as its sole outlet. As well as reducing the seat capacity of individual showrooms, multiplexes substantially shortened screening times for individual movies, often additionally circumventing the complicated screen quota regulations by programming national releases in unpopular matinee and afternoon slots, reserving evening sessions for high-grossing international blockbusters. Whereas at the beginning of the 1990s, national distribution companies such as SAC and Coll-Saragusti still controlled between 60 and 70 per cent of the market, their share had dropped below 10 per cent by 2003, the remaining 90 per cent now in the hands of transnational multiplex operators. These programme on the basis of screening packages dominated by Hollywood blockbusters which, by the time they arrive in Argentina, have already recovered their cost at the US box office, thus in fact turning additional copies for overseas exhibition into a net-gain deal – one that, in addition to the low import duties raised on foreign films as a consequence of Menem's free-market reforms, amounts to a highly unequal competition by price-dumping against the national film industry.[34]

From the mid-1980s, Argentine cinema attempted to respond to this changing landscape of film exhibition and consumption through international joint ventures, as a way of maintaining and re-accommodating the previous model of medium-sized productions aimed at national middle-class and international arthouse audiences alike. While some of these – notably Alejandro Agresti's El amor es una mujer gorda (Love is a Fat Woman, 1987), co-produced with the Netherlands, Adolfo Aristarain's Un lugar en el mundo (A Place in the World, 1991), co-produced with Spain, or Eliseo Subiela's El lado oscuro del corazón (The Dark Side of the Heart, 1992), with Canada – resulted in formally complex and interesting films, on the whole the co-production model only accentuated the aesthetic and political dead ends faced by the cinema of the democratic transition. The demand of having to cater to foreign audiences' expectations for recognisably 'Argentine' plots and situations (often additionally complicated by contractual obligations to cast one or more foreign actors) conspired against attempts to move beyond the by now conventional, token representations of social or political types derived from television aesthetics, leaving little or no room for innovating cinematic language. This failure became especially acute when trying to move beyond the topic of dictatorial repression and focus on problems of the present such as social decline and marginalisation, for which this kind of film language proved singularly inadequate.

Yet at the same time, even before hyperinflation had reached its peak, filmmakers had also started exploring alternative forms of production such as cooperative financing, as a way of escaping the constraints of the industrial mainstream. In this system, pioneered by directors such as Bebe Kamin and Alejandro Doria in the 1980s, all crew members were simultaneously shareholders in the film venture, working for free until, following the film's completion and distribution, any resulting profits would be divided among participants.[35] The cooperative model also became an important factor in the resurgence of documentary cinema from the second half of the 1980s, with films such as Raúl Tosso's *Gerónima* (1986) or Miguel Mirra's and Eulogio Frites' *Hombres de barro* (Mud Men, 1988) addressing the oppression of native populations, or Marcelo Cespedes' and Carmen Guarini's *La noche eterna* (Eternal Night, 1991) and Alejandro Fernández Mouján's *Banderas de humo* (Flags of Smoke, 1989) investigating the plight of Patagonian miners and plantation workers in the tropical Northwest, effectively anticipating fiction film's interest in the social and ethnic margins of the nation a decade or so later. Under the umbrella of documentary cooperatives such as Cine Ojo (Film Eye), a new kind of political cinema emerged, now not actively immersed – as Fernando Solanas' and Octavio Getino's *Cine Liberación* or Raymundo Gleyzer's *Cine Grupo de la Base* in the 1960s and 1970s – in the struggles of the militant Left but attempting to reconstruct in the observation of, and empathy with, local situations and actors, an unprejudiced and non-didactic political reading of society at large.[36]

Whereas, then, multiplexing, VHS and private TV largely dissolved not only the more homogeneous mainstream audience the cinema of transition had sought to address but also the film-club circuits of traditional cinephilia (centred on classic European avant-garde fare), it also had the effect of diversifying interest in contemporary non-Hollywood genres, for instance by bringing previously unavailable non-western cinemas into the reach of Argentine film viewers. At the same time, the rise of commercial television produced a surge in audio-visual professionalisation, largely through the growth of the advertising sector – the relatively low production costs as compared to Europe and the USA and high standards of technical expertise even resulting in major international campaigns (such as a Renault ad directed by Wim Wenders) being shot in Argentina. Following on advertisement's heels was mainstream cinema itself: not just Alan Parker's 1996 adaptation of the Lloyd-Webber musical *Evita* but also less site-specific blockbuster fare such as the *Highlander* sequel *The Quickening* (1991) or the Brad Pitt vehicle *Seven Years in Tibet* (1997) being shot in the country (both in the scenic Lunar Valley just east of the Cordillera). A side-effect of the rising demand for audio-visual professionals was the creation (or re-emergence) of film education institutions, foremost among them the Fundación Universidad del Cine (FUC) founded in 1991 by Manuel Antín after the end of his tenure at the National Film Institute. Many of the protagonists of new Argentine cinema are FUC graduates – including directors Pablo Trapero, Albertina Carri, Lisandro Alonso and Juan Villegas; editors Nicolás Goldbart and Alejo Moguillansky; or sound engineers Catriel Vildasola, Enrique Bellande and Jésica Suárez. The University also plays a key role in promoting new talent through its series of compilations of shorts *Historias breves* (Short stories), now in its fifth edition, which showcases work from recent graduates of FUC and other institutions in well-produced, cinema exhibition-ready copies – the first release from 1995 including the debuts of Daniel Burman, Jorge Gaggero, Bruno Stagnaro, Ulises Rosell, Lucrecia Martel and Israel Adrián Caetano. Other important film schools, if not as powerful in their impact as FUC, include the National School of Cinematographic Directing and Experimentation (ENERC), run by the INCAA – where directors such as Lucrecia Martel and Julia Solomonoff learned their trade – the Centre for Research and Experimentation in Film and Video (CIEVYC), directed by film critic and director Aldo Paparella, as well as the film schools of the Universities of Rosario and Córdoba, among others.[37]

This milieu of a resurgent film literacy outside the traditional circuits of *cineclubismo* was further enhanced by the appearance of critical journals, following the lead of Fernando Martín Peña, Sergio Wolf and Paula Félix-Didier's *Film* (which appeared between 1993 and 1998). Apart from print journals such as the influential *El amante de cine* (Film Lover), *Haciendo cine* (Making Cinema) and *Kilómetro 111* (Km 111, a homage to an Argentine film classic), others such as *Cineismo, Grupokane* and the now defunct *Otrocampo* and *Citynema* make use of the internet, appealing to younger, IT-literate readers and have played an important role in promoting 'New Argentine Cinema' as a generational battlehorse. Finally, the re-opening of the Mar del Plata film festival in 1996, following a 25-year hiatus, and the creation of the Buenos Aires Independent Film Festival (BAFICI) in 1999 – focusing particularly on emerging work by restricting its competition to first- and second-feature releases from debuting directors – provide an institutional platform for these new film audiences which have sprung up over the 1990s. At the same time, they offer an important showcase for national talent, marked by the awarding of the Jury's Special Prize to Caetano's and Stagnaro's *Pizza, birra, faso* (*Pizza, Beer and Cigarettes*) at the 1997 Mar del Plata Festival, and of the best director and best actor awards to Pablo Trapero's *Mundo grúa* (*Crane World*) at the 1999 BAFICI.

Among the more interesting effects of this resurgent audience interest in, and institutional platforms for, national and international off-mainstream cinema has been the way in which it prompted and made viable new combinations of production models beyond the co-production/cooperative divide that prevailed earlier in the decade. Although access to state funds remained limited until recently due to the freezing of INCAA subsidies between 1997 and 2002 under economic emergency legislation, many younger film-makers now routinely apply to international foundations such as the Sundance Institute, the French Fonds Sud Cinéma, or the Dutch Hubert Bals Fund, for credits and advances to start shooting rather than, as had been the norm in previous years, to first await INCAA approval – often in the cheaper digital video format, subsequently transposed to 35mm thanks to further income generated through festival exhibitions and prizes. Unlike in the previous co-production model, these subsidies do not come with any contractual obligations as concerns a film's script or cast: although the older models remain in use as well, more often than not co-production is now merely one aspect of film financing among various others. Frequently stretched out over several years, film production becomes, in Gonzalo Aguilar's words, 'an adventure': a segmented process with different sources of funding generated along the way for the stages of script writing, shooting, editing and distributing a work.[38] As a consequence, many film professionals – not just directors but also editors, cinematographers and sound engineers – now also have their own production companies, foremost among which are Daniel Burman's and Daniel Dubcovsky's *BD Cine* (co-responsible for, among others, Marco Bechis' *Garage Olimpo* and Anahi Berneri's *Un año sin amor*), Pablo Trapero's and Hugo Castro Fau's *Matanza Cine* (co-producers of Enrique Bellande's *Ciudad de María* and Albertina Carri's *Géminis*), and Hernán Musaluppi's *Rizoma Films* (producers of Martín Rejtman's *Sílvia Prieto* and *Los guantes mágicos*, and of Pablo Trapero's *Mundo grúa*, among others). Expertise, contacts and prestige are thus being shared among film-makers across aesthetic divides, also frequently exchanging resources and moonlighting in each other's work in a number of roles, in a way unthinkable only a few years ago.

If, then, new Argentine cinema can to an extent be thought of as a generational project, it is more for these concrete and multifold networks of collaboration in the production process than for any shared aesthetic or political preferences (as in the transition cinema of the 1980s). If there is an aesthetic break with previous film-making practices, it is in the way many recent films have sought to incorporate this segmented, improvisational production process into their formal solutions, rather than trying to camouflage the lack of Hollywood production standards under a polished editing veneer. As Gustavo Aprea asserts:

> we have come from a model of mass production on a national scale to a fragmentation, which can connect elements of local production with certain audiences at international level. Over twenty-five years, we have exchanged the possibility of imagining a mass audience with shared interests [...] for the presence of a variety of audiences disconnected and often opposed to one another. Perhaps the strongest element of the crisis experienced by Argentine film from the late Eighties to the mid-Nineties was its attempt to keep thinking of itself as a spectacle with universal appeal, in a moment when the ways of watching and understanding cinema were changing.[39]

New Argentine cinema, then, can be thought of as the contingent and heterogeneous outcome over the last decade and a half of the profound changes in film circulation and consumption – boosted by festivals and film journals – with the resultant emergence of new, diversified audiences, the possibilities offered by cheaper, lightweight technologies such as digital video and editing software, the consolidation of film schools raising levels of formal and technical expertise, the introduction of new, fragmentary and improvisational rhythms of production and, last not least, the ways in which these have made cinema contemporaneous with, and curious about, its own present.

Zero hour, 1994: Raúl Perrone's Ituzaingó trilogy

Although not altogether parallel with the nation's socio-economic fortunes, this process of innovation nonetheless had to invent new – formal, but also logistical and financial – answers to the economic crisis surrounding it. To an extent, its success can therefore be related to the way in which production process, subject matter and film form have been collapsed into one. As writer and film critic Alan Pauls puts it: 'nowadays, film form and mode of production are one and the same problem. To think about form is to think about production. This does not necessarily produce good movies, but at least it generates a disinhibited cinema. In this, it differs from the previous kind of Argentine cinema, which had been the victim of everything it couldn't be and couldn't have.'[40] In other words, political crisis is encountered now not necessarily at the level of film content but, rather, any sort of content becomes actively and self-consciously political in the way it is taken through a production process and its formal resolution, in which cinema inscribes, at one and the same time, its contemporariness and reasserts its autonomy. Even where there is, as in many fiction and documentary films released in recent years, a resurgent interest in the social, ethnic and geographical margins of the nation, this 'ethnographic' curiosity is at the same time a formal statement about cinema's departure from the previous model of totalising narrative or allegorical synthesis – a declaration of the autonomy of film from politics as understood by the mainstream cinema of the 1980s. Perhaps its most graphic example is an oft-cited sequence from Pablo Trapero's *El bonaerense* (2002), in which Zapa – the young protagonist about to join the provincial police force – runs into a protest march of the unemployed, only to turn the other way, the camera joining him rather than staying with the protesters. Conversely, even in highly experimental films that omit any direct reference to the socio-political present – indeed, for the most part, to Argentina as such – such as Aldo Paparella's *Hoteles* (Hotels, 2003) or Luis Ortega's *Monobloc* (2004), the very disavowal of locality and contemporariness also obliquely reinscribes the latter as a question about form and legibility.[41]

As Gonzalo Aguilar has suggested, to distinguish between two major strands in contemporary Argentine cinema in terms of an opposition between realism and experimentation may therefore be a futile task, an attempt to tie these back to modernist film aesthetics which, on the contrary, recent films have left behind.[42] Rather, I shall argue below, there are now different modes of inscribing *indexicality*, the way in which shot composition and montage point to the profilmic, transforming the sound-image into 'the junction between two portions of experience'[43] – shooting and acting. Nevertheless, the opposition between realism and experimentalism is still useful not just to describe the present of cinema in Argentina but also the models from the early 1990s it has cast as its precursors – the ways in which, in the midst of socio-economic crisis and on the margins of mainstream production, certain directors developed new modes of film-making that signalled alternatives to the status quo. The names of Raúl Perrone and Martín Rejtman spring to mind most immediately, pointing as they do towards, on the one hand, a 'socio-realist' film aesthetic and, on the other, a 'modernist' or metacinematic one – as well as to the limits of such a classification. More importantly, both Perrone and Rejtman also developed new routines of shooting and editing which, in their radical and self-reflexive break with pre-existing ones, remain unsurpassed, as both have refined their oeuvres over the last decade and a half.

Perrone had made his first incursions into cinema in the late 1970s, when he directed several shorts in Super-8 and participated in the short-film contests organised by UNCIPAR (Unión de Cineistas de Paso Reducido, or, the Syndicate of Film Buffs of Short Breath), an organisation of amateur film-makers whose peak of activities had been towards the end of the dictatorship and the first years of *alfonsinismo*.[44] Around 1980 he gave up film to become a professional cartoonist, only to take up experimental movie-making once again in 1988 when home-video equipment became widely available, resulting in numerous shorts and, from 1992, the medium-length features *Ángeles* (Angels, 1992), *Jimidín* (Jimmy Dean, 1995) and *La película del taller* (The Workshop Movie, 1998), the latter a collective project directed, acted and edited by participants of the film workshop Perrone now regularly runs in his home town of Ituzaingó, on the far outskirts of Buenos Aires.[45] His work – already of a certain cult status – became more widely known with the release of *Labios de churrasco* (Beefsteak Lips, 1994) in late-night screenings at downtown Cine Lorca, followed by the sequels *Graciadió* (Thankgoodness, 1997) and *5 pal' peso* (Five Cent Short, 1998), all three integrating 'la trilogía de Ituzaingó' for its continuity in terms of cast, location and time. Although all of Perrone's work – most notably the slacker comedy *Zapada* (1999), the social-realist screwball *La Mecha* (The Flame, 2003), featuring the amazing 85-year-old pensioner Nicéforo Galván in the lead role, and the love-and-exile romance *Canadá* (2006) – is set in and around Ituzaingó, a bland suburb on the western periphery of Greater Buenos Aires, the trilogy nevertheless stands out in the way it marks the crystallisation of a particular aesthetics, taken over from video experimentation into feature-length narrative, the possibilities of which for radicalisation and genre variations all of Perrone's subsequent oeuvre explores and develops.

Labios de churrasco starts with a shot-sequence which, recurrent throughout the film like a visual refrain, also functions as a statement of intention. It establishes a time and place, a particular diction, body posture, audio-visual rhythm and their relation to a set of cultural values and references, both cinematic and non-cinematic, both local and global: a poetics. The first frame has a fixed camera looking down, in grainy black-and-white and with only scant focus length, an unremarkable suburban street. A subtitle appears at the bottom of the image: 'Ituzaingó, Buenos Aires, 1994', as Juan (Fabián Vena) walks into the shot from the left, until his face from close-up occupies one half of the frame. Wearing a slightly ridiculous woollen cap, making him appear like an adolescent smurf, he takes a few puffs from a cigarette and blinks, looking up at the sky. A shot of clouds from bottom-up follows before Perrone cuts back to the initial shot, then, to a medium-distance reverse shot of Juan, looking towards the camera as he stands in the middle of the road, the point of flight now behind him. The shot sequence thus establishes a movement in and out of the character's point of view, a free-indirect-speech narration. The film then cuts back to the initial shot, as Juan begins to speak – or better, recite, in a theatrical, non-realist version of 'cool', a plea to a rosary of local folk saints: "The only thing I ask of you, my dear God, little Virgin of Luján, San Cayetano, Ceferino Namuncurá, is to have a good day. Thanks." [Lo único que te pido, Diosito querido, Virgencita de Luján, San Cayetano, Ceferino Namuncurá, es que tenga un buen día. Gracias.] Blues chords and a hummed, cracked voice appear on the soundtrack, as Perrone cuts to a rear shot of Juan walking slowly forward into the distance as the image fades into black through a diaphragm, referencing the presence of the lens – an indicator that will remain onscreen for almost the entire film, except for the 'refrain' sequences spliced in-between, where Vena recites little variations on his opening prayer, with the images of street, sky and face occupying the full screen space.

The diaphragm also indicates Perrone's preference for a certain type of lens, the extreme wide-angle, allowing him to develop narrative action with a static camera and long takes, characters walking in and out of the shot while keeping camera movement and montage reduced to a minimum. In particular during a sequence of Juan and Gus (Gustavo Prone) playing the flippers in a game arcade, shot with a fisheye lens which permits Perrone's camera to take in the reduced interior space in its entirety, the diaphragm also signifies the appropriation of the cinema screen by a low-fi technology, further emphasised by the apparently casual and 'careless' (but actually highly elaborate and composed) rhythm of jump cuts and non-chronological progression between sequences. The opening of *Labios de churrasco*, then, posits a number of elements to which the film and its sequels will add new variations without changing its overall proposition: a temporality – the present, as experienced through the lives of a bunch of adolescents, and thus as pure emergence, a here-and-now devoid of a past; a locality – the outskirts, the neighbourhood, an autonomous, self-enclosed space the characters never leave (a proposed trip to downtown Buenos Aires in *Graciadió* to watch a movie never materialises). This autochthony is marked in a form of speech as much as by a set of unremarkable locations – bars, shops, street corners – yet it is at the same time plugged into global circuits through radio and TV – as when Juan and Pao (Violeta Naón) in *Labios de churrasco* passionately discuss the latest Madonna record, or when El Mendo (Mauro Altchuler) enthuses about *The Simpsons* in *Graciadió*. In fact, with nothing much happening in the manner of an 'adventure', a lot of the time is spent telling each other about films – an alternative universe of genre and indie movies found at the local video store (a key space of sociability in Perrone's Ituzaingó) from which both the characters and the films themselves construct their identities and filiations: in *Graciadió*, Gus enquires at the videoclub about Larry Clark's *Kids* (1995), sparking an angry discussion about unprotected sex in times of Aids; in *Labios de churrasco*, Pao and Gigí (Gigí de la Mota) get aroused reminiscing about the masturbation scene from Abel Ferrara's *Bad Lieutenant* (1992). While breaking radically with any Argentine or Latin American antecedents, then, Perrone reinvents and emplaces in his suburban chronotope the narrative and compositional models found in US indie cinema, in particular the juvenile slacker movies of Clark, Richard Linklater, Gus Van Sant, Harmony Korine or the early Jarmusch. With *Labios de churrasco*, Perrone asserts, 'I found my own place and iconography: the video store, the kiosk, the low houses. Ituzaingó turns into a nucleus with its own identity. I built my own Seattle or Portland, Oregon, where I could make my own "indie" movies.'[46]

Perrone's cinematic experiment then proceeds by a particular *reductio ab initio* – a DIY ethic of film-making modelled on US indie cinema and on its antecedents in French *nouvelle vague*, codified in Perrone's own famous 'Decálogo' (an ironic riff on the Dogma movement's founding statement), where he sings the praise of low-fi technology ('Don't bother about the format: if what you have to say doesn't stand up in VHS, it won't do in Beta, Super-8, 16 mm or 35 mm either'), unpolished sound ('Use direct sound. If it's too good, contaminate it') and quick, improvised shooting ('Shootings will take, at most, eight days').[47] By stripping narrative down to its minimal core, what is brought to the fore is the poetic potential of situations: with hardly any variation, the same storyline is taken over from one part of the trilogy to the next, pairing a girl and two boys – not so much in the classic form of the love triangle but, rather, as a way of staging an alternating rhythm between, on the one hand, the homosocial friendships of childhood (with its games, confidences, the simple joys of hanging out together) and, on the other, the threshold of adulthood – the betrayal and recomposition of the couple invariably building up towards the both threatening and life-changing prospect of teenage pregnancy. Between friendship and the couple, the drama of adolescence is being played out here as the difficulty of coming to terms with 'love', as the both longed-for and feared horizon where the openness and potentiality of adolescence comes to an end. In the trilogy, different couples embody this 'invariant' story, the sidekick characters from one movie (played by Gustavo Prone, Mauro Altchuler and Micaela Abidor, respectively) becoming central ones in the next. Continuity of place, meanwhile, apart from the ubiquitous street corners, bars, and post-industrial ruins, is entrusted to a cast of secondary characters, foremost among them the caricaturesque neighbourhood vigilante El Cana (The Cop), played in all three films by Carlos Briolotti (also responsible for the cinematography in *Labios de churrasco*), as the hapless yet brutal, parastatal authority threatening the lovers' bliss and the friends' petty infractions.

Thus El Cana, even while he represents a nebulous and undefined external threat to the adolescents whose lives he polices, nonetheless still belongs, in his overacted slapstick brutality, to this very universe of youth culture, made up of cartoonish poses and cut-piece representations, whose ultimate shattering by the forces of the real the trilogy both wards off and prepares for. Indeed, Perrone's films *work*, they derive their aesthetic coherence and persuasiveness from the way in which they incorporate into their formal make-up a set of cultural references they share with their characters: above all, the aesthetics of cartoons and rock 'n' roll music. *Graciadió* features a long sequence from Matt Groening's *The Simpsons*, filmed in a long take of El Mendo's TV set, shot from the viewpoint of the sofa on which the characters spend much of their time together (and where we subsequently see them gathering, in reverse shot, after Gus has sold off the TV, telling each other episodes from the series, 'now that we can have a real conversation'). Scattered throughout *Labios de churrasco* are close-ups of black-and-white comic magazines, often from the point of view of characters browsing through them. Rock music, meanwhile, not only accompanies much of the action on the soundtrack (pride of place being given in all three films to local blues combo Los Caballeros de la Quema [Knights of the Waste Incinerator], who also contribute the title song of *5 pal' peso* and whose lead singer, Iván Noble, appears in supporting roles). It also features intradiegetically, as characters play and discuss their latest tapes with one another – in *Graciadió*, Gus and El Mendo embark on a long discussion of fictitious, outlandishly named neighbourhood bands parodying the real ones on the soundtrack. But rather than being merely youth-cultural trophies exhibited like exotic specimens, here 'the merging of image and music appears natural.

Rock is not merely background music [but rather] symbolizes the destiny of the characters and their geography [...] the musical flow chosen by Perrone succeeds in expressing space. The monotonous cadences and rugged, moribund paucity of chords, collaborate in modulating the coarse and sorrowful space exhibited in each frame.'[48]

Cartoons and rock songs are, then, structuring principles of composition in the trilogy, the former as a way of organising the frame – which Perrone started using, he explains, as a mobile cartoon frame: 'you construct a camera view, and the actors enter as if it was a drawing that moves'[49] – in the relation between foregrounded characters and background space, summarised by a few easily recognisable features. Characterisation of actors and locations occurs through the repetition of one or two key features (Pao's blowing chewing gum bubbles, Gus' acrobatics with his lighter that never works). Their cartoon origins are also marked by the handwritten names superimposed on the image in *Graciadió* to introduce characters, with little arrows pointing to them ('Pao', 'El Mendo', even 'Girl in the swimming pool'). The rules of rock 'n' roll songwriting, meanwhile, provide a template for the editing of shots: sequences repeated with few variations, such as the opening prayer in *Labios de churrasco*, function in the way of choruses, while the long travellings following the characters as they walk down the suburban roads – a Perrone trademark, punctuating in each of the films the falling-out and coming back together of the couple – provide harmonic bridges between the choruses and the narrative 'strophes', each section's musical identities highlighted (and thus made immediately intelligible to a rock-literate audience) by the melodic sequences illustrating and punctuating them. In *Graciadió*, for example, a fight between Pao and Gus after he has cheated on her is rendered in a sequence of travellings following the two as they walk down the streets, discussing and turning away from each other, while '5 pal' peso' (the Caballeros de la Quema song) refers their story on the soundtrack ('He first met her at a street corner kiosk...'), building up to the instrumental bridge – an acoustic guitar solo – to which Perrone cuts alternating close-ups of Pao's face in tears and slow-motion panning shots of Gus walking past graffiti-covered walls, and ending in a shot of clouds racing across the sky while the music slowly fades out.

The relation between music and image here is not so much that of the pop video (referenced in *Graciadió* through a sequence where Pao watches a video clip of the pop group A-ha, which famously used black-and-white cartoon animation), a relation where the image remains supplementary and subservient to the song structure. Rather, they are being merged into a single, musical-cinematic whole. In Perrone's trilogy the blues and rock elements are themselves being cut and pasted back together according to the rules of cinematic editing, while the editing also respects the rhythmic and melodic protocols of the material it incorporates. Gonzalo Aguilar has commented on the increasing sophistication of this filmic language from one 'chapter' of the trilogy to the next, reading it as an unacknowledged turning-away from Perrone's self-professed amateurism.[50] But in fact, this gradual 'maturing' – manifest on the level of the format itself, in the progression from H8-video to Betacam and finally to 35mm in *5 pal' peso* – is entirely in tune with the trilogy's narrative movement towards its tragic climax, the shooting of El Mendo by an outraged neighbour as he attempts to retrieve a football that has fallen into the latter's backyard. Referenced, *on the level of film form itself*, through the move, first, from black-and-white to colour and, even more so, from the daytime skies of *Graciadió* to the sublime, crepuscular cloudscapes that open *5 pal' peso*, this movement from *bricolage* to fully-fledged cinematic expression also runs parallel with a gradual realisation, on behalf of both the characters and their narrator, of the impossibility to hold on to adolescence as a threshold of potentiality and indetermination. In his prolific post-trilogy oeuvre, Perrone has emphasised this elegiac and melancholic dimension of his interest in youth culture, either by revisiting – as in *Ocho años después* (Eight Years Later, 2005) – the characters from the Ituzaingó saga as they struggle with adult life, or – as in *180 grados* (180 Degrees, 2008) – by narrating new versions of their story, now filtered through the musical and technological references of subsequent generations of adolescents (here, the entire film is shot – beautifully – using the video functions of mobile phones and cheap digital cameras).

In her reading of 'postgeneric film in Argentina', Joanna Page argues that the use of classic genre templates in the 'peripheral' context of Argentine film, rather than – as Fredric Jameson has famously argued for the postmodern cinema of the USA – turning into purely self-referential surfaces and thus into allegories of the very impossibility of representing social totality,[51] become re-politicised as a way of exposing Argentine and Latin American film's 'position at the margin of the film-producing and film-distributing centers of North America and Europe, which have also historically been the centers of genre production'.[52] I shall return to the question of 'postgenre' in chapter 6; what interests me here is instead the way in which, in importing an *already marginal* (or 'subcultural') genre aesthetic – the slacker movie – Perrone's trilogy also recovers the former's political implications, yet not so much as a critique of the unevenness of global production and distribution networks but, rather, as a way of opening up in Argentine cinema itself a 'marginal space' set free from the testimonial politics of the cinema of transition. Nicolás Bermúdez rightly points to the politically charged character of the trilogy's diegetic present, the year 1994 marking the presidential re-election of Carlos Menem at the peak of the privatisation and specularisation of the national economy.[53] The past- and future-less, indeed *orphaned* space-time of the trilogy's suburban youths, is in fact plainly contemporaneous with the 'end of history' of neo-liberalism, the moment of closure of politics under the imperatives of globalised markets as sanctioned by the Argentine electorate and as summarised in the infamous Thatcherite slogan 'There is no alternative'. This, indeed, is the 'experience of history' as pure exteriority into which the characters of the trilogy are about to grow up – or rather, into which they *refuse* to grow up, adolescent refusal turning, as in the case of their slacker cousins north of the Río Grande, into a kind of anti-politics. The trilogy's struggle to ward off the end of adolescence, for all its (fully acknowledged) romanticism, is at the same time an attempt to hold on to this politics of refusal, in the face not just of the demands of consumer society but also, and just as importantly, of the prefabricated answers and conventional wisdoms of the 'political cinema' which had predominated in Argentine film for over a decade.

Martín Rejtman: the political economy of the sitcom

Suburbia, adolescence and the refusal of the politics of the nation, as predominant in the cinema of the democratic transition, are also the points of departure for Martín Rejtman, the other emblematic figure who started shooting in Argentina in the early 1990s and whose oeuvre has been adopted as model and precursor by directors debuting a few years later. Rejtman had, in fact, taught several of these at CIEVYC, the film school where he gave directing and screenwriting classes after returning to Argentina following studies and assistant directorships in Italy and the USA. *Rapado* was shot in 1991, on a shoestring budget part-financed through the Dutch Hubert Bals fund, following Rejtman's earlier, failed attempt to complete a feature-length film, *Sistema español* (Spanish System, 1988), co-produced with Otto Grokenberger, the US indie producer who had worked with Jim Jarmusch in *Stranger than Paradise* and *Down by Law*.[54] Just as *Labios de churrasco*, *Rapado* – which was not commercially released until 1996 due to its classification as 'without interest' by the INCAA, thus in fact depriving it of access to institutional distribution channels – was a laconic, largely uneventful story narrating the hapless efforts of suburban youth Lucio (Ezequiel Cavia) to compensate for the theft of his scooter by stealing one himself. Yet rather than to add, like Perrone, new versions and variations to this minimal plot, thereby bringing to the fore by means of repetition its critical dimension as a politics of refusal, Rejtman in his subsequent feature-length works *Silvia Prieto* (1999) and *Los guantes mágicos* (*The Magic Gloves*, 2003) elaborates on the comic element already present in *Rapado* through the character of Damián (Damián Dreyzik) as taciturn Lucio's clownish sidekick.

Once more forming a trilogy, these films gradually extend to the entire cast rather than an individual actor a form of deadpan humour achieved through proficiently timed, non-naturalistic delivery of dialogue and straight-faced, emotionless acting, the repetition and flattening-out of actions and locations and the potential for hilarious confusions and mishaps all this generates. These are, of course, the classic mechanisms, of Hollywood screwball comedy (Howard Hawks, Preston Sturges) and even its anarchic forerunner, slapstick. But in Rejtman's film, these are also filtered through their postmodern, televisual version – the US sitcom, as practiced by comedians Jerry Seinfeld or Larry David – *and* through their 'postgeneric' pastiches in the work of global indie filmmakers including Hal Hartley, Aki Kaurismäki or Alex van Warmerdam. The sitcom, Emilio Bernini argues, 'provides Rejtman with a model of great narrative economy and, at the same time, allows him to construct a fictional universe completely set apart from the conventions of realism. […] Thus, the genre converts economic limitations into effective aesthetic choices; the scarcity of material resources for filming becoming a conscious staging decision.'[55]

But – as in Kaurismäki – this auteurial re-appropriation of classic genre to a different geographical and historical context in fact implies the virtual reinvention of this form in terms of locations, mannerisms and comic timing which, for all their active elimination of a mimetic realism, nonetheless have to retain some sort of anchorage in the profilmic for their humorous effects to succeed. One of Rejtman's main procedures, both regarding the construction of narrative space and progression and of reference to the out-of-field, is the ellipsis, a figure of speech by omission of which he is a veritable master. But in incorporating the unsaid and unseen into the narrative texture, Rejtman's cinema also turns the ellipsis into the device of a particular 'ethnography', a way of observing and exposing the present. In Rejtman's hands, the sitcom becomes a way of caricaturing and critiquing, through the medium of form, the economics of neoliberalism and its socio-cultural effects and preconditions – a post-Brechtian device of apprehending the real through defamiliarisation.

In fact, then, and against the by now well-established division in critical readings of contemporary Argentine cinema, between a 'neo-realist' recovery of indexical transparency and its (post)modernist critique by recourse to genre and pastiche, both supposedly harking back to Perrone and Rejtman as their respective founding fathers, I would argue that a comparison of their trilogies confronts us instead with different *modalities of realism* – both of which remain influential to this day. Neither Perrone's nor Rejtman's cinema falls squarely into the modes of forging transparency or of critiquing the mechanisms of illusion, which Fredric Jameson has described as the twin poles between which the dialectical force-field of realism opens up.[56] In different ways, the two directors deal in both strategies: whereas Perrone manufactures transparency by eliminating rehearsals and recording his actors' spontaneous improvisations in long takes – including elements of surprise such as the stray dog in *Graciadió* suddenly bursting forth from a garage and barking at Violeta Naón as she walks past – Rejtman on the contrary annuls not just the out-of-field but any kind of adornment or artifice not immediately related to the situation unfolding onscreen, such that every frame becomes self-contained and self-sufficient, painterly rather than photographic: 'Everything has to be said in the frontality of the location. That's what it takes, you don't need anything else. I'm more interested in working through bi-dimensionality than tri-dimensionality,' Rejtman has explained and (purloining a line from Hal Hartley)[57]: 'My entire theory is a single sentence: "cinema is surface", because there is nothing beyond the screen.'[58]

A comparison between the way in which both directors employ panning shots makes the difference clear: whereas, in Perrone, the camera travels backwards in front of a character walking down the road, or following from behind – different modalities of opening up the frame towards surrounding space – in Rejtman (as in a sequence in *Rapado* where Lucio runs down a sidewalk, persecuted by another boy whose motorcycle he has tried to steal) the camera is almost always beside him, limiting the spatial context to what is immediately necessary and functional to the narrative situation. This flattening-out of space in Rejtman, combined with the anti-emphatic, non-emotional delivery of dialogue (during the filming of *Sílvia Prieto*, Rejtman reportedly supervised the shooting of particular scenes from a distance, listening to the dialogues over a pair of headphones), amounts to a critique of the mimetic conventions of expressive realism – or, as Bernini calls it, 'a conscious and precise work of dis-attribution of the cinematographic image'.[59] In Perrone's cinema, the marked presence of genre elements (cartoons, rock) likewise emphasises the mediated, representational character of onscreen action. Both directors, then, critically depart from the mimetic, televisual realism which to different degrees predominated in Argentine cinema of the previous decade. But whereas Perrone turns to youth and subcultural formats in search of an 'outside' from which to recover lyricism and spontaneousness, Rejtman on the contrary proceeds by the radical subordination of indexical registers under the self-sufficiency of the onscreen situation.

As in *Labios de churrasco*, the milieu of suburban youths in *Rapado* (the film is set in an unspecified area of Buenos Aires' affluent northern periphery) serves as a blank slate on which to start from scratch, radically eliminating any references to historical or social context through the extreme reduction of the frame, suppressing the out-of-field. As Rejtman has stated: 'I had the impression that Argentine cinema wasn't contemporary. The basic need I felt was to make a contemporary film [...] For instance, I never liked the dialogues of Argentine films. So I proposed myself to begin from zero [...] I tried to reduce everything [...] to be more primitive. Not to dismember the scenes, not to provoke them through montage. It isn't about using longer shots but about observing the scene and not to construct it through montage.'[60] The purging of dialogue from all traces of psychological expressiveness and the intrinsic

Figures 1 and 2   A panning shot from Raúl Perrone's Labios de churrasco *(above) and from Martín Rejtman's* Rapado *(below). Whereas the former opens up towards the out-of-field, the latter eliminates it.*

duration of situations, marked off against one another by slow fades-into-black, provide the basic grammar of a filmic language the effect of which is the theatricalisation of real locations, making them stage-like, while the non-naturalistic acting deliberately distances interpersonal exchanges from the affective realism of the 1980s. Yet this departure from a mimetic or indexical realism – since what is eliminated in Rejtman's flattening-out of the frame into 'bidimensionality' is precisely the aleatory dimension of the depth-of-field – also allows for a different, more indirect and complex, mode of reference that exploits this 'irreality' to comic effect, exposing the absurdities of late capitalist everyday life. Lucio's theft of a scooter, for instance, is narrated in a sequence which deliberately avoids the creation of suspense, let alone moral dilemmas: a long panning shot of Lucio walking past shop-windows on a commercial street – the camera travelling sideways, focusing only on Lucio and the merchandise displayed behind the glass – is followed by several shots of the interior of a record store, where he browses through a box of long-plays before spotting the unlocked scooter parked outside. A medium-length shot of the unclaimed scooter from the street follows, before Lucio enters the frame, mounts the scooter and drives away, the camera turning to follow him down the street. In the next shot, Lucio pulls up at a traffic light beside a cyclist, and a short dialogue between the two ensues, the cyclist asking: "How much, one of these?" – Lucio: "New?" – Cyclist: "Yeah, how much?" – Lucio: "Two, three hundred dollars." – Cyclist: "And how does it run, fine?" – Lucio: "Yes." Of course, the scooter is used rather than new, and Lucio himself has just contested its supposed value by stealing it. As it turns out, it also doesn't work, being worth – as a female mechanic tells Lucio after the bike has broken down on a test-drive into the countryside – "nothing at all. It's scrap. Your cheapest option is buying a new one."

There is, then, a disparity between words and the things or actions they refer to, a crisis of meaning which centres, in *Rapado* as in Rejtman's subsequent films, on the problem of value. Firstly, the film could be read as functioning entirely along a series of running gags, first and foremost about motorcycles and their propensity for being stolen (the sole obsession, it seems, of Lucio and his friend Damián, who fails dismally in his attempt to copy the theft of Lucio's motorcycle, in a slapstick caricature of the film's opening sequence). But it is also a kind of anxious self-presencing of the object of desire itself, motorcycles being forever parked, locked and unlocked wherever the friends go, Damián at one point scolding an incautious motorist: "Do you think this is a safe place for leaving a bike like this one?" Secondly, there are the false banknotes that start to proliferate, apparently with a cross- rather than straight-eyed founding father on them (we are never shown the supposedly obvious piece of fake, only its effects: Lucio having to walk 40 blocks for not being allowed onto a bus, Damián settling for five tokens at the video arcade in exchange for a banknote supposedly worth 800 tokens). In a particularly hilarious scene, the two friends buy aspirins at a kiosk, paying with game tokens for lack of money and getting their change back in sweets, since the shopkeeper doesn't have any either. Joanna Page suggests that this scene could be read as a prescient anticipation of the 'primitive' barter economy that ensued on the financial default of 2001, pointing to a Buenos Aires 'caught between two forms of society that we might variously express as First World and Third World, market and nonmarket'.[61] I would suggest instead that the crisis of value, as a hollowing-out of things' and words' affective contents – which Rejtman's subsequent films stage as a frantic, precipitous circulation of objects, names and people – points to a structural affinity between the sitcom genre and the functioning of neo-liberal society (in a fully mercantilised rather than 'nonmarket Third World'), exposing the latter's flaws *through a realism of the form* rather than its content.

Sílvia Prieto (1999), Rejtman's second film, could superficially be described as narrating the couplings, emotional anxieties and professional dead-ends of a bunch of urban twenty-somethings gathered around the title-giving character (played in a wonderfully low-key, deadpan performance by rock songstress Rosario Bléfari). Yet right from the start, the film turns away from the well-groomed, existential angst treatment the same material might have received on the hands of another director (indeed actively turning its back on a tradition of urban existentialism harking back to such early-1960s' classics as David Kohon's *Tres veces Ana* [Three Times Ana, 1961] or Rodolfo Kuhn's emblematically titled *Los jóvenes viejos* [The Old Young Ones, 1962]). To shots of an unremarkable bar, Bléfari's faux-naive voice-over informs us of the protagonist's decision, having reached age 27, to make radical changes to her life which she claims has run out of purpose. To this effect, she takes her clothes to a laundry shop and gets a job as a waitress in a café. Next, we see her having a coffee with her ex-husband, Marcelo (Marcelo Zanelli), who looks at her with concern: "You've put on weight." She replies: "The blouse is a size too small – at the laundry, they gave me someone else's clothes." To which she adds, after a pensive pause: "I'll have to go on a diet." This double disparity – between great aspirations such as a life-change and trivial actions such as getting a McJob, and between short-size clothes and their consequences (to go on a diet rather than exchange them for the right-size ones) – establishes the tone and narrative logic of the film, in which bland, unremarkable characters with hardly anything to distinguish them but their names are prompted into action by objects circulating, and losing their way, among them.

Immediately after his encounter with Sílvia, Marcelo meets Brite (Valeria Bertuccelli) – a girl handing out samples of a brand of soap called Brite. He asks her out and later picks her up at a sit-in protesting against the death of another soap-promoter run over by a bus ("She was crushed against the wall and the passers-by took all the samples," Brite explains to Marcelo). While they have dinner at a pizza chain, Marcelo recognises among the contestants of a lonely hearts show on the TV his ex-schoolmate Garbuglia (Luis Mancini), declaring himself to his TV fiancé Marta (Susana Pampín).

Meanwhile, Sílvia has continued her quest to 'find herself' by giving up pot-smoking (and receiving an answering machine as a farewell present from her dealer), acquiring 'a canary which doesn't sing' and rewarding herself with a trip to the seaside with her first salary from the café. At a frosty boardwalk bar, an Italian tourist offers her his Armani jacket, which she promptly takes with her as he makes a trip to the bathroom. Back in Buenos Aires, she receives a call from 'Armani' who reclaims his jacket and, asked how he found her, informs her that there are only two Sílvia Prietos in the phonebook. "Another Sílvia Prieto?" she exclaims, shocked. Events start to accelerate from here: Sílvia quits her job at the café (she has lost count of the coffees she has served) and, being introduced to Brite by Marcelo, starts working with her as a soap promoter (she is given the dead girl's uniform to which, she informs us, "they only had to make a few adjustments"). Brite also sets her up with her ex-husband Gabriel (Gabriel Fernández Capello, aka *Vicentico* – lead singer of the band *Los Fabulosos Cadillacs*), who turns out to be another ex-schoolmate of Marcelo's who has just returned from Los Angeles and has nowhere to stay. Their supposedly love-at-first-sight romance is narrated in another sequence of deadbeat humour: a shot of the indifferent-looking Sílvia and Gabriel entering her apartment is followed by another of a still-inexpressive Gabriel putting on his shirt, Sílvia informing us in her voice-over that "he woke up with his back all scratched because I forgot to take off my nail extensions". As they leave for breakfast, Gabriel wears the Armani jacket; immediately afterwards he sells it to Marcelo, also presenting him with a painted porcelain statue he brought from America, "as a present for Brite". Brite hates the statue and gifts it to Sílvia since, she says, "she looks a bit like you". Sílvia calls the other Sílvia Prieto and arranges to meet her, having surmounted – after several failed attempts – the difficulties of getting into a dialogue ("Sílvia Prieto!" – "Yes?" – "Sílvia Prieto." – "That's me. Who is there?" – "Sílvia Prieto!" – and so forth).

All the while, the accelerated circulation of more or less trivial objects imposes a kind of parallel rhythm on the making and unmaking of personal relationships: Sílvia, wondering what she could give her alter ego for a present, puts together a 'bottle-lamp' with a lampshade and an empty whisky bottle left behind by Gabriel; on being dissuaded by Brite (who recommends shampoo) she gives it to Gabriel instead, who – having moved in with Garbuglia in the meantime – is unwittingly reminded by the latter that 'bottle-lamp' was the name they used to tease him with as a child. 'Armani', meanwhile, turns up, in shirtsleeves, at the Chinese restaurant where Brite and Marcelo are having dinner (all dinner scenes in *Sílvia Prieto* take place at the same table of the same unremarkable restaurant identified by shots of its neon-sign 'Tokyo Chinese restaurant'); recognising his jacket, he buys it back from Marcelo for twice the price the latter had paid Gabriel. Sílvia, back from her meeting with Sílvia Prieto 2 – an amiable if slightly patronising older woman (Mirta Busnelli) – throws the little statue (representing 'herself', according to Brite) out of a bus window, in a burst of rage over having to share her name with someone – or something – else. After spending some time in the gutter (the camera staying with it, in a series of close-ups recording the changes of light, weather and ambient noise), the Sílvia Prieto statue is picked up by a youth who takes it home before going out to a rock concert of the band 'El Otro Yo' (The Other I), whose bass player turns out to be the second Sílvia Prieto's daughter. Other objects going astray include Sílvia's and Marcelo's wedding video, shown three times during the film (each over a dinner of chicken cutlets previously hacked to tiny bits by Sílvia), the last as a stand-in for Marta's and Garbuglia's televised wedding ceremony Sílvia couldn't manage to record for Gabriel, imprisoned at the time for smoking marijuana in public – only that Gabriel had mistakenly been released the day before Sílvia was supposed to pick him up in place of his cellmate Walter, who instead shows up at their meeting-spot and is taken home for dinner by her to watch the (wrong) video together. The film concludes with a quasi-documentary sequence of real-life Sílvia Prietos having tea with Mirta Busnelli – the film's Sílvia Prieto 2 – and recounting their lives to each other and the camera.

In *Los guantes mágicos* (*The Magic Gloves*, 2003), which chronicles the impending mid-life crises of a bunch of thirty-somethings, things and effects circulate at a similarly frantic speed – including a depression and subsequent pill-addiction and detox cure at a Brazilian spa, passed on between one female character and the next, a dog which is forever obsequiated and loaned out, complete with dog-walking vouchers, and a series of medical afflictions suffered by several characters after being treated to a full-blast demonstration of amateur rocker Piraña's (Fabián Arenillas) musical skills. Centrally, the film revolves around the title-giving ploy conceived by Piraña, of importing a shipment of Chinese rubber gloves to take advantage of a record winter, resulting in spectacular failure when the ship is delayed in heavy seas and temperatures rise back to tropical heat by the time the gloves arrive. This results in the loss of minicab driver Alejandro's (another bravura performance by Vicentico) beloved old Renault, which he had been persuaded to give up for sale by Piraña following a series of increasingly absurd lease and buy-back arrangements to raise capital. Yet if, even more than in Rejtman's previous films, it is almost impossible to summarise the plot of *Los guantes* (which was awarded the national FIPRESCI critics' prize for best film of the year), it is because none of its actions can be 'synthesised' into larger formations of meaning beyond their shared propensity for repeating themselves with slight diversions and digressions, in the process suffering a kind of hollowing-out, a loss of the singularity which had been their only distinctive feature.

If indeed, as Rejtman has suggested, all his films 'talk about economy, in every possible sense',[62] it is by incorporating into their (comic) form a kind of inflation that is reflected in the accelerated rhythm of sequences repeating the lines, poses and locations of earlier ones. Yet instead of thereby acquiring density and depth, the films work onto these quasi-repetitions an increasingly hollow surface-quality, their almost compulsory nature tending towards pure slapstick. Yet comedy is being used here (as in the classic slapstick of Chaplin and Keaton) as a means of exposing the inner logic of capital at a particular moment of its history and in a particular location in the global economy. As Beatriz Sarlo has argued, it is possible to read Rejtman's cinema (as well as his literary oeuvre)[63] as a particular kind of sociology exposing the contemporary erasure and hollowing-out of social identities based on class or profession, characteristic of an economy of virtualisation and precarisation of labour. 'Constructed on the principle of non-identification,' she suggests, Rejtman's cinema 'offers us "cold" forms', which sidestep the demands of televisual affective realism. In Rejtman, she concludes:

> there is no discrepancy between narration, type of shot, structure and setting, the absence of music. There is no mismatch between subject and treatment. A world without qualities, a world of post-work, of flat identities that occupy no space just like the portrayal and dialogues of the film itself.[64]

Yet rather than offering us merely a peculiar kind of social diagnostics, Rejtman's counter-realism of the everyday is after something else, a poetics. The poetic dimension emerges by containing the hyperreal associations of brand names, modes of speech and musical references in the self-sufficiency of the situation. Thus, the everyday is made to release its absurd and hallucinatory qualities by closing off the wider frame of (socio-cultural) reference, the out-of-field, as soon as it is invoked – producing an intrafilmic real that is shot through with figments of contemporariness, but isolated, set free from their usual contexts. The relation between one and the other, between filmic and external 'reality' (the non- rather than profilmic) is re-asserted time and again by the long fade-into-blacks separating one sequence from the next and thus ensuring the self-containedness of every situation. This black screen, as an absence that makes its presence felt, could thus be understood as the silent centre of Rejtman's poetics: the abyss of meaning, which both renders the 'situation comedy' form possible and inscribes in it its own limit, the darkness that envelops it.

Chapter Two

Locating Crisis
Compositions of the Urban

Try entering 'Argentinazo' into your YouTube browser. Among the clips retrieved – and expect there to be quite a few, from individual amateurs' footage of the 20 December 2001 uprising to the more sophisticated narratives of video-activist collectives and professional documentary film-makers – many will probably follow a similar storyline. Cutting from TV images of (soon to be deposed) President Fernando de la Rua, announcing a state of siege in response to the previous day's food riots, to grainy photographs and video shots of the darkening city, they show the crowds assembling on street corners and outside apartment blocks, first only a handful, then rapidly becoming so numerous that they fill up the entire street. Many are banging rhythmically on pots and pans, syncopating the chants that begin to appear: '*Que se vayan, que se vayan…*' ('away with them, away with them'). The crowds begin to move, some of the cameras right in the midst of them, others frantically crossing the city by car or on the back of a motorbike, as if they wanted to take it all in at once: crowds at the Obelisco, on the corner of Callao and Corrientes Avenue, marching down Diagonal Sur.

Eventually, they all converge on Plaza de Mayo, the central square opposite Casa Rosada, the presidential palace. Many of the videos, not just the more elaborate ones, cut back and forth from TV footage to their own recordings, as the marchers clash with police: initially, there will be contrast between the two images – the newsflashes seeking an intermediate vantage point in order to get both sides of the battle into frame, the amateur footage filmed from the crowd's point of view. Frantic zoom-ins and telescopic lenses are in frequent use here to highlight moments of tension between the marchers in the foreground, in their shorts and trainers, and the police in the back in their full battle gear, firing shots that subsequent close-ups reveal to be combat ammunition. Yet at some point during the night, the two kinds of images merge to become almost indistinguishable except for the TV channels' logos, the 'official' ones being drawn into the crowd, losing their distance. This, it seems, is also the moment when the balance of power topples over, a 'power vacuum' that is not so much represented in this suddenly ubiquitous audio-visual form as it *is* this very form: a breaking down of boundaries between infotainment and counter-information, between performance and spectatorship, viewing and action.[65] Indeed, one of the most chilling examples of this blending into one of image and action was the killing, a week later, of three young men who were watching – and loudly cheering – news footage of another *cacerolazo* march by a streetcorner kiosk in the Floresta neighbourhood and were shot on the spot by an incensed ex-cop.[66]

Needless to say, this time window of indetermination remained open only for the briefest of instants. In fact, it is possible to time it more or less exactly by watching the documentaries of edited news footage such as Roman Lejtman's *El estallido* (The Uprising, 2002), released a couple of months later, where it becomes clear that normal business was resumed almost from the moment of de la Rua's departure by helicopter from the roof of the Casa Rosada – an event which, although it may have appeared for an instant to seal the victory of the crowd, also transferred media protagonism back to the suits emerging from committee backrooms. However, as an audio-visual hiatus, collapsing politics and the politics of the image into one, the December 2001 events would remain a point of reference for Argentine cinema in years to come. This is particularly true, for obvious reasons, for a new militant, combative brand of documentary cinema and video-activism, for which the December uprising was in many ways a foundational event (see chapter 4). But in a wider sense, this spectacular eruption of discontent also provided a remarkable visual archive of urban crisis in motion, cutting from a large panoramic of the moving crowd (shot from atop lamp posts and bus shelters) to individual faces, from the epics of street fighting to zoom-ins on barricaded banks and the red lights of cars stuck in traffic. During these two days in December, from the suburban food riots to the *cacerolazo* marches and the battle of Plaza de Mayo, the inhabitants and locations of a city in crisis were brought into each other's gaze – not only because the uprising put them on the move and brought them face to face with one another but, also, because of the real-time images streamed through the internet and television.

Siegfried Kracauer's classic characterisation of the street as the locus of history in film, made in respect of Italian neo-realism of the 1950s – 'When history is made in the streets, the streets tend to move onto the screen'[67] – seems to apply equally well here, although the screens now tend to be those of televisions, computers and mobile phones.

Cinema was slower off the mark than its small-screen rivals (although, as I have argued in the introduction, it had already started capturing the worlds of marginality and discontent long before they erupted into prime-time TV).[68] One of the most interesting filmic reflections on the 2001 crisis, turning this belatedness into a formal choice and, thus, into a meditation on cinema's – and art's – relation to the event of history, is Alejandro Fernández Mouján's *Espejo para cuando me pruebe el smoking* (A Mirror for when I try on the Dinner Jacket, 2005). Mouján's documentary observes the sculptor Ricardo Longhini during the production of a piece commemorating the victims of police violence during the uprising. Longhini's work, titled *Argentinitos* (Little Argentines), incorporates the leftovers from the battle which he found on returning to Plaza de Mayo a day later: bullets and tear grenades, stones and marbles (used by protesters – Longhini explains – for toppling the horses of mounted police). Eventually, he assembles these into an allegorical arrangement loosely modelled on the Argentine flag, cast in an asphalt panel.

The film closely and patiently follows each step of Longhini's complex process of object-making, at the same time as it emulates the latter's archaeological approach to the event both commemorate: like Longhini himself (who, he confesses, spent 20 December in a neighbourhood bar watching things unfold on TV, having fled the Plaza scared and nauseated by the tear gas), the film makes a belated return to the locations of the revolt, cutting video footage of the street fights to Longhini's voice-over explaining his formal decisions and their allegorical purposes. Thus, a complex relation of distance and empathy emerges between the two artists reworking the materials of the immediate past each in their own medium and its discontinuous temporality, yet also in confrontation with one another. At one point, Longhini compares his own work using *objets trouvés* with the Dogma group's self-imposed film-ascetism, explaining that he will never add anything to his rescued material for the purpose of sculptural effect. Likewise, Mouján's film hardly ever strays from Longhini's workshop, patiently watching the assembly of his counter-monuments. Yet it also subtly installs this inner space of reflection and reworking in the social and political world with which it engages. In one sequence, the camera pans over objects in various states of completion while on the soundtrack the radio (a constant aural presence of the outside world in Longhini's workshop) reports the point-blank killing by police of the *piquetero* protesters Kosteki and Santillán during a rally in June 2002. Rather than to confront these events directly – as do activist video-collectives such as Indymedia Argentina in *Piquete Puente Pueyrredón* (2002) or Ojo Obrero in *¡Piqueteros carajo! La masacre de Puente Pueyrredón* (2002), using their footage of police repression – Mouján chooses to engage with them through the mediation of *another* aesthetic (and, in its own way, documentary) process. Thus, inverting its title – alluding to another Longhini piece – Mouján's film finds *mirrored* in Longhini's artistic practice its own difficult relation with a society riled by poverty and repression. His film asks about the possibility of maintaining cinema – and art – as spaces of reflexivity and critique: as a *monument to*, rather than just a *document of*, the present.

Contemporary Argentine cinema, I argue in the following chapters, comes down at either end of the opposition sketched out here: at times it locates crisis directly in the fabric of the real, working with non-professional actors and shooting in real life-worlds; at others, it seeks out critical locations allowing for a more detached, reflexive approach both to the social present and to its filmic representation. Here I shall observe the way in which these different options capture – and stage – the big city, Buenos Aires, as a key site of crisis, indeed as the eye of the storm.

Through the speed barrier: shooting the city's margins

Of course, the city itself is always already cinematic. Pioneers of modern cinema from René Clair to Eisenstein already noticed film's particular affinity to (modernist) architecture, particularly as concerns montage and point of view. Among film theorists, Kracauer and Benjamin were the most alive to the structural equivalences between the haptic gaze of the film viewer and that of the street *flâneur*. Both of these collect and conjoin space-time fragments in acts of traversal, in a constant counterpointing between the movement and stillness of these snippets of the real and that of their own mobile gaze. Hence, too, the affinity from very early on between urban camerawork and engine-powered means of transportation such as tramways, buses and cabs, which seem to endow the gaze of every city-dweller with cameratic power. Or, better, it is film that takes its codes for the spatio-temporal organisation of shots into sequences from the perceptual habits of the modern city, of which it thus becomes a kind of idiosyncratic cartography. As Giuliana Bruno puts it: 'The panoramic views, the shifts in viewing position, the traversal of diverse spatio-temporal dimensions and the movements of the spatial consumer have linked the city to travel to film. Cinema, born out of the theatre of urban motion, exhibits a fascination for the very means that produced the modern, moving visual space.'[69]

Contemporary Argentine film frequently uses the camera-in-transit device as a means of interconnecting the disjointed urban worlds of the postmodern metropolis, at the same time as introducing into the continuity of the plot an 'empty' time-block that corresponds to the city's spatial divisions. In Ariel Rotter's *Sólo por hoy* (*Just for Today*, 2000), near-abstract shots of lights flashing by, taken from a hand-held camera travelling – the sequence suggests – on the back of bike-messenger Ailí's motorcycle, provide a notion of simultaneity and spatial continuity between the episodes narrating each of the five characters' working day. In Martín Rejtman's *Los guantes mágicos* (*The Magic Gloves*, 2003) the nightly car ride of minicab driver Alejandro listening to techno music on his stereo transmits the pleasure of surfing an urban exterior transformed into pure visual surface by the speed of movement. Yet it is in the breaks and intersections of this accelerated and abstracting movement which, detaching itself from the concreteness of place, is also the speed at which (literally, in the case of Ailí's deliveries) global finance-capital traverses the city, that cinema catches a glimpse of the social margins, of what has been cast aside.

The opening shots of Israel Adrián Caetano's and Bruno Stagnaro's *Pizza, birra, faso* (*Pizza, Beer and Cigarettes*, 1997), prior to the start of the action proper, are a kind of founding manifesto of a cinema literally relocating itself on the other side of neo-liberalism's speed barrier. Further to grainy footage of a police operative, foreshadowing the film's tragic and violent ending, Caetano and Stagnaro cut to a black screen with the film's title underlaid by the first beats of a *cumbia*. Cumbia, of course, is the musical form favoured by the migrant underclass from the interior and adjacent countries; the kind of music, too, playing at the *bailanta*, the dance hall the film's band of hapless young criminals will attempt without success to assault. Next, we see the city in the distance, shot from the side window of a car moving along the urban motorway. The film cuts to a group of common people waiting at a bus stop; then, in reverse shot, to buses on the move. The female voice of a radio taxi operator joins the *cumbia* beats on the soundtrack; the shot of a traffic jam is followed by that of a street preacher, as if glimpsed by a passing pedestrian: "You have to fight to win," he shouts into a microphone, "you have to fight to make history!" Quick shots using a telescopic lens follow, as if by association: a bag lady, a beggar by the subway entrance. Cut to the city from the motorway: now we see the high-rises in the centre, with the Retiro shantytown in the foreground; the camera panning upwards as it passes a particularly high tower as if to underscore the distance between the two planes of the image. Interrupted from time to time by black screens carrying the opening credits, with the music and radio voices continuing on the soundtrack, the following shots alternate between street and motorway views (now increasingly through the car's windscreen, as if signalling a forward movement into the city and into action) and people glimpsed, as it were, in the interstices of traffic: window cleaners and beggars moving in-between cars, working the traffic lights, *cartoneros* (rubbish collectors) carrying their bulky freight, homeless people sitting on sidewalks, street kids, a platoon of riot-gear police. Towards the end of the credit sequence, this visual prologue gradually makes way for diegetic action, or rather is embedded in it, as two of its adolescent protagonists walking through the traffic and a taxi passenger are being identified as the carriers of these counterpointed gazes. The sequence ends with the two space-times clashing, while on the soundtrack a newsreader recites the latest unemployment statistics. Or rather, one domain invades the other, as the taxi is assaulted by the two young marginals, Pablo (Jorge Sesán) and El Cordobés (Héctor Anglada), the violence of their intrusion being signified, rather than by their physical handling of the passenger, through their loud, fast slang language and a hand-held camera hectically panning to and fro (rather than cutting from one speaker to the next).

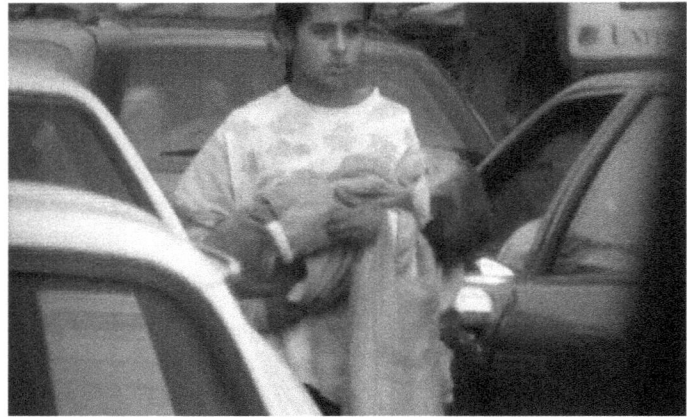

Figures 3 and 4 Opening shots from Pizza, birra, faso *(Bruno Stagnaro and Israel Adrián Caetano, 1997), mapping out the contemporary city as composed of uneven velocities – a space of traffic flows, in the interstices of which are the places occupied by marginals and castaways.*

During the opening shots, then, the taxi, if only implicit in the mobile gaze it carries through the city, figures as a time capsule of the kind also featuring in Rotter's and Rejtman's films. Its self-enclosedness is warranted by the music and radio messages on the soundtrack, which convert it into an imaginary inner space, a sonic interior bracketed from the derelict life-worlds glimpsed on the outside. These, if only apparently, remain at a safe distance thanks to their inaudibility, their transformation into purely visual surfaces. Drawing on Paul

Virilio's philosophy of speed, film critic Christian Gundermann argues that the acceleration of physical and cultural space in Argentina during the neo-liberal government of Carlos Menem in the 1990s, through the exponential growth of private motorway and television networks, was crucial to the imposition of a new kind of authoritarian politics, based on the impossibility of challenging an accelerated circulation of signs and bodies that poses as history itself, a speed-regime which Virilio calls *le globalitaire*.[70] *Pizza, birra, faso* shows this spatio-temporal sound/vision barrier to be a fiction and a reality at the same time: the social underworld is always already inside the enclosures of the globalised city inhabited by the taxi passengers (both of the film's taxi-raid victims, incidentally, are on their way to the airport to board a plane). Both the music and the radio-messages, while keeping the material city at bay, also constantly refer to it, drawing it back inside; meanwhile, in terms of the plot, the 'assault' is but a kind of living theatre directed by the taxi driver (who provides the essential stage requisites: the guns) and acted out by his accomplices, the youths. Yet the final shot of the sequence, of a jet plane taking off, also signals the utter irrelevance of these small interruptions on a systemic scale: the taxi passenger may have lost his money and missed his plane, yet none of this amounts (as the street preacher's battle call at the beginning might lead us to expect) to an act of rebellion or disturbance that is even so far as noticed by 'the system'.

Joanna Page has noted how, in *Pizza, birra, faso*, a sensation of contemporariness, of presence, is actively produced by constantly calling attention, through the film's composition and editing of frames, to the contrast between motion and stillness in urban public space. Referring to the long sequence of the youths hanging out in the middle of the Obelisco roundabout, waiting for their friends to return with some pesos for food, traffic rushing past them on both sides, Page suggests that 'the film as a whole attempts to carve a hole in the frenzied time of the city, through which we may glimpse the lives of those who are not integrated into the space-time of global capitalism [...] Marginalization in *Pizza, birra, faso* is explored primarily as a kind of temporal disjuncture rather than a spatial displacement – more out-of-phase than out-of-place.'[71] Page is right to insist on the film's active, indeed 'archaeological', production of a historical present, yet this latter is also crucially bound up here with the fate of place – and especially urban, public places, *plazas* – under neo-liberal modernisation. These, we could argue with Mike Davis, increasingly become the location of those deprived of access to the velocities of communication and transport networks, which qualify for participation in the (more than ever virtual) 'market-place'.[72] To be seen sitting aimlessly in public places, as the youths in *Pizza, birra, faso* often are, is to be identified as belonging to an underclass of outcasts from the city, at once invisible and absolutely exposed to everyone's gaze. *Pizza*'s most interesting achievement is perhaps the way in which this split in the urban texture is woven into the narrative and compositional structure of the film itself: the way in which, after first showing us these 'marginal worlds' from the usual vantage point of a mobile viewing platform (which also means: from the safety of the other side of a screen, be it a car or train window or a television set), Caetano's and Stagnaro's camera then relocates, as it were, into these interstitial worlds themselves, with their very different demands on the duration and framing of the filmic image.

This stepping over the speed barrier of the neo-liberal city, signalled at the end of the assault sequence by a static camera on the side of the motorway observing the taxi disappear into the background of the image, is thus also a break with a particular form of staging, practised by Argentine urban films of the early 1990s such as *Últimas imágenes del naufragio* (*Last Images of the Shipwreck*, Eliseo Subiela, 1989) or *El verso* (The Riff, Santiago Oves, 1995). Despite also registering the crisis of *porteño* society, which they narrate through traumatic experiences of loss and social descent of middle-class characters, these films nevertheless held on to an aesthetic model that seemed to belie their own content, as if despite this very crisis the narrative conventions of psychological realism preferred by middle-class audiences still held good. Both films featured well-known lead actors (Lorenzo Quinteros, Luis Brandoni) as targets of affective identification, using references from the literary canon (Roberto Arlt's existentialist novels in *Últimas imágenes*; the *sainete*, a popular form of grotesque comedy, in *El verso*) to allegorise the estrangement of their characters. In terms of shot composition and acting styles, these films deployed a pastiche of earlier genre forms and cut-piece representations of social types, as well as iconic locations to signify, ironically enough, a city in which the protagonists had supposedly lost their footing. If anything, then, these films could be credited with a certain self-reflexivity in signposting the crisis of a kind of *mise-en-scène*, inherited from the 1980s and based on the incorporation of expressive forms proper to literature and to television, which *Pizza, birra, faso*, by contrast, resolutely breaks with.

Or rather, Caetano's and Stagnaro's film incorporates a *different* kind of television image, that of the new sensationalist, private news channels such as *Crónica TV*, with their cast of real-life poor talking unscripted street-lingo into the outstretched microphones of onsite news-units, and their *temps morts*, with the camera lingering outside some anonymous and miserable crime scene awaiting 'new developments'. Film theorist Ana Amado has suggested the concepts of exhaustion and precipitation to think about this new temporality pervading the filmic image. These, she suggests, are also the modes in which, towards the end of the millennium, history itself has been experienced in Argentina.[73] One of *Pizza*'s main innovations on earlier films of the decade, then, was to introduce this temporality oscillating between boredom and eruption, not only through the rhythm of montage and camerawork but also through the semi-improvised acting of its non-professional leads. It is the unpredictability of their actions, the always lingering possibility of a sudden, unmotivated outburst that determines the 'unconventional' composition of shots – as, literally, when during the preparations for an assault, Megabom (Alejandro Pous) fires off the gun he had been toying with. Conversely, it is also this quasi-documentary, explorative construction of the shot which produces the effect of a seemingly unstaged, real-time event.

In its choice and treatment of locations, *Pizza* – as do other, somewhat less accomplished films about disaffected youths including Ezequiel Acuña's *Nadar solo* (*Swimming Alone*, 2002) and Diego Lerman's *Tan de repente* (*Suddenly*, 2002)[74] – also goes some way towards de-iconising the city. Instead of recognisable points of orientation, the action transcurs on anonymous street corners, among cheap food stalls and in suburban wastelands by the river. Only two elements of a postcard Buenos Aires are included, both inscribing the film in an urban cinematic and literary tradition evolving around the centre vs neighbourhood (*barrio*) opposition at the same time as it disavows it: the Obelisk – visual shorthand for the centre of commerce and entertainment ever since the modernist photography of Horacio Coppola in the 1930s – and the riverfront at La Boca, the working-class neighbourhood whose iron bridges provided a picturesque backdrop for legions of social melodramas all the way down from *Riachuelo* (Luis J. Moglia Barth, 1934) or *Puente Alsina* (José A. Ferreyra, 1935) at the very beginnings of sound film. Yet in *Pizza*, the Obelisk is literally turned inside out, its monumental surface visibility undermined by social rot, not only by being found to be hollow inside but, furthermore, to contain a makeshift shelter for the homeless, wallpapered with porn magazine cuttings. What is more, the ascent of the monument by the youths does not yield any panoramic shots across the city below, as a kind of momentous and compensatory visual empowerment of the disenfranchised (an image that recurs instead, as we shall see below, in night-in-the-city films such as *Vagón fumador* and *Ronda nocturna*). In fact, it is actively withheld from us here as Frula (Walter Díaz) stands by one of the window openings, turning his back on the spectacle of lights we can only just glimpse behind him. On the other hand, the melodrama's affective connotations of La Boca and the riverfront – as a simpler, more honest and authentic world than the treacherous centre – are being mobilised in *Pizza* to signify El Cordobés and Sandra's fleeting dream of another life,[75] only to be crossed out by the final shot over the muddy waters from the departing ferry, while on the soundtrack a police radio confirms the death of El Cordobés and all the other youths involved in the failed *bailanta* raid. Only at first, this extremely long shot can be attributed to a subjective camera observing from the place of Sandra. Instead, its sheer extension as it slowly recoils from the scene draws attention to the distance and exteriority in which *our* own gaze is caught in relation to the marginalised youths, and calling into question our capacity to empathise, previously teased out by the La Boca sequence.

Pizza's 'archaeology of the present' (Page), then, both reinscribes and crosses out a previous cinematic Buenos Aires, its crisis becoming visible in the process. Two other films, both produced in 2001, the year in which the crisis of neo-liberal economics peaked, also approach the city's new margins. Both Luis Ortega's impressive debut *Caja negra* (*Black Box*) and Ana Poliak's *La fe del volcán* (*The Faith of the Volcano*) share Caetano's and Stagnaro's 'neo-realist' strategy of casting non-professional actors in real locations, using light camera equipment and an almost total absence of staging to produce 'reality effects' of an uncanny directness. Both films, moreover, resort to the device – also employed in *Pizza* – of introducing a 'real' actor (Dolores Fonzi, Jorge Prado) among its non-professional cast, thus calling attention, as in a Brechtian alienation effect, both to the artifice, the *work* of acting – and thus to the staged, fictional character of the narratives – and, by contrast, to the individual and historical experience borne out by the non-actors and real-time locations.

In both films, moreover, this fictional emplotment of real characters and situations is related to some form of bridging the social gap dividing urban society. In *Caja negra*, the impressive Eduardo Couget – a homeless street beggar from the San Telmo neighbourhood – plays a character of the same name who, on his release from prison, seeks refuge at the Salvation Army and makes his living begging for alms outside the Shell gas station on Paseo Colón (the same spot where the real-life Couget works). There, he is tracked down by his daughter Dorotea (Fonzi), who works at the local dry cleaners and cares for her elderly grandmother (Eugenia Bassi, the director's neighbour in real life, at whose home the film's interiors were shot). Without revealing anything about the characters' past (the traumatic and violent character of which it nonetheless signifies in an intercalated dream sequence of Eduardo's naked, emaciated body writhing in pain), the film follows Dorotea's patient, and mostly silent, attempts to reunite her family, dressing and taking her sick father to a doctor and, finally, organising dinner for all three of them at her grandmother's home. Although the film is not without weaknesses (such as the non-diegetic music, which introduces an aesthetics of affect unjustified by either narrative or composition), it is nonetheless remarkable in the way it stages crisis simply by inserting the weak, ravaged body of Eduardo into the urban flow. Thus, his pedestrian crossing of the city from the Devoto prison to San Telmo is narrated in a quick succession of shots observing him inside the crowd, from which he is at the same time set apart by his laborious and shaky pace. The rhythm of editing exposes the frailty and exteriority of Eduardo as it syntonises with a space-time continuum from which he is excluded, as if he inhabited another dimension. Further on, when he and Dorotea meet during her lunch break, a subjective camera spots him waving at her from the other side of Paseo Colón boulevard, the telescopic lens underscoring the contrast between his immobility and forlornness as he sits on a bench and the relentless flow of the traffic rushing past.

La fe del volcán employs similar shots to single out its two protagonists, the middle-aged knife-grinder Danilo and the adolescent hairdressers' apprentice Anita, as they find solace in each other's company during lunch breaks and on their way home after work. Just as *Caja negra*, Ana Poliak's film takes the real-life city as its location, a hand-held camera following the characters as they walk or cycle down streets and squares bustling with traffic and people, with staging kept to a minimum. Once again, too, this indetermination between a documentary style of narrative and the fictional plot unfolding inside it is mirrored by the contrast between Mónica Donay's more naturalistic, restrained representation of the young Anita and Jorge Prado's theatrical performance as Danilo, calling attention (though without ever interrupting diegetic continuity) to the film's own affinities with street-theatrical experimentation. In one scene, Danilo attempts to cheer up Anita, who has just been fired from her job for accidentally arriving late for work, by acting out a fantasy journey of the two of them to Europe, as they sit on a bench overlooking the basins of Puerto Madero harbour. In another, he role-plays his own imaginary twin brother when the young girl visits him at home. This contrast between acting styles at the same time points to an opposition between the biographical temporalities of the adolescent Anita, in her attempt to cope with the harsh realities of the 1990s, and of the middle-aged Danilo, whose monologues return almost compulsively to the dictatorship as (we are left to guess) the traumatic origin of his damaged personality. This unresolved past, which inside the narrative returns as an 'over-acted' theatricality, also frames the plot in a sequence of autobiographical reflections on the director's own depressive crisis in her youth, which had led her to attempt suicide. Set to a voice-over of Poliak's mother remembering the events, the film starts with a camera exploring the bleak, derelict interior of an abandoned house (the director's own childhood home). Further on, Poliak returns to the interconnectedness between internal – psychic – and external – social – crisis, which arguably is the very subject of *La fe del volcán*, through intercalated shots of opaque, misty windows in the director's flat through which we glance at the city. In a particularly harrowing take, all we see are Poliak's own hands on the other side of a wet shower glass-pane. As Joanna Page argues:

> many of these shots suggest ideas of interiority and exteriority, and of transparency and opacity, which are crucial to the film's use of the image. […] If the image here obscures as much as it reveals, it is perhaps because for Poliak, visibility does not necessarily bring knowledge or understanding: her characters must deliberately remain 'other' to us, and meaning resides in the out-of-field, the offscreen, in past events and

inner experience that are inaccessible to us. [...] The film hangs back from imposing a narrative because it constructs the relationship between past and present as indeterminable and as a site of trauma.[76]

Poliak herself has referred to her work as 'a cry of despair in the darkness of *menemismo*, when I felt that something just had to burst, that it was going to burst'.[77] If her film could then be understood as the performative re-enactment of a relation between internal and external crisis, the origins of which are shown to be historical as well as biographical (although the relation between the two remains a mystery, both with respect to the fictional character of Danilo and to Poliak herself, who can only return to the wound at the core of her own self by projecting it outward), the final shot nonetheless provides, if not a solution then at least a way forward. In a dissociative cut from a close-up on Anita's hand resting on the quilt cover of Danilo's bed, the film moves to a several minutes-long tracking shot moving alongside Anita, as she walks on a dirt track running parallel to a motorway, perhaps returning to her home in the suburbs. At first, a voice-over from Danilo accompanies her walk, riffing away on the theme of Kafka's short story 'The Departure': "away from here, that is my destination" – perhaps in a last, desperate attempt to explain himself to her. Yet when he finally falls silent, the shot goes on for several minutes more, as if opting to stay with Anita's present – and presence – in an image that has finally freed itself of all verbal, allegorical and theatrical ballast, to turn instead into pure observation.

Reconstructing community

Gustavo Aprea observes that many of the narratives of recent Argentine cinema feature small groups having to face a hostile reality confronting them from the 'outside'.[78] Although this is perhaps an over-generalization, Aprea is right in claiming this model for a particular form of narrative which articulates plot constructions with wider patterns of historical experience in present-day Argentina. Specifically, it obtains with regard to a host of films addressing the crisis of the urban from a different social and cultural location than the ones studied in the previous section of this chapter: that of a more accommodated middle class threatened with financial decline. Rather than focusing on the margins of urban society, as places in relation to which the camera remains in a position of exteriority that forces us to observe attentively, the films I study next relate to place as a sphere of belonging that must be defended against a hostile exterior, and around which a community can assemble with regained strength. The shared flat in *Sólo por hoy* (*Just for Today* – Ariel Rotter, 2000), the shopping arcade in *El abrazo partido* (*Lost Embrace* – Daniel Burman, 2003), the neighbourhood club in *Luna de Avellaneda* (*Moon of Avellaneda* – Juan José

Campanella, 2004), the debt-stricken upper-class condo in *Cama adentro* (*Live-in Maid* – Jorge Gaggero, 2004), the family restaurant and the tango bar in *El hijo de la novia* (*Son of the Bride*, Juan José Campanella, 2001) and *Bar 'El Chino'* (Daniel Burak, 2003), are examples of such places of shelter and reconstruction of community.

In these films, urban space is experienced differently from the ones discussed above, also resulting in a different relation between screen space and film-theatre space. If, in the films concerned with the margins of urban society, this relation is one of separation and exteriority, where our gaze is actively denied the means of identifying with the onscreen world, being forced to remain – along with the camera itself – in the position of an external observer, the films I study here are all concerned with reconstructing spaces of community. This also endows them, I shall argue, with a particular self-reflexivity (more explicitly marked in Burak's film than in Burman's and Campanella's) as the stories they tell are always also about cinema and its audience. Gonzalo Aguilar has argued that an opposition between nomadism and sedentarism underwrites contemporary Argentine cinema and its relation to social, affective and geographical space.[79] Whereas the nomadic movement follows bodies-in-motion that have lost their anchorage on their journey through precarious space – the unbound, the margins – sedentarism is 'a spiralling movement toward the inside' that reveals the decomposition of those former places of shelter, of which the home is both the origin and model. Aguilar's proposal is highly suggestive, though we can probably sharpen it further by adding two provisos: firstly, that it is an opposition which also speaks to the fundamentally different ways in which socio-economic crisis has been experienced by different social classes; and secondly, that 'sedentarism's' focus on the home and its prosthetic extensions always entails at least the possibility of narrating not just its crisis but also its recomposition – a possibility of 'return' that is decidedly not available for 'nomadism'.[80]

As 'structures of feeling', then – to use Raymond Williams' expression – these different compositions of urban space as the setting of national crisis also speak to cinema's capacity for incorporating real historical experience through the medium of form.[81] Giving the lie to euphoric readings of a 'multitudinous' cross-class alliance between *piqueteros* (the unemployed) and *caceroleros* (middle-class protesters), contemporary Argentine films through their dissimilar narrative and formal solutions made it clear that, if 'crisis' was (and is) indeed a phenomenon that traverses the whole of society, it does so by widening, rather than reducing, the rifts between different social sectors. Thus, cinema calls into question, as Aguilar suggests, the very idea of a single 'people'. As I have argued, moreover, it is the 'nomadic' strand that incorporates this erosion of the popular bond as the very principle of aesthetic composition, as a gap between viewers and actors. Meanwhile, the 'sedentary' strand is not just about the reconstruction of community onscreen but also that of the cinema as an affective space, inviting us to re-engage, to deposit our trust once more in the camera and let its gaze be ours: a politics of the image, then, which stakes its bets on the recomposition of a (middle-class) audience.

Indeed, some of the films discussed here are among the biggest box-office hits in recent years: according to figures reported by Octavio Getino, Juan José Campanella's *El hijo de la novia* (*Son of the Bride*, 2001) was screened in over 30 countries, with some 1.6 million viewers in Europe alone, making it the biggest commercial success of Argentine cinema in recent years, closely followed by Fabián Bielinsky's *Nueve reinas* (*Nine Queens*, 2000) and *Luna de Avellaneda* (*Moon of Avellaneda*, 2004), also by Campanella, with 1.2 million tickets each sold at the box office.[82] However, what makes these films interesting is the fact that, in order to achieve the desired emotional – and commercial – effect, they first have to acknowledge crisis both diegetically, as part of their spatio-temporal setting, *and* formally, as an erosion of viewers' trust in the conventions of cinematic affect (a side-effect, perhaps, of this same audience's new-found scepticism about the solidity of their bank deposits). As we shall see, the link I suggest here between monetary bust-up and cinematic productions of affect is less fanciful than it might seem. Juan José Campanella's films in particular are intriguing in the way they mobilise spectatorial empathy by first taking us through disaffection. Thus, they register the crisis of the social bond both in terms of diegetic action *and* as a crisis of cinema's traditional role as a 'dream factory' capable of releasing viewers, albeit temporarily, from the constraints and frustrations of everyday experience. Reminiscent of Frank Capra's cinema during the United States' Great Depression, Campanella expertly wields elements of melodrama and comedy to forge a mode of social commentary at the same time as promising us that, however grave the problems society faces, they can still be emotionally resolved within a classical genre framework. Thus, they both situate cinema in a critical dialogue with the social present *and* offer it up as an alternative to, or escape from, the latter – an interior space of dreams akin to the ones which are in a sense the real heroes of onscreen action: the family restaurant in *El hijo de la novia* and the neighbourhood social club in *Luna de Avellaneda*.

In *El hijo de la novia*, this ambivalent and complex relation between realism and genre is marked through the subplot that has the two male leads – Rafa (Ricardo Darín) and Juan Carlos (Eduardo Blanco) – take part as extras in a film shooting: incidentally, as customers in a restaurant scene, in a kind of mirror image of the 'real' family restaurant where much of the action takes place. At one point, Campanella's camera takes up the viewpoint of the fictional camera, as we watch Rafa and Juan Carlos ruin the take by clashing violently in the background of the image; all the while the 'main actor' in the foreground unsuspectingly recites his vapid, pseudo-Shakespearean monologue. The scene is a clever pun on genre and the eruption of the real: for, of course, even while it relegates its heroes to mere extras in 'another' film, *El hijo* in fact never ceases to build the scene around them, and their interruption of the fictional scene is not so much that of an external 'reality' bursting through the celluloid fantasies of cinematic illusion but rather returns us to classical melodrama, the motive of their fight being Juan Carlos' infatuation with Rafa's girlfriend Naty (Natalia Verbeke). Earlier on, Juan Carlos (who actually makes a precarious living from stunts as a film extra) had introduced himself to Rafa, his childhood friend, as 'an actor', prompting the latter to admit that "I don't watch Argentine cinema … you know how it is, running around all day just to pay the bills." To which Juan Carlos replies, after a theatrical pause: "I don't watch Argentine reality."

Much of the success of Campanella's movies builds on they way in which they manage to cross the gap ironically acknowledged in this little dialogue: while indeed they do 'watch Argentine reality', the latter is incorporated here not in the observational, documentary fashion associated with contemporary Argentine cinema but by taking it through the motions of classic Hollywood-style melodrama, centred on the crisis and recomposition of the couple and, by extension, the community at large. With an almost identical cast, *El hijo de la novia* and *Luna de Avellaneda* are but two variations of the successful formula inaugurated by the former: the mid-life crisis of its male lead (played both times by Ricardo Darín) providing the reference point of recognition and affective investment for crisis-stricken audiences. In both films, moreover, it is precisely the larger-scale, socio-economic crisis of Argentine society as a whole which precipitates the Darín character's personal crisis, pushing it to its dramatic climax and subsequent resolution. Darín – and the audience with him – has to hit rock bottom in order to reconnect with the 'true values' of love, friendship, truthfulness and so forth, which he had forsaken in his increasingly desperate, daily struggle to 'be someone' in the hectic, competitive consumer society of the 1990s. As the embattled manager of the Italian restaurant founded by his immigrant parents or as spokesman of the neighbourhood club where his mother had given birth in the midst of a ravishing tango night, Darín is faced in both films with the tempting choice of selling off the debt-ridden venues to foreign investors (a mafia-style Italian restaurant chain in *El hijo*, a faceless consortium seeking to transform the premises into a casino in *Luna*, represented by the career politician Alejandro, his one-time amorous rival). At the same time, his fatalistic resignation alienates Darín from his loved ones – his girlfriend, divorced wife and little daughter in *El hijo*; his wife Verónica (Sonia Kutica) and their children in *Luna* – pushing the family to the brink of dissolution until, following an emotive re-encounter with the material leftovers from a better past (the family portraits decorating the restaurant; the long-lost club membership card), he decides to take a stand and start again from scratch: setting up a new restaurant in the rundown café opposite the old one, or starting a new club with the remaining small band of friends from the neighbourhood. In both films, moreover, this rebirth of faith from the ashes (which also draws Darín's character back into the arms of his female love interest) is prompted by the silent plea of someone who 'has had it worse': Juan Carlos in *El hijo*, who has lost his wife and child in a car accident, and the shantytown girl Dalma in *Luna*, for whom the club's ballet classes (and canteen food) provide a glimmer of hope in a life of hardship.

The political allegory carved out by both films is hardly subtle: in reconnecting with the plight of others ('the poor'), the self-estranged middle-class hero rediscovers his mission in life, which is none other than to save the couple, the family and the nation through love, trust and patriotism. This re-entitlement of the hero is simultaneously a re-empowerment of cinema itself to speak for and on behalf of the nation – a claim which, as we have seen, is being called into question by many of the films exploring the margins of society. Indeed, the self-proclaimed capacity of Campanella's films to allegorically represent the nation's plight sustains itself precisely on the *occlusion* of the margins and the poor: the only image in *Luna* of the shantytown where Dalma lives is shot from afar, literally 'from across the river' from where Darín's Ramón calls her after deciding to allow her free access to the club. The interior spaces where the action transcurs, then, represent 'Argentine reality' at the same time as protecting us from having to 'watch it' – an allegorical dimension that is more explicitly thematised in *Luna*'s club hall than in *El hijo*'s restaurant dining room. Painted in the national colours (which also happen to be those of the club), the sports arena is where the decisive membership assembly takes place, culminating in an oratorial duel between Ramón and Alejandro which restages their former clashes in student politics at university (the moment, Verónica recalls, when she fell in love with Ramón). Here, the antagonism between Alejandro's slick managerial discourse about the need to 'adjust to the times', and Ramón's emotive response about the primacy of immaterial values over cash, is shot in a slow pan that brings into tangible presence the elements of the space dividing them: the national flag and the audience of listeners ('the people').

Daniel Burman's trilogy of films protagonised by Daniel Hendler adopt the same allegorical-affective mode of sentimental comedy in order to narrate and imaginarily resolve 'crisis'. Here, however, the spatial interior standing in for, as well as protecting against, the city of disequality and fear is not so much the allegorical inner *sanctum*, the treasure chamber where the nation's core values have survived intact, as it is a diasporic space of internal difference. First and foremost, it is that of the Jewish community which, faced with the decline of country and city, must reassess its Argentineness and Jewishness – its attachment to place. In *El abrazo partido* (*Lost Embrace*, 2003), Hendler's Ariel must decide on whether or not to emigrate to Europe, taking advantage of his grandmother's (a Holocaust survivor's) Polish passport. In the end, his decision to stay and confront his ties to community and nation is prompted by the return of his father Elías (Jorge D'Elia), whose own decision to emigrate to Israel and enroll, as a volunteer in the battle of Yom Kippur, Ariel discovers, had been provoked by jealousy rather than patriotic fervour: the inability to cope with his mother's fling with a *goym*. As in Campanella's films, then, politics in *El abrazo partido* turn into the politics of the couple; and as in Campanella the sentimental core story is simultaneously framed in that of the crisis and resurgence of the very space that shelters it: here, the rundown shopping arcade where a closely knit community of immigrants (Jewish and others) ply their trade. Yet unlike the unambiguous sentimentalism of *Luna* and *El hijo*, here this spatial enclosure is simultaneously a place of shelter *and* of claustrophobia, its unresolved relation to the city outside marked by Ariel's frantic escapes, the camera panning alongside him as he runs down the busy streets. Unlike Campanella's films, *El abrazo* concludes by conceding the insufficiency of its own politics of figuration: in order to stay, Ariel must confront the story of his parents, but he must also find a way of reconnecting with the surrounding city beyond the false alternative of his mother's self-enclosure in the arcade and his father's escape overseas.

Campanella's – and, to an extent, Burman's – films, in short, simultaneously invoke and disavow the crisis of the city and the nation, which they 'resolve' through their retreat into interior spaces sheltering a core of values that are found to have remained intact at the end of all three films. These values – which the films (*Luna* more explicitly than *El hijo* and *El abrazo*) *claim* to be the same as those voiced by the Argentine people at large – the assembly scene in *Luna* more than once explicitly cites the language of the *asambleas populares* following the December 2001 uprising – are actually none but those of a classical cinema of affect. Yet, interestingly, both Campanella films, as transnational ventures, also counteract in their own production model the affective nationalism they preach. They actively solicit the favours of a global audience by their typified representations of the national (for instance, through the invocation of a gilded age of tango in *Luna*) and by inserting the experience of social crisis into plot structures that maintain an orthodox adherence to rules of genre. Both films were produced by Pol-Ka, the transnational production company part-owned by the Clarín group, Argentina's largest multimedia empire with an important presence of Spanish shareholders, and controlling the majority of private television channels and other news media. The films also received public and private subsidies through the Argentine and Spanish film institutes, and from Spanish television.

Daniel Burak's *Bar 'El Chino'* (2003) offers an interesting counterpoint. In Burak's film, the relation between the crisis of the nation as a socio-affective space of belonging and cinema as a traditional production instance of national-popular affect, which now finds itself caught up in the demands of a *transnational* audio-visual economy – a relationship Campanella's films reference only to disavow their own implication in it – is instead the work's very subject. The title-giving bar, one of the city's last traditional tango hangouts, provides the equivalent here of Campanella's (and Burman's) interior places of shelter, where a vanishing Argentineness (or Jewishness) persists. Yet in Burak's film its authenticity – or rather, our own spectatorial consumption of it – is problematised by the way in which it is shown to be solicited, as a commodity, by highly asymmetric and exploitative global networks. The film, then, critiques the way in which globalisation engages and *places* the local, but without giving up on it altogether. As in Campanella's neo-populist melodramas, the struggle for place is articulated here with the love story plot of the production of the couple. The relation is between the young TV producer Martina (Jimena La Torre) and the seasoned *auteur* Jorge (Boy Olmi) who, in a moment of personal and national crisis (Jorge loses his bank deposits in the 2001 disaster, Martina is unceremoniously fired by her TV station's US mother company), decide to embark together on a documentary on Carlos 'El Chino' Fernández's old tango bar in the far south of Buenos Aires, where they first meet each other. The fact that the real-life El Chino had died in 2001, cutting short an earlier documentary project (archive footage of which is edited into *Bar 'El Chino'*), and the use of real TV footage of the December insurrection, only adds to the complex, refractory relation the film constructs between 'authenticity' and 'fiction' in an inexorably commodified image-world.

As in many of the films discussed above, the lovers' bliss is threatened here by the appearance of a foreign intruder, Jorge's cheesy Spanish agent and financier Jesús, who not only woos Martina with the promise of a well-paid overseas job but also demands prompt delivery of the project supposed to finance the couple's cinematic declaration of love for one another and for their long-lost national roots. This turns out to be a promotional video for the Spanish-owned private highway operator 'Autopistas Argentinas', in which a slick corporate executive with an unmistakably peninsular accent waxes lyrical about the holding's 'spirit of leadership' and 'creation of employment [...] on our journey into the future', to an upbeat tango-fusion soundtrack, while in the background a digital landscape of suburban dirt tracks morphs into a postmodern paradise of lawn-enclosed motorways. It is during their joint struggle to meet the video's delivery deadline, in a frantic three-day editing marathon, that Martina and Jorge become amorously involved – 'national solidarity' in facing the demands of global capital once again blossoming into cinematic affect. Meanwhile, outside the sheltered space of Jorge's home studio, national crisis reaches boiling point: while the lovers put the final touches to their corporate fairy tale, national TV broadcasts the looting of supermarkets by the suburban poor and, finally, de la Rua's on-air declaration of the state of siege. Juxtaposing the video's hollow soundbytes of progress and modernity with TV footage of police repression against protesters, *Bar 'El Chino'* forges an eloquent, self-reflexive statement on the way contemporary image-making industries (TV but also cinema, including independent arthouse) are actively implicated in producing the (dependent) capitalist present, even when – as Jorge's and Martina's documentary on El Chino, or prime-time TV 'exposing' the state's repressive action – they come down on the side of 'the people'.

But, having thus signposted its own implication in the speculary economy it decries, Burak's film nevertheless ends on a different note, in which – similar yet different to Campanella's and Burman's uplifting endings – the crisis of neo-liberalism represents an opportunity for reconnecting with a deeper and more genuine dimension of experience. Unlike in the films discussed earlier, here the reconstruction of the couple shipwrecks under the pressures of economic realities – Martina eventually gives in, if not to Jesús's erotic advances, to his offer of a stable job in Spain – but the values on which their short-lived romance thrived are reasserted in a video-greeting she sends the grief-stricken Jorge through his son Nacho (himself an economic émigré). In this 'other' transnational image travelling the opposite way, she exhorts Jorge to finish their documentary love child and gifts him some extra footage: a declaration by Spanish actor José Sacristán, who insists on the need to pass on to forthcoming generations how, 'regardless of folklorism, tradition, or musical significance, in some moment and at some point on this fucking planet a bunch of humans understood something about friendship, solidarity and affection, as did the people who inhabit, and pass through, El Chino's bar'. Sacristán's statement, counterpointing the Spanish exec's previous video-discourse about the global progress and modernity incarnated in traffic and communication flows (read: capital), reasserts the potential for resistance upheld by locality and place, a resistance that withstands even the threat of being turned into a commodified image. Beyond folklorism – beyond the affect-image of the national so expertly mobilised by Campanella – place as understood by Sacristán and as exemplified in documentary footage of El Chino, as a network of solidarities, retains in Burak's film a universal significance beyond the local, announcing a different kind of globality from the one whose ruinous consequences the film narrates.

Cruising crisis

There is yet another group of films that depict the crisis of the speculative economy and consumerism of the 1990s as one in which their own gaze is deeply implicated: films dealing with the city as an eroticised location, one that is immediately – and intensely – connected with its character of a marketplace, as a stage for the spectacle of the commodity. Cristian Bernard's and Flavio

Nardini's satire *76-89-03* (1999), narrating – in what rather too openly aspires to be a parable of *menemismo* – the cocaine-fuelled nightly adventures of a trio of friends frantically trying to gather an impossible sum of money in order to gift themselves the favours of a TV starlet and high-end prostitute, exemplifies this ambivalence in its formal flirtation with the same televisual grotesque it purportedly criticises. A more subtle and aesthetically satisfying approach to the nocturnal city as, at one and the same time, the dark side of neo-liberalism, and a dream surface of fantasy and flight, is found in several films engaging with the urban experience of sexual minorities. Lesbian, gay, *travesti* and transgender themes have only been taken up very recently in Argentine cinema, partly as the result – explicitly thematised in Santiago García's *Lesbianas de Buenos Aires* (2002) – of gay-lesbian rights struggles over the last few decades. As I have argued in chapter 1, this emergence of 'minority issues' in Argentine film also has its condition of possibility in the diversification (and globalisation) of audiences ensuing from the demise of the last remnants of a national film industry and the rise of video/DVD and cable TV as potential outlets for 'niche productions'.

The emergence and viability of a 'gay-lesbian cinema', then – just as the growing visibility of, and concern for, gay-lesbian 'issues' themselves – is in itself an effect (albeit a positive one) of the neo-liberal fragmentation of society. Thus, also, the attitude towards the 1990s as a moment of crisis is often more ambiguous and complex in these films than in 'straight' ones, where the break-up of a more homogeneous past of clear-cut boundaries is nostalgically decried in terms of loss. Here, instead of the single thread of national history, more complex and contradictory temporalities appear, as well as forms of experiencing and coding urban space which are irreducible to simple oppositions between centre and margin, rich and poor. In films such as Anahí Berneri's *Un año sin amor* (*A Year Without Love*, 2004), Verónica Chen's *Vagón fumador* (*Smokers Only*, 2000), or Edgardo Cozarinsky's *Ronda nocturna* (*Night Watch*, 2005), a more ambivalent relation with the mercantilised city is staged in the gay cruiser and taxi-boy (male prostitute) characters' trawling through multiple urban worlds, from the high-rise apartments of rich clients and friends to rundown street corners and night bars. But rather than – as in Alejandro Chomski's descent-into-prostitution drama *Hoy y mañana* (*Today and Tomorrow*, 2003) – merely as exploitative and reifying, this fluid nightly space of casual encounters is experienced also as an adventurous stage for sexual experimentation and self-performance, in which the appreciation of paying customers induces a raised sense of self. As Andrés, the taxi-boy protagonist of *Vagón fumador*, asserts: "If you don't have a price you have nothing to offer. No value. You're worth nothing. And I love being paid. Being appreciated, being enjoyed."

Rather than remaining external to their characters' joyful display and use of their bodies as commodities, these films actively incorporate the gaze of the market in the way they take us through a stage-like city of erotically charged locations, encouraging our own gaze to indulge in voyeuristic visual pleasures as it targets nocturnal bodies in motion as potential sex objects. Although less convincing than the other two films for its rather wooden acting, *Vagón fumador* is nonetheless interesting in the way its adventurous editing both incorporates the exchange of gazes between sex-workers and their clients in a city that is already spectacle, *and* constructs in this fluctuation of looks a critical, observant distance towards its visual surfaces. The two central characters – the punk *chanteuse* Reni (Cecilia Bengolea) and the bisexual taxi-boy Andrés (Leonardo Brzezicki) – first meet each other here as she watches him having sex with a male client in an ATM cabin: an illuminated fish tank in the urban night, pleasure deriving not so much from the sexual act in itself as from the thrill of its being witnessed by anonymous passers-by. "Everyone can see you here," Reni says to Andrés later on in the film, having tracked him down at another cash dispenser, "doesn't it bother you?" "You also like it when they watch you," he counter-attacks, "don't you?" Both scenes incorporate this pleasure of self-exposure, alternating a camera position outside the cash box – identified with Reni's gaze through a reverse shot of her face – with CCTV footage from a surveillance camera inside, whose presence Andrés' theatrical self-exhibition half-acknowledges, as he puts himself up for visual consumption, a commodified body posing and performing as in a shop window or a film set.

Vagón fumador is at its best in the passages in which it gives itself over to this interplay of gazes in the seedy nocturnal world of the *microcentro*, only loosely connected to the storyline of the two characters seeking each other out, or of Andrés and his taxi-boy friends working the streets: the camera alternating, to a pulsating tango-fusion soundtrack, between hand-held tracking shots of the crowd in motion and close-ups of individuals walking down the pavement or standing on sidewalks and street corners, their 'cool' poses and ambiguous glances echoing Mel Gibson's icy stare from a billboard behind them. A traffic of ambivalent gazes and looks, then, in which our own gaze gets caught up, and in which the look becomes the agent of an always already commodified desire, assessing the merchandise on offer or inviting passers-by to come out as sex-punters, to make their bids. The city becomes an eroticised surface, a libidinal scenography with billboards, neon advertisements and shop windows serving as stage requisites.

Though much slower-paced than *Vagón fumador* – the former's tango-fusion soundtrack, incidentally, giving way here to a more classicist *tango nuevo* score reminiscent of the 1960s, a bandoneon improvising on the syncopated patterns laid out by piano and strings – Edgardo Cozarinsky's *Ronda nocturna* likewise takes us through a nightly melodrama of poses and exchanged glances. Even more than in Verónica Chen's film, the visual rhythm of Cozarinsky's narrative (marking the veteran director's return to the country after almost 20 years working in France) is produced in an alternation between shots of various nightspots loosely based, in a kind of indirect free speech narration, on the taxi-boy Víctor (Gonzalo Heredia) – criss-crossing of the city, and takes of Víctor and his co-workers posing for potential customers, shot from the position of a car moving slowly down the street where they have lined up. Here, then, the shot-reverse shot sequence characteristic of cinematic productions of an affective constellation, in which the viewer's gaze is – albeit in an illusory way – incorporated (the mechanism critical screen studies have analysed through the concept of suture),[83] is actively and immediately associated with the money-form. The interchange of gazes is a sexual bargaining: the negotiation of the value of the encounter which visual pleasure here anticipates – unlike cinema – not just figuratively but literally. The gaze is a prelude to sex, and to sex as a commodity, as Cozarinsky states by intersecting into the street prostitution sequence a combination of shots – edited in exactly the same order – that has Víctor admire a display of shiny trainers in a shop window, complete with their price tags beneath them. Later on in the film, Víctor himself and his friend and ex-colleague, the taxi driver Manuel (Rafael Ferro), drive around the transvestite prostitution district, taking pleasure in the inversion of their role from performers to spectator-consumers – a kind of visual foreplay before they go to bed with each other. But if the city is therefore an erotic space – a space of arousal of mobile bodies through visual stimuli: a *cinematography* – the taxi-boy as the inhabitant of this traffic network of flows of cash and desire is also, literally, an urban emblem. Cozarinsky captures this iconic dimension of the taxi-boy beautifully in a shot of Víctor's face and torso set against the background of an illuminated subway map, anticipating several of the 'stations' he will pass through on his journey through the night.

Figure 5   The taxi-boy (Gonzalo Heredia) as an urban emblem in Edgardo Cozarinsky's Ronda nocturna *(2005).*

Both Chen's and Cozarinsky's films, then, refrain from victimising their taxiboy characters, their agency as performers and seducers being asserted in the way they are granted access, in both *Vagón fumador* and *Ronda nocturna*, to panoramic viewing platforms – a rooftop, a glass elevator – literally lifting their gaze over the city below. Rather than power, the elevated viewing position here connotes unboundedness, the way in which the taxi-boy, as a star performer, the object of the gaze and desire of others, nevertheless remains a free agent, literally above the streams of affect represented by the movement of lights in the city below. But this elevation from the profane goings-on on ground level, the way in which Chen's and Cozarinsky's films are themselves very much in thrall to their taxi-boy protagonists' magic, also makes their own relation with the city somewhat distant and abstract. And even if, as in *Ronda nocturna*, Víctor's nightly odyssey is counterpointed by the appearance of a family of *cartoneros*, rubbish collectors, who he runs into several times on his way from one encounter to the next, these appearances of 'the social' here remain purely ornamental and without any real bearing on the main plot: pure surface images of an otherness which, if anything, serve as contrast highlighting the beauty and grace of Víctor and his friends. As the night progresses, the spectre of Aids (and thus of transience and death, the invisible 'downside' of prostitution) likewise appears briefly in Víctor's and Mario's conversation – but *Ronda nocturna* prefers not to go there and to stray, instead, into tango allegories which, rather than surreal, come across merely as self-indulgent. Just as *Vagón fumador*, it is finally an ambiguous fragmented film – its refusal to cohere into a single story being, in part, justified by the characters' own ambivalent, both immersed and distant, attitude towards the city they inhabit.

Anahí Berneri's *Un año sin amor* is a more substantial exploration of the gay city, despite being considerably less of an 'urban' film than Chen's and Cozarinsky's. To quote Martin Lefebvres' useful distinction, Buenos Aires throughout *Un año sin amor* remains a *setting*, a space subordinate to the story occurring inside it, and only very rarely turns into *landscape*, as 'space freed from eventhood', the 'camera's lingering making [it] pregnant with significance'.[84] Here, this 'lingering' gaze is not external to diegetic action but is itself identified with the central character's plight: its excessive duration – its lingering – is akin to a desiring gaze seeking fulfilment in the object of visual pleasure, yet it is simultaneously the gaze of an 'ethnographic' curiosity (the camera's and our own) longing to enter and to behold a space of otherness. As Catherine Russell suggests, ethnography and pornography in cinema often coincide in a kind of scopophilia – a longing to see – in which the 'other' who is posited as the object of the gaze can be both controlled and contained as an object of possession and release despite this containment 'a supplementary discourse of violence and wildness. The field of the Other is rendered exotic and erotic precisely by virtue of the apparatus of vision.'[85]

Yet in *Un año sin amor* this lingering gaze exploring the terrain of the other is also a line of visual flight from the film's central concern with a body in pain, an anxious body. Pablo Pérez (Juan Minujín), the film's central character (and the author-hero of the autobiographical novel on which it is based), is a young, gay poet and HIV-positive. Months ago, he has returned from Paris, where his former lover has died from Aids-related diseases, trying to remake his life in Buenos Aires by publishing, and responding to, relationship ads in gay magazines, while he consults various doctors and experiments with self-medication in an effort to restore his own rapidly deteriorating health. The year is 1996, the moment when the drug cocktails, which (at least for those with medical coverage) transformed HIV from a death sentence into a chronic condition, were first introduced. After some initial resistance Pablo agrees to participate in a trial of the new medication, his new-found motivation to live stemming from an initiatory, transformative encounter with the gay SM subculture where he eventually finds – and almost immediately loses again – an object of love.

Pablo's anxious obsession with his own body and its signs of deterioration or recovery (which he records on forms and charts, along with the diary he keeps of his self-medicating experiments) is echoed in the film's predilection for close-ups, and more generally in the extremely well-composed, orderly set-up of most shots. Berneri's camera, in other words, takes up a position approaching Pablo's own self-obsession – the way in which little things, mostly medicines and herbal extracts, take on an emotional value as the external deposits of his struggle against, and intimacy with, death. Yet at times this proximity not just to the objects surrounding him but to Pablo's own body also refers to the medical gaze and its apparatuses, which fragment, cut up and reframe this body in a fashion that is (as Walter Benjamin already knew) not unlike cinema's own. In this alternation between two forms of visual discipline, which is also one between two interior spaces – Pablo's flat and the clinic – and which lends much of the film an extremely clean, almost antiseptic appearance, Pablo's escapes to go cruising in the nightly city are the only moments of release from this tense, anxiously maintained order. Just as for Pablo himself, these sequences of short, hand-held shots of people, signs and lights in the street provide brief moments of flight for our gaze, freed from the cocoon of discipline and introspection in which it had been caught. Here, moreover, the 'street scenes' also serve as a visual prelude to the similarly mobile and fragmented sequences in which the camera explores (once again loosely identified with Pablo's own curious, voyeuristic gaze) the underworld of the sadomasochist orgies taking place in specially fitted basement torture chambers under the auspices of the patriarchal Comisario (Osmar Nuñez), where Pablo meets his love-interest Martín (Javier van de Couter).

Berneri's portrayal of the SM community is one of considerable delicacy, avoiding the freakish and showing us instead a closely-knit space where friendship and love but also altogether more mundane emotions such as jealousy and narcissism hold sway. Yet, even more than the street scenes, the orgy sequences (with their stark, if only glimpsed at, displays of real sex shot, as Berneri and Pérez have explained, at an SM party specially convened for the purpose of the film) also introduce into the film an excess, a 'wildness' uncontainable in the 'ethnographic', *cinéma-vérité* protocols of jump cuts and hand-held pans. Although their liminal and transformative function is ultimately re-conducted into the diegesis (serving as a kind of awakening for Pablo who, through these rituals of physical and visual pleasure of violence and punishment, advances towards a more open and forward-looking relationship with his own body, eventually accepting to try out the new medication), in these sequences the profilmic perforates narrative closure in much the same way as do the bodies of the poor in Poliak's and Ortega's films discussed earlier in this chapter. But if, in these, the 'naturalist' image of the other's body called forth an extreme experience of socio-economic crisis as utter destitution and expulsion, here 'naturalism' alerts us to *other temporalisations, other histories*, in which this same crisis intersects with the tension between curiosity and containment, sexual exploration and self-enclosure in a body in pain, experienced by a young gay man in the mid-1990s.

Cities in transit

If cinema, as I have argued in this chapter, encounters in the city a way of locating crisis – of staging, at the intersection of multiple trajectories and temporalities, the dislocation, yet also reassertion, of what Doreen Massey calls 'the event of place'[86] – then films dealing with experiences of migration, diaspora and exile capture this fragmentary and disjointed character of the cinematic city better than any other. During the consumption-based economic bubble of the 1990s, maintained through the heavily subsidised monetary parity of 'one peso, one dollar', Argentina became the destination of a sizeable community of economic migrants, not merely from neighbouring countries such as Paraguay, Bolivia or Peru – from where Argentine middle classes have for a long time sourced their domestic personnel, as well as builders, waiters, sweatshop workers and other low-pay, untrained manual labourers – but also from such faraway places as Korea, West Africa or the former Soviet Union (several ex-members of which signed an immigration treaty with Argentina in 1992 to alleviate the Eastern bloc's post-1989 economic breakdown). During the crisis leading up to the default of Argentina's economy and the massive devaluation of the national currency, the total of emigrants (including former immigrants returning to their home countries as well as Argentines leaving theirs) once again exceeded the number of those arriving, yet another indicator of the country's changing fortunes. Many, however, simply could not afford to return or had nowhere to go to, leaving them with no choice but to adapt to a suddenly impoverished and less welcoming city.

The migrant stranded in a place which, rather than a safe haven, suddenly turns out to be afflicted with socio-economic turmoil, suffers a double dislocation, cut off both from the home he left behind and from the destination which, at some point, seemed to hold a better future. Indeed, one of cinema's starkest images of Argentina's implosion in 2001 is a shot from Eva Poncet, Marcelo Burd and Diego Gachassin's *Habitación disponible* (Room for Rent, 2005) following Ukrainian immigrant Natasha Dimytriuk, as she and her little son walk silently past the crowds assembling on Plaza de Mayo during the December uprising, a puzzled expression of curiosity and disbelief on her face. A trained psychologist at home, in Buenos Aires Natasha can barely scrape together a living as *cafetera*, or selling coffee on the street, and it is perhaps her own shattered dream of a better life elsewhere, which she recognises in the scornful expression of the pot-banging protesters. Yet this shared plight does not necessarily forge a space of solidarity and understanding, as the camera panning around her in a circular movement insinuates, singling her out from the crowd rather than including her in the latter as she slowly walks away from the square, urging her excited little boy away from a fight in which she seems to feel she has no part.

The migrant experience, in Poncet, Burd and Gachassin's documentary as well as in Israel Adrián Caetano's fiction feature *Bolivia* (2001), offers a displaced vantage point on a city and country in crisis, literally putting these into perspective as it inserts them into alternative trajectories and temporalities, allowing Argentine audiences an (auto-)ethnographic view of themselves as seen from elsewhere. But elsewhere, as Martín Rejtman's masterful documentary *Copacabana* (2006) on the Bolivian community living in the Flores neighbourhood west of centre demonstrates, is also right here, a semi-autonomous and self-enclosed portion of the city that is connected to different economic and affective networks than the rest, and where Argentines (such as Rejtman himself and the gaze his film works onto his audience) rather than Bolivians are the 'outsiders'.

Both *Habitación* and *Copacabana* are documentaries that fall squarely into what Bill Nichols calls the observational mode, in which the production of insight is delegated exclusively to the camera rather than an omniscient narrator's voice-over, yet also without any reference to the camera's presence in, and impact on, the world into which it ventures, as in the interactive and reflexive modes of documentary film-making.[87] Yet this absence of explicit markers of the film crew's interference here turns itself into a powerful trope of reflecting on the radical disjuncture between the migrants' urban experience and the city of the locals, a way of capturing, on the level of the cinematic form, the exteriority of the former and of making strange the familiar settings of the latter. Observation serves as a way of incorporating into the documentary form itself the distance and strangeness between, on the one hand, the city inhabited by film-makers and audience and, on the other, that of the subjects of the narrative: parallel worlds, literally, despite sharing the same streets, shops and apartment blocks.

An emblematic location in both *Habitación* and *Copacabana* – as well as in *Bolivia* – of this 'other', migrant space is the *locutorio*, or telephone centre, from where the immigrants make contact with their loved ones at home. In both *Habitación* and *Copacabana* the immigrants' solitude and isolation is doubly marked in these emotionally charged sequences, the camera remaining on the other side of the telephone cabin's glass panels, while on the soundtrack we witness one half of a conversation, the speakers often frantically trying to sound upbeat and reassuring, attempting to unmake in the course of a few minutes the distance and absence that is at the same time highlighted through the very construction of the shot. A particularly striking sequence in *Habitación disponible* shows Natasha and her son on the phone to relatives or friends in Ukraine, their separation from us and them doubly marked by the glass panel and by the used-up telephone cards Natasha's son presses against it, displaying a stylised world map. Spliced in between these shots of mother and son, while

Figure 6 Natasha and her son at the telephone centre in Habitación disponible (Room for Rent – E. Poncet, M. Burd and D. Gachassin, 2005). *The migrant experience of displacement and diaspora, and its relation to economic globalisation, is emblematically captured here in the shot-reverse-shot sequence of the telephone cabin from the outside and the street seen from inside the cabin.*

the conversation continues on the soundtrack (impenetrable to us due to their use of Ukranian), are views from the cabin onto the street outside, deliberately out of focus as if to underscore the withdrawal from external space experienced by the intrafilmic bearers of the look. These shots, then, draw us into an affective interior whose language we cannot understand, being able only to guess potential meanings from the inflection of a voice or the smile on a face. Reflected in the glass in one of these shots from inside the phone cabin is a sentence in Spanish from a sign, perhaps a traffic education poster, urging 'the entire family to please use safety belt' – an enigmatic response, the cross-editing of both shots suggests, to the little world maps Natasha's son had pinned against the other side of the same glass barrier, the two together offering a kind of subtitle, framing the scene as in a baroque emblem card, a sign-language conferring a secret meaning on this incomprehensible sequence. Or rather, in our exclusion from communicative exchange – which in fact fashions upon us the very essence of the migrant experience – we are urged to construct meaning from discrete objects and figments of reality, in a kind of ad-hoc bricolage, just as Natasha and the other exiles do on a daily basis.

Habitación disponible follows the daily routines of its three central characters (often, literally speaking, the camera hard on their heels as they walk down streets and corridors). Apart from Natasha, there is Favio from Paraguay, an estate agent and amateur musician, and Giuliana from Peru, a trained engineer who works as a maid and housekeeper for an old retired judge. Their trajectories never cross, inhabiting as they do entirely different spaces of work and lodging, from Favio's posh downtown office and the balconied apartment he shares with his Argentine girlfriend, to Giuliana's cramped, plastic-furnished flat and the judge's tasteful upper-class residence, and to Natasha's single room in the backyard of an orthodox church. In fact, one of the film's main achievements is to bring out, through the cross-editing of its three stories, the diversity of the migrant experience, the characters' lives having little in common apart from an essential infrastructure of foreignness such as the telephone centre. At the same time – and certainly unplanned in the film's original project – the social unrest sparked by rising unemployment and the freezing of bank deposits affects all three characters, prompting them to decide whether to stay or to return: to define the degree of their belonging, an affective as well as economic decision, as Favio's discussions with his girlfriend reveal (the two are planning, at one point, to open a Paraguayan-Argentinian restaurant). Just as Fernández Mouján's documentary through Longhini's sculptures, *Habitación disponible* encounters in the plight of its characters a dislocated vantage point from which to observe the crisis of the city – indeed, one reviewer praised it as the most original and creative documentary on Argentina's economic collapse[88] – which is literally in the background of the image (as when Natasha, on her way to the supermarket, cycles past a street assembly discussing education policies).

Wisely, in editing their material, the directors grant Natasha slightly more screen time than Favio and Giuliana, who are cast in supporting roles: her struggle with the language, moving between Spanish and Ukrainian and sometimes mixing both, and her work in the street make her the richest character from a cinematic point of view, allowing the camera to construct a *spatial expression of cultural distance* as it follows her through the city. Perhaps the most brilliant sequence in this quest is her long conversation – again, in Ukrainian – with her husband midway through *Habitacíon*, the camera attempting to forge a different kind of understanding, in the absence of a linguistic one, by essaying a series of framings, from medium distance shots of both sitting at opposite ends of a table, to over-the-shoulder and frontal views edited in shot-reverse shot sequence, and even to close-ups of objects on the wall or around the table, or shots framed by a half-open door. Here the camera *performs strangeness*, in a way that it cannot in the cases of the more 'assimilated' Favio and Giuliana: but all the same the stories of the other two are necessary in order to provide us with an insight into the way the city and country in crisis are experienced from a foreigner's perspective, thanks to their greater (linguistic) proximity to it and to local cinema audiences. Thus, the attention with which Giuliana listens to, and comments on, the news reports from Peruvian and Argentinian TV (including one, in chilling detail, of the Kosteki and Santillán killing also featured in Fernández Mouján's documentary), and which, despite her indictment that "over there, it's worse than here … people are starving", finally makes her attempt a return to Peru, provide a different measure for assessing the scale and impact of national crisis, as do Favio's discussions with his girlfriend. Interestingly, in the final credits we learn that it was Natasha, of all three, who managed to succeed in Buenos Aires, reuniting her family and finding a flat and employment, whereas Favio returned to Paraguay and Giuliana to Buenos Aires, after a failed move to Peru.

Whereas *Habitación disponible*, then, conveys the migrant experience by following its protagonists – fashioning in the way the camera relates to, yet also departs from, their negotiation of the city, a mode of discourse akin to the free indirect speech of verbal narrative – Martín Rejtman's documentary debut *Copacabana* opts for a different approach to incorporate strangeness and exteriority. Rather than, as in *Habitación*, granting our gaze access to the characters' privacy, gradually building up empathy even though observational distance is never breached by direct engagements of character-to-camera, in Rejtman's film the separation between performance and spectatorship, community and camera-eye, is rigorously marked and maintained throughout. In his account of the feast of the Virgin of Copacabana – the Bolivian community's most important feast – Rejtman makes this separation almost tangible in the medium distance and fixity of the frame registering this highly mobile event and its preparations (the only exception being the long panning shot along a street market, which opens the film). Unlike the camera in *Habitación*, Rejtman's never singles out individual characters, and only rarely provides establishing shots of the Bolivian *barrio*, the medium distance favouring instead the observation of mid-sized groups in particular locations: streets, bars, a sports arena, a basement.

This rigorously composed, indeed photographic, shot – a Rejtman trademark, as we saw in the previous chapter – in being deployed not, as in his fiction features, on a bunch of local urbanites, but on a 'foreign' culture and its rituals, achieves the opposite effect. Rather than 'flattening' the frame suggesting an impoverished, two-dimensional existence, here depth of field is positively enhanced in the way the distance and contrast between the rhythms of camerawork and spectacle urge us to perform an observant, 'ethnographic' viewing. In denying our gaze the visual cues to, literally, find its feet in the dance routines, Rejtman's film actively obstructs any possibility of folkloric typification – the way of 'taming' non-western cultural forms cinema inherited from its nineteenth-century forerunners such as world fairs and dioramas.[89] A masterful example is Rejtman's account of the procession in honour of the Virgin, in which the succession of relatively short, fixed shots of different dance ensembles going through their moves, separated by fades-into-black, establishes a subtle counter-rhythm to the Andean dances of the performers. At the same time as underscoring the non-synchronicity between both – the exteriority of the editing rhythm with respect to the spectacle it contains – this counter-movement nonetheless has the effect of heightening our sensibility for the intricacy and sheer power of the performance it makes us witness.

If the composition of shots in *Copacabana* establishes an insurmountable distance between observation and action, the editing of these in a sequence

Figure 7 The relation between the static camera that never leaves the medium distance and the intensity and movement of the dance procession in Martín Rejtman's Copacabana (2006) works onto the gaze the distance and exteriority city inhabitants experience with regard to immigrant communities, their neighbourhoods and cultural practices.

moving backwards from the procession to its preparations over the year adds to this distance by introducing a counter-temporality. From the parade Rejtman takes us back to the training shifts of dance squads following a labour day in textile sweatshops, preparatory meetings among the 'fraternities' to decide on the marching order, all the way to a bus crossing the Argentine-Bolivian border: a backwards migration in time. This narrative counter-movement or rewinding, which goes against not just the conventions of continuity editing but also, within Rejtman's film itself, the forward direction of individual shot sequences, eventually associates itself with the time of memory, through the film's only voice-over spliced in about midway through *Copacabana*. Here a Bolivian musician (who we never see on camera) displays an album of postcards featuring the national monuments and natural marvels of his native country. *Copacabana*, then, presents us with a mnemonic, idealised Bolivia, crafted for the sake of having something to hold on to in the distance – a diasporic dreamland. Yet Rejtman's own time-travel back to the charmless border town of Villazón does not simply reveal 'the truth' underneath this mythical narrative. Rather, his shot composition and editing incorporate the counterpointed rhythms of memory and performance to register from a critical third space of observation the construction of diasporic community, including the way in which it perforates and redraws the boundaries between the two countries.

Whereas *Habitación* and *Copacabana* construct the space of migration as one that unbinds and fragments the city, *Bolivia*, Israel Adrián Caetano's low-budget migration and racism drama, concentrates the tensions of this impoverished city haunted by unemployment and social descent in the theatrical, interior space of a bar – not the tastefully decorated Italian restaurant of *El hijo de la novia* but an unpretentious neighbourhood hang-out, refuge to an underclass microcosm of cabbies and drunkards. Caetano splits his attention more or less evenly among the denizens of this little urban crossroads: Enrique (Enrique Liporace), the owner, Rosa (Rosa Sánchez), the Paraguayan waitress, Freddy (Freddy Flores), the Bolivian cook and illegal immigrant whose arrival, negotiation of life abroad and ultimate death provide the film's baseline, Marcelo (Marcelo Videla) and El Oso (Oscar Bertea), two coke-snorting, debt-ridden taxi-driver regulars, the latter of whom will shoot Freddy in a sudden outburst of violence after being ejected from the bar on Enrique's orders. The film narrates the gradual build-up of the tension resulting in Freddy's death, in an almost orthodox observance of neo-realist protocols: filmed on location, using mostly non-professional actors playing 'themselves' (all characters and actors have the same names), with camera movement mostly restricted to pans from one character to another, interspliced with panoramic shots of the bar from above – the place of the wall-mounted TV set, which at times absorbs everyone's gaze. The only sequences shot outside the bar follow Freddy, who is thus singled out from the rest and granted a dimension of depth and complexity beyond the reduced sphere of his work: making a phone call home, being stopped by police, taking Rosa out to a *bailanta*.

Apart from these few exceptions, however, the film's action transcurs entirely inside the bar. *Bolivia* is in many ways a film about place – not in any nostalgic or allegorical fashion, such as the films by Campanella, Burman and Burak analysed above, but using spatial enclosure as a way of studying how people are *emplaced*, being cast into social roles and token representations of themselves by the capital relation in which they are all caught up. Just as the chauvinist xenophobia of El Oso (drawing a superb performance from Bertea), Freddy's own proneness to drink, anger and sexual philandering – as in the night he spends with Rosa at the *bailanta* – are forms of releasing the abuse and pressure both are constantly subjected to under a regime of precarious labour. As the dialogue between Freddy and Enrique at the beginning of the film anticipates – and several of his customers will insist throughout – the latter's preference for illegal immigrant personnel is due to the fact that he can pay them even more exploitative wages than fellow Argentines.

This link between place as locality and as the function assigned to humans in the capitalist production chain – place being where the effects of capitalist accumulation and value extraction are actively embodied, *located* in physical subjects and affective constellations – is established from the outset of the film. The opening dialogue, in which Enrique explains the work routine to Freddy, is set to close-up shots of the empty bar and its work spaces and tools, in a state of rest (it is a Sunday): the coffee machine, the barbecue, a knife with some meat leftovers next to it, the gas cooker, a shelf with salt, oil and vinegar flasks, all presided over by a wall clock marking an exact four seconds while Enrique goes through the bar's opening times. Throughout the film, Caetano will use these close-up shots of objects – now in motion – to remind us that we are in a space of work, the surfaces, tools and elements bearing the marks and scars of years of wear, as if reminding us of their endurance beyond the circumstantial humans operating them. In a second sequence of close-ups, just after Freddy has made his first phone call home, the grill and coffee machine are re-encountered churning out hamburgers and espressos, worked by Enrique, Rosa and Freddy, sweating under their peak-time workload. What makes the sequence stand out is not just its propension to single out objects and faces – the close-up representing, as film theorists from Béla Balász to Gilles Deleuze have insisted, a way of incrementing affective intensity through isolation from surrounding space, making us see things and faces in their singularity[90] – but also the slow-motion projection of the entire sequence as well as, finally, its setting to a Bolivian *huayno* sung in Quechua by the band Los Kjarkas (the same non-diegetic music which, at the beginning of the film, had counterpointed the TV transmission of a football match between Bolivia and the victorious Argentinians, insisting, as it were, on the former's dignity in defeat).

Figure 8 A shot from the slow-motion sequence in Israel Adrián Caetano's Bolivia (2001), following Freddy's telephone conversation with his family at home. Time and space are out of joint, as the editing itself mimics the migrant experience, at the same time as it reveals the alienated and exploitative relationships transcurring in Enrique's bar.

Among film scholars, the sequence has prompted some debate. Christian Gundermann suggests that close-ups, temporal and sound/image disjunctures here operate an effect of defamiliarisation, which cuts 'right through the conventionality that has constructed the world for us as commodity and as consumer object'. Defamiliarisation – making the everyday strange – he argues, is foremost among new Argentine cinema's 'strategies that aim at interrupting the flow of desire in late capitalism, attempts at providing a critical interstice'.[91] Joanna Page, contesting Gundermann's reading, suggests instead that 'the defamiliarising effect of this technique [...] is less at the service of contesting commodity fetishism and more in the interests of according human dignity to human labor [...] in a redemption of the material and the everyday for the purposes of lyricism'.[92] While both critics have a point – the sequence certainly disrupts our perception of the bar space, as constructed by the rest of the film's more conventional continuity editing, and yet it has a lyrical rather than Brechtian rhythm – neither of them repairs on the folkloric musical score, which associates this and other sequences to Freddy, as well as the fact that it comes right after his telephone conversation with his family at home. Taking into account its double association, by editing sequence and soundtrack, with 'somewhere else' – Bolivia – the sequence also acquires an intradiegetic motivation which, if it does not contradict the critical and counter-illusionist function ascribed to it by Gundermann and Page, nevertheless re-attributes it, as a dimension of the experience of alienness and exile, to Freddy. Defamiliarisation and strangeness, in other words, are concepts that obtain here because the space of the familiar – the neighbourhood bar – is already defamiliarised as one of uneven encounters between multiple trajectories between place and the out-of-place. Estrangement is at the very root of the violence that explodes in the film's final moments, yet it is also shown in *Bolivia* to produce its very opposite, the all too familiar: the stereotype. Strangeness and familiarity co-inhabit, and thus indeed produce, place: as in *Habitación disponible* and *Copacabana*, relations of closeness and distance in the composition of the shot provide a way of negotiating, in film form itself, the dimensions of strangeness and uprooting experienced by migrants and *porteños* alike. But if the former suffer from their effects because of their displacement from home, the latter – as I have argued in this chapter – experience estrangement because the city they thought they were inhabiting has all but collapsed.

Chapter Three

Margins of Realism
Exploring the Contemporary Landscape

The landscape, film historian Martin Lefebvre suggests, makes its appearance in film where narrative comes to a halt. As distinct from the setting – 'the scenery of and the theatre for what will happen' – landscape for Lefebvre 'is space freed from eventhood',[93] similar to the emancipation of the landscape genre in Renaissance painting from its subordination to religious or historical anecdote. This appearance onscreen of space in and for itself requires *another* way of seeing, just as, in painting, the acknowledgement of landscape as an autonomous aesthetic object had come about as the result of a new, critical engagement with visual form rather than religious content alone. In an analogy with feminist screen studies' model of the double framing of the (female) star's body, Lefebvre suggests that different modes of spectatorship – one narrative, the other spectatorial – are simultaneously put to work in the construction of cinematic space, which they behold alternately as narrative setting and as autonomous, idiosyncratic landscape. In contemporary cinema, landscape therefore often manifests itself 'according to two distinct strategies: landscapes appear either during lulls in the story *(temps morts)*; or they appear in moments free of any diegetic motivation. In the first case, it is the story's space, the setting, which becomes autonomous and acquires the value of landscape; in the second, the story's space gives way to another space, a space that is "displaced" or arbitrary in terms of the narrative progress.'[94]

I would add that, in Argentine cinema as much as elsewhere, the landscape is also already invested with a repertoire of cultural, historical and political meanings even *before* it becomes filmic space – and this iconographic dimension inevitably permeates both the diegetic setting and the landscape which envelops and exceeds it. In Argentina's cultural tradition, rural and natural locations signal not just an opposition to the city and the values of modernity and cosmopolitanism associated with it, but they also, from the writings of twentieth-century philosophers and cultural theorists such as Carlos Astrada, Ezequiel Martínez Estrada or Rodolfo Kusch, promise a more truthful and substantial insight into the reality and plight of the nation, unvarnished with the port-city's superficial and delusive mirages of civility. During the frantic sell-off of state assets in the 1990s, resulting in the wholesale closure of the national rail network as well as of sugar refineries, mines and oilfields and dragging entire regions to the brink of abandonment, the interior was also the place where the social impact of neo-liberal 'structural adjustment' made itself felt long before city-dwellers found their bank deposits confiscated in 2001, adding a sense of urgency to the mid-century, high-modernist images of a more 'real' and 'authentic' interior. Incidentally, it was also from the interior that social resistance against the neo-liberal model originated in the roadblocks of laid-off oil and railway workers (*piqueteros*) in Patagonia, Salta and Jujuy in 1996 and 1997 and in civic uprisings in Catamarca and Santiago del Estero between 1993 and 1997, which eventually succeeded in overthrowing the criminal camarillas, allied with the Menem government, which had ruled these provinces since the dictatorship of 1976.[95]

Contemporary Argentine cinema is once more being drawn to this interior space of misery and rebellion in what Gonzalo Aguilar has called a 'nomadic movement', manifest through 'erratic itineraries and displacements towards the world of leftovers, vagrancy, and delinquency (all that which capitalism aims to place, imaginarily, at the margins)'.[96] Rural space had been a constant screen presence right from the outset of national film-making. Works such as Humberto Cairo's silent movie *Nobleza gaucha* (*Gaucho Nobility*, 1915), Argentina's first blockbuster, loosely adapted from the national epic *Martín Fierro* praised the simple and honest country folk under threat from greedy and lascivious urbanites. This became an oft-repeated formula in works such as José Agustín 'El Negro' Ferreyra's *La gaucha, un poema de los campos* (The Gaucho Girl, a Country Poem, 1921) or Mario Soffici's *Viento Norte* (*North Wind*, 1937), based on an episode from Lucio V. Mansilla's literary classic *An Excursion to the Ranquel Indians*.[97] However, also from very early on, a different image of the interior as the violent frontline of capitalist accumulation emerged in films such as Alcides Greca's expressionist *El último malón* (*The Last Indian Attack*, 1917) – one of the few surviving Argentine silent movies, which re-staged with native extras the 1904 uprising of the Mocoví Indians of Santa Fe[98] – looking forward to the depiction of rural labour and oppression in Soffici's *Prisioneros de la tierra* (*Prisoners of the Land*, 1939), based on short stories by Horacio Quiroga and partly shot on yerba plantations in the tropical north, or Hugo del Carril's *Las aguas bajan turbias* (*River of Blood*, 1952), where the bleak realities of rural misery, oppression and sexual exploitation are counterpointed by the dream of a better life 'further south', leading up to a violent climax of rebellion and flight. Fernando Birri's *Los inundados* (*Flooded Out*, 1961), in its semi-documentary realism accompanying a family of displaced rural poor on their odyssey to the city, marks the high point of this naturalist strand of cinematic ruralism.[99]

Both tendencies – costumbristic and expressive-naturalistic – would be fused together in the militant cinema of the 1970s, prompting an allegorically coded, politicised re-reading of the national-popular tradition in works such as Leonardo Favio's *Juan Moreira* (1973) or Fernando E. Solanas' *Los hijos de Fierro* (*The Sons of Martín Fierro*, 1972–75), both of which draw on the nineteenth-century epic of social banditry in order to narrate the political plight of the working class and their leader-hero, Perón. Here rural space becomes an allegory of historical time, its vast, empty extensions literally opening up the stage for revolution. Likewise, the epic flight towards the Cordillera of Patagonian working-class strikers escaping violent military repression in Héctor Olivera's *La Patagonia rebelde* (*Rebellion in Patagonia*, 1974) employs the natural sublime as a utopian image of historical redemption.

A weak echo of these politically-charged images of landscape returns in post-dictatorship road movies such as Carlos Sorín's *La película del rey* (*A King and His Movie*, 1986) or the final part of Solanas' *Sur* (*The South*, 1988) – now, however, the images of rural emptiness are not so much a figure of futurity as a space where to come to terms with historical defeat, a refuge from, as well as a site of mourning for, experiences of exile, solitude and loss. Sorín returned to Patagonia in 2002 to make the wonderfully laconic *Historias mínimas* (*Minimal Stories*, 2002), an anti-road movie shot almost entirely with local non-actors and drawing in its interweaving of experiences from different classes and generations a subtle portrait of society in this far-off, near-deserted region. Yet just as Solanas himself a decade earlier in *El viaje* (*The Voyage*, 1990), Sorín in his subsequent films *El perro* (*Bombón: El Perro*, 2004) and *El camino de San Diego* (*The Road to San Diego*, 2006) relapses into the conventions and clichés of the genre, reducing the presumably 'documentary' images of places and their inhabitants to mere token illustrations and exoticist stereotype, the more emaciated and weather-beaten the better. In other films including Eduardo Milewicz's *La vida según Muriel* (*Life According to Muriel*, 1997), veteran director Adolfo Aristarain's *Lugares comunes* (*Common Ground*, 2002), or Lucía Puenzo's debut *XXY* (2007), the use of remote, solitary natural settings remains likewise conventional, if now in a psychologising rather than social-realist fashion.

The more interesting examples of contemporary Argentine cinema, I would argue, revisit the cinematic, literary and political archive of landscape in a double movement: on the one hand, in a critical redeployment of its genre elements (the road movie, the rural melodrama), their conventions clashing with the intrinsic rhythms of place; on the other, by reinventing an expressive naturalism in order to reveal the impulsive, violent underpinnings of history. In its most radical expression – the films of Lisandro Alonso – this neo-naturalism, immersing itself into the 'otherness' of marginal places, also returns to the ethical and political questions first raised by the militant cinema of the 1960s and 1970s, about the possibility of forging empathy and solidarity from the distance in which, as viewers, we find ourselves with respect to the object of our gaze.

North / South: ends of the road

Pablo Trapero is among the most prolific of young Argentine film-makers who have made the reworking of genre traditions their way of apprehending the social present of the nation. Among these, the road movie seems a personal favourite: three of Trapero's six feature-length films employ elements from the genre. Yet whereas *Familia rodante* (*Rolling Family*, 2004) falls squarely into the road-movie category, *Nacido y criado* (*Born and Bred*, 2006) and, previously, *Mundo grúa* (*Crane World*, 1999) draw on its grammar merely for particular segments of their stories, only to then depart radically from it. It is no coincidence that their journeys are also headed in different directions, pointing to opposite ends of the road, or ways of employing landscape as a setting and as an autonomous image conveying a particular mood: to the lush, subtropical north, in *Familia rodante*, and to the barren deserts of southern Patagonia, in *Mundo grúa* and *Nacido y criado*.

Although filmed after *Mundo grúa* (and *El bonaerense*), *Familia rodante* was Trapero's first feature-length script. Arguably, it is also the one closest to the mainstream cinema of the 1980s discussed in chapter 1, in the way it deploys easily recognisable elements of narrative genre and typecast acting in order to forge an allegorical story of national self-estrangement and re-encounter. Even though by no means Trapero's strongest work, the film – released in, and speaking to, a moment of optimism when Argentina appeared to have surmounted the peak of the default crisis – works nonetheless thanks to its light comic touch and the committed ensemble performance, led by the magnificent Graciana Chironi (Trapero's own grandmother, who had already appeared in supporting roles in his previous two films). Chironi plays Emilia, the family matriarch who, having been invited to act as bridesmaid at a niece's wedding in distant Misiones on the tropical frontier with Brazil and Paraguay, gently bullies her two forty-something daughters Marta (Liliana Capuro) and Claudia (Ruth Dobel) into joining her with their husbands, adolescent children and grandchild, all of them packed into son-in-law Oscar's (Bernardo Forteza) battered Chevrolet Viking mobile home. As the clunky engine falters, the conflicts simmering among the multitudinous cast squeezed into the narrow space of the caravan break into the open. Claudia's philandering husband Ernesto (Carlos Resta) makes moves on his sister-in-law, her hippie daughter Pao (Laura Glave) splitting up and getting back together with her boyfriend Claudio (Federico Esquerro), while the hormonally-challenged younger cousins frantically seek sexual release in the van's tiny toilet.

Filmed largely in short close-up shots that replicate the exchange of glances inside the caravan's living quarters and cabin, *Familia rodante* employs landscape mostly as background space rushing past, seen not so much from the individual point of view of any particular passenger as from that of the Chevrolet itself, as a kind of collective exterior in which the gradual passage from the open pampas into subtropical woodlands is registered in a visual counterpoint and commentary on the conflicts heating up on the inside. Landscape remains largely just that: an external, detached and foreign natural scenery in the distance, any actual interaction being cut short by the speed of movement, registered in the shot through the disappearance of the foreground into a mere green blur at the bottom of the image. At the same time, this perspectival distance also figures the containment of interpersonal conflicts and passions while the family remains suspended in movement. Conversely, conflicts explode into the open whenever its members are obliged by engine failure to immerse themselves into concrete locations on the side of the road, the landscape suddenly morphing from a distant wallpaper into an actual place to be negotiated and engaged with.

The locations of those moments when the speed barrier between inside and outside, the family mobile home and surrounding space, breaks down, are anything but accidental. The first roadside camp, where the family is forced to spend much of its first day on the road, comes close to resembling a nativist *locus amoenus*, willow-flanked stream and all, with country boys on horseback trotting past. This benign, pastoral nature sets the scene for young Yanina's (Marianela Pedano) erotic advances on her cousin Matías (Nicolás López). Later, when the family is forced to seek overnight accommodation, the village they arrive in happens to be in the midst of a folk celebration, machete-flashing gauchos appearing in the headlights like ghosts from a remote past (or indeed from silent-movie ruralism). Immediately afterwards, the family heads for the nearest town, as Claudia needs an emergency molar extraction – only to arrive at Yapeyú, birthplace of José de San Martín, the national founding hero, whose museum the youngsters duly pay a visit (although the liberator's belongings hardly take their minds off more pressing, bodily matters).

The journey to the north, then, brings the hapless, stressed-out urbanites back in touch with a primordial Argentineness, forcing them to face up to the multiple desires and self-deceits which had been governing their lives. Although Trapero manages to stay within the limits of costumbristic comedy and, thus, to maintain a self-ironic distance towards national allegory, the cathartic moment of conflict between the two adult couples just prior to their arrival in Misiones also references a moment of national crisis and self-reckoning, which is resolved here by reconnecting with the interior's alternative – tropical, mestizo – Argentineness. The Misiones wedding party at the end of the film (on a forest clearing next to a hillside church) is a kind of ritual refounding of the nation 'in the spirit of love', in a once again self-ironic (but not overly critical or deconstructive) nod towards Latin American literature's 'foundational fictions' of the nineteenth century.[100]

Familia rodante closes with a sweeping pan from the hilltop across the lush woodlands and rivers below, cut against a slow zoom-in on Emilia's wrinkled face as she looks into the distance, having decided to stay behind in the place of her youth as her family departs back to Buenos Aires: a sequence connecting landscape and memory, the location and duration of the gaze and the mode of remembrance into which Emilia, in what is finally revealed to have been a deliberate, pedagogical rite of passage, has gently introduced her family. Of all characters, she is the one who has achieved her aim, exchanging the city once more for her native countryside; whether her children and grandchildren have learned their lesson remains – as her long, doubtful gaze seems to imply as she sips on a *maté* – an open question.

In contrast with the bucolic natural scenery of the north, the barren desert landscape of Patagonia in *Mundo grúa* and in *Nacido y criado* offers a setting not so much for the refashioning of identity as, on the contrary, its dissolution and erasure. In *Mundo grúa*, migration southward is simply the only option Rulo (Luis Margani) has left after being sacked from his job as a crane operator in the capital – sacrificing the company of loved ones and friends for the prospect of a regular job, in a virtual self-banishment that is emphasised by the opposition between his lonesome journey into the desert and the noisy gaucho festival he visits on his last day in the city together with his friends and his mother (once again played by Graciana Chironi). In marked contrast with the utopian connotations of Patagonia in a political cinema descending from Del Carril's *Las aguas bajan turbias*, as an open space where the oppressive mechanisms of patriarchal society and of capitalist exploitation can at least potentially be overcome, here the solitary construction site near the oil port of Comodoro Rivadavia is only the most extreme expression of labour's exploitation in the age of neo-liberal crisis. Working extended hours, day and night, interrupted only for meals in the ramshackle canteen, food rations arriving notoriously late, and sleeping in overcrowded dorms, the road workers resemble nothing so much as a prison colony or a chain gang – associations the film actively encourages in a sequence of shots of the men arriving at the barracks after their shift, their uniforms coated in dust. But even so, Rulo is happy, even relieved, to have recovered not just a stable job but a rhythm, a temporality organised around the working shifts of heavy machinery, and for the sake of which he is ready to renounce his affective ties to his neighbourhood, family, and even his new lady friend Adriana (Adriana Aizemberg). As Gonzalo Aguilar argues, to hold fast at any price to an eroding working-class identity (anchored in the operation of heavy machinery) is Rulo's desperate response to a world increasingly slipping out of control and threatening all certainties – "Yo laburo todos los días" – "I work day in, day out" remains his mantra throughout the film, despite all evidence to the contrary.[101]

Echoing the character's own point of view, in *Mundo grúa* the landscape – except for two instances – vanishes almost completely behind the construction site, which from the moment of Rulo's arrival occupies the screen, relegating the surrounding plain and mountains in the distance to a mere background with scant importance for the construction of the shot. The frame is organised, rather, around the movement of the machines – cranes, diggers, drills – and of the workers operating and adjusting them, the camera's movements and the rhythm of editing blending in neatly with the mechanical choreographies of construction work (indeed, to explore the affinities between cinema and the already vanishing, classic forms of industrial labour, is a driving idea of the entire film). Typically these images of labour, which take up considerable time throughout the second half of the film, are composed – just as, previously, the crane shots at the construction site in Buenos Aires – in sequences that alternate between close and medium–long shots of machine parts in motion, cut against others of Rulo and his co-workers operating them, and shots from inside the drivers' cabin, before all are wrapped up in a panoramic long shot of the site as an almost organic whole, a network of mechanical acts and processes that intersect with one another.

This work rhythm, which has become the film's own just as it has completely taken over Rulo's existence, is only interrupted twice, allowing the surrounding space to emerge in its own right. The first of these landscape views is prompted by the arrival of Rulo's chums Torres (Daniel Valenzuela) and Walter (Roly Serrano) in their self-made car, re-introducing into the film a more personal and passionate relationship with machines and mechanics which, along with rock 'n' roll music, also provides the very core around which their friendship is built. Just as in the first, urban section of the film the shared memories of Rulo's band 'Séptimo Regimiento' had presented an alternative, affective space of memory and socialising to the routines of the workplace, here the couple's arrival in their makeshift car briefly opens up the possibility of another, more adventurous and artisanal relationship between machinery and landscape – the road movie. The brief trip on which the two take Rulo during a break between shifts, all three wearing old-fashioned pilot goggles as they cruise through the barren landscape, and somewhat later hanging out together in a chalkstone canyon, their dark-clothed bodies forming a stark contrast against the white canyon walls (a shot reminiscent of the Cleveland lakeside images in Jim Jarmusch's *Stranger than Paradise*), not only provides a moment of release for Rulo and for the viewing audience from the monotony of his work routine – it also lets us glimpse, if only for an instant, the possibility of *another* film, in which the landscape and its emptiness would offer a horizon of escape, of flight into space.

In *Mundo grúa*, however, this road-movie alternative is signposted only to be immediately withdrawn: upon the travellers' departure a different series of landscape shots ensues, now depicting the roadworks themselves in a state of stasis; the motionless, silent machines set against the vast horizon as if asleep or as if they were the remains of prehistoric creatures under the drifting clouds. Rather than one of harmony, the scene is revealed as one of desolation, as Trapero cuts to a workers' meeting inside the barracks, anxiously discussing how to resist the persistent food shortages and imminent closure of the site. The landscape, in fact, is what remains after work has ended: just as in Dani Yako's photo-essay on the crisis of industrial and agrarian labour in Menem's Argentina, suggestively titled *Extinction: Last Pictures of Labour in Argentina*,[102] with which the film's grainy black-and-white cinematography bears remarkable similarities, the landscape view in *Mundo grúa* is what emerges from the stillness of post-work, once production has ground to a halt. More than an image of space, here it is one of the exhaustion of time: of the rhythms of the working day but also, in a more general sense, of the history of the working class, in many ways the very history of modern-day Argentina – the country being thus returned to its primal, prehistoric state of desertion and emptiness.

Nacido y criado, Trapero's fourth film, has been hailed by critics as the maturing of his previous cinematographic storytelling into a more fully achieved, novelistic expressiveness. Thus, it has been read as signalling the advent of a

Figure 9 The landscape in Mundo grúa (Pablo Trapero, 1999) comes to the fore when work has ended: as an image of post-labour, of the desolation caused by neo-liberal economics.

'second wave' of new Argentine cinema less immediately concerned with social chronicle and more with the extension of the filmic languages crafted in the context of the former into wider constellations of human experience, including new dimensions of intimacy and anguish, as well as a more comprehensive exploration of film genres. This goes in particular for the ways in which *Nacido y criado* literally expands the gritty black-and-white 16mm format of *Mundo grúa* and the short-take editing of *Familia rodante* into the epic, 2:35 widescreen cinemascope format of Guillermo Nieto's magnificent camerawork.[103] The film's central argument revolves around successful interior designer Santiago (a remarkable Guillermo Pfening), whose picture-perfect urban middle-class life with wife Millie (Martina Gusmán) and daughter Jose (Victoria Vescio) is suddenly plunged into tragedy by a traffic accident, ejecting him, in ways we only gradually discern towards the end, into the desolate, frozen wilds of a remote country outpost in southern Patagonia. Much more than in Trapero's previous films, the landscape in *Nacido y criado* turns from a mere scenic backdrop into an active bearer of meaning, its snow-covered wastes and dark, motionless forests echoing the sadness and silence inside Santiago's mind, his inability to come out of his state of shock and face up to an almost certainly unbearable loss.

As already in *Mundo grúa*, landscape as 'space freed from eventhood' (Lefebvre) interrupts and suspends temporal continuity. But here it also, and much more forcefully than in Trapero's earlier work, resonates with a state of mind, the sheer extremity and inhospitality of its ruggedness paradoxically providing a spiritual refuge, a point of anchorage, for the character's state of immobilisation by traumatic loss. As experience ceases to be communicable, space itself becomes enigmatically significant through visual correspondences, flashbacks and ominous forebodings. Throughout the film, there is a subtle yet pervasive use of colour and its absence, in particular the relationship between white, black and red. The films starts with a slow pan across the immaculate white wall of Santiago and Millie's city apartment, decorated with (mostly black-and-white) family photographs, while Palo Pandolfo's title track, 'Sangre' (Blood), plays on the soundtrack, indicating the absence of colour in its most visceral, both life-enhancing and threatening incarnation. The action then starts with a shot-sequence of an insomniac, nightmare-struck Santiago getting up at dawn to get a glass of water from the kitchen, fading into a white screen that slowly reveals itself as a bird's-eye panning shot over a snow field, abruptly giving way to a deep ravine which opens the view across a dark, desolate plain, snow-clad peaks towering on the far horizon. The same shot occurs again later in the film, immediately after the (red) family car has crashed off the road and caught fire, the screen fading into black while Santiago's desperate screams ("Millie! Jose!") are heard on the soundtrack. As these fade out themselves, the black screen in turn gives way to another image of whiteness turning into a flight across dark-grey desolation. Landscape shots then follow from a train travelling alongside a glacier's edge, once again counterpointed by tracking shots of black earth rushing past beside the tracks, before the sequence ends in a vertical top-down pan from leafless black treetops against a dull light-grey sky into the dark undergrowth of a forest, where the camera eventually 'finds' two hunters – one of them a ragged, long-haired Santiago.

Landscape in *Nacido y criado* is then quite literally a denial of narrative, standing in the way of temporal continuity. Both for Santiago and for us viewers, its wintery stillness actually enshrines – sheltering but also keeping at bay – the moment of violent rupture of the family's car accident. Indeed, the whiteness of the Patagonian winter contains a kind of frozen echo of the now-irrecoverable family home, actively impeding the traumatised Santiago from moving beyond his personal state of shock and beginning the work of mourning. But here, too, it is once again the red of blood which interrupts and cuts through the monochrome white of snow-clad nature (which is also a figuration of death), most notably in a close-up shot of the blood of a slaughtered sheep dripping onto the snow – just as Santiago's own solitary self-confinement is being interrupted by phone calls from his mother-in-law arriving on a friend's mobile phone.

But the landscape in *Nacido y criado* is crucially not just a spatial figure for Santiago's inner desolation and shock – a mindscape projected outward when it cannot be turned into words or actions. Rather, it is simultaneously registered as social space, as *place*. Trapero masterfully deploys the possibilities of free indirect speech, moving in and out of the central character's perspective in order to register the plight of the hamlet's dirt-poor natives. Foremost amongst these are the two co-workers at the airfield where Santiago has enlisted as an odd-job man: young Robert (Federico Esquerro) who struggles with the responsibilities of an imminent paternity, and El Cacique (played in an impressive performance by folk musician Tomás Lipán), an older, indigenous man who drowns his sorrow over his wife's terminal illness in alcohol and prostitutes. The affection of these men, with the very real problems and pain of their own, eventually rescues Santiago from the brink of suicide, enabling him to move beyond self-destruction and towards confronting the task of mourning and reconstruction. The film's title – 'born and bred' – refers to an expression native Patagonians use to distinguish themselves from newcomers moving in from elsewhere; indeed, it is the double vision of Patagonia as space and as place to which the saying alludes – its vast emptiness serving as projection surface for anxieties and desires, yet all the same representing for its inhabitants a place of lived experience – which Trapero's film puts to productive use. Here, too, Patagonia – a region particularly hard-hit by the industrial decay of the 1990s, the closure of mining and oil-drilling sites, and one of the early hotbeds of *piquetero* struggle – functions as a spatial allegory of melancholy, but it is the lives and deaths inhabiting it, as place, which save both Santiago and the film itself from the immobilising effects of melancholy and allegory.

Landscape's irreducible double-presence onscreen, as a spatial image open to metaphoric or allegorical inscription, and as experiential place apprehensible only through close observation, is also explored in several other recent films, most notably Sandra Gugliotta's drama *Las vidas posibles* (*Possible Lives*, 2007) and Mariano Donoso's documentary *Opus* (2005). Despite their differences, in both films – as in numerous other recent releases, including María Victoria Menis' *El cielito* (*Little Sky*, 2003), Juan Solanas' *Nordeste* (*Northeast*, 2005), or Ulises de la Orden's *Río arriba* (Upriver, 2004) – the distance between a foreign gaze and local histories of place produces an ominousness, a mystery, which cannot be resolved because of the ambiguous and uncertain nature of the gaze sustaining it. Thus, these films could be linked to a discourse of counter-travel – *Las vidas posibles* in the register of fictional drama, *Opus* in the one of ethnographic and geographical documentary – questioning the capacity of the gaze to render places knowable as landscapes.

In an open reference to the road movie genre, the landscape in these films often appears framed through a car windscreen – in *Las vidas* with protagonist Carla's (Ana Celentano) face in the rear-view mirror, as she drives around Patagonia searching for her husband Luciano (Germán Palacios), a geologist who has suddenly disappeared on a field trip to the far south. Decided to take matters into her own hands, Carla drives down from Buenos Aires, calls in at the hotel where Luciano used to stay during his fieldwork, and begins exploring the forlorn lakeside town, when she stumbles upon Luis (also played by Palacios), a local estate agent identical to, *if not in fact*, her husband. Luis, who is separating from his wife Marcia (Natalia Oreiro), does not appear to recognise Carla, who pretends to be house-hunting as an excuse to spend time together, visiting abandoned, half-empty properties – all the while the police searches for Luciano who, it soon turns out, has almost certainly, and fatally, crashed his car off the road and into the lake.

Gugliotta's script bears some similarities to the plot of François Ozon's *Sous le sable* (*Under the Sand*, 2000), a film to which *Las vidas* pays homage in the almost identically shot morgue scene. Yet unlike Charlotte Rampling's character in Ozon's film, Celentano's Carla in *Las vidas* is not (just) haunted by the ghost of her vanished lover but rather challenged by the very real presence of Luis, whose 'identity' with Luciano is very much a fact – or at least a fact of the gaze which may or may not be Carla's subjective fantasy. Vision's uncertain epistemological status, its dangerous proximity to voyeurism and daydreaming, is indeed one of the film's central themes: the very problem of attention and distraction, which, if indeed the body in the lake were his, might also have killed Luciano.

Lucio Bonelli's cinematography constructs the film's visual space as fragmented and disorientating, yet not – as in recent cinematic narratives of perceptual crisis such as *Memento* (Christopher Nolan, 2000) – as a visual puzzle of clues in need of being edited back into the right order. Rather than through fragmented, non-chronological montage, uncertainty is being produced here on the level of the shot itself. Throughout the film, Carla's own point of view – whose insecure, searching gaze structures the perception of the landscape and its inhabitants, at times (as in the subjective shots peering into Luis' and Marcia's home from outside the windows) to the point of merging character and camera view – is counterpointed by a peculiar kind of 'reverse shot', visually preying on Carla in an equally intrusive and voyeuristic way, from an ominous vantage point without anchorage in the diegesis, generated through the use of telescopic lenses and hand-held camera. Violating the classical rule book for constructing a continuous and coherent narrative space (the positioning of figures within the scene and in relation to the camera's movement, anticipating and accommodating the action by leaving more space to the front than to the back of the actor),[104] the medium-length frame in *Las vidas* dislocates our gaze from its comfortable position of narratorial omniscience, instead thrusting it into one of implicatedness and proximity towards the characters' own confusion and desire. Much more than Carla's visual exploration of the enigmatic landscape that has swallowed her husband and thrown up an enigmatic double of him, it is this exploration of Carla herself from an ominous vantage point, neither close nor far, which imbues the film with mysteriousness. Yet, much in the same way as in Michael Haneke's *Caché* (*Hidden*, 2005), the mystery is not so much about the bearer of this gaze as about its target: the mystery, Sílvia Schwarzböck suggests, 'is Carla, not the man (or the men) who has (have) abandoned a woman [...] The spectator comes up against the same enigma as Carla herself, both ask themselves the same question: does she really desire a new man identical to the previous one, or is she seeking to recover the lost one?'[105]

In Mariano Donoso's *Opus*, the peculiar relation between traveller and landscape challenges the epistophilic protocols of documentary in a similar way as *Las vidas posibles* challenges those of the mystery thriller. Here it is the travel documentary that is under scrutiny as a means of bringing the space of the 'other' into visible presence and under representational control. But Donoso also draws on a national literary tradition of allegorising the landscape, turning it into a cue for deciphering national history and identity (fragments from Argentine nineteenth-century as well as from Spanish, Latin and Greek classics are abundantly cited throughout the film).[106] However, even while the conventions of cinematic and literary artifice in the production of space are ironically acknowledged by thus playing them out against each other, the film's unravelling – its failure to cohere into a single, well-rounded 'opus' – paradoxically reinstates the landscape and the journey as a valid mode (perhaps the only one left) of capturing a society in crisis. By performatively re-enacting, in the documentary form itself, the fragmentation and dispersal that have grasped the film's subject(s), *Opus* becomes, *malgré soi*, a sequel to the great geopolitical essays for which its chief literary referent (nineteenth-century writer, politician and educational reformer Domingo Faustino Sarmiento) was renowned. Incidentally, *Opus* sets out as a documentary on the crisis of education in Sarmiento's (and Donoso's) native province of San Juan, as a way of beholding the wider context of social and political emergency in Argentina. Yet the projected case study of the way social reality impacts on the education system never materialises, as schools in the province are found to be perennially on strike in protest against unpaid wages. The crisis of its object, then, literally sets Donoso's film adrift, 'effectively roll[ing] several shorts into a chaotic and often flawed whole', according to *Variety*'s stern judgement.[107]

Epistophilic desire is ironically referenced in the film by a voice-over in (US-accented) English from producer Jerry Rubin – Donoso's real-life uncle – impersonating, in self-consciously stereotyped fashion, the exoticist viewer from the north demanding some real-life poverty and breathtaking scenic surroundings: "We've already seen your *cacerolazos*", Jerry tells Mariano, over a black screen. "I wanna see some real landscapes of your country … maybe in the West. You're from there, you must know. How is the West? Are there any jungles or pampas?" Mariano informs him that there are deserts and mountains. "Good", concludes Jerry. "I want a child on a long walk to the school in the desert. That works, that's beautiful, isn't it?" Donoso's film does not so much confront this caricatured foreign viewer as it critiques the voluntary auto-exoticism of certain social documentaries. Its principal storyline is the film crew's quixotic attempt to complete the assignment and satisfy exoticist curiosity, in an ironic and self-conscious turning of attention towards documentary's own staging devices. As Emilio Bernini suggests, and as I will discuss more extensively in the next chapter, this self-reflexive turn has to an extent inverted and turned the documentary form itself from a 'discourse on the other' into a 'discourse on the self'.[108]

The landscape which, for the most part, is seen rushing past through the windscreen of Donoso's car is thus doubly framed – through the intradiegetic story of the film crew's ramblings through provincial Argentina, in search of a subject, and through the conventions of constructing the exotic 'other' space of the documentary journey. This multiply refracted, stage-like quality of the landscape is wonderfully summed up in a panoramic shot of San Juan city, which recurs several times in the film – first as conventional establishing shot (complete with voice-of-god commentary on the soundtrack, running through geographical data and population statistics), then as visual counterpoint to archival footage of the destruction wrought on the city by the 1944 earthquake. In between the two, we witness the crew on location, constructing the shot – which turns out to be taken from San Juan's most infamous landmark, the giant, never-completed government palace: an empty, concrete monolith towering above the skyline, the ruin of a modernity that never arrived. This paradoxical, future preterite space is also the one which, thanks to its height and central location, provides the ideal vantage point from which to shoot the city and its surroundings. Yet, precisely for that reason, it is also an epistemological location, a site of enunciation where cinema's own incapacity to transform comprehensive visibility into narrative coherence can be staged. Once again, then, the view is framed by multiple layers of critical self-reflexivity – literally speaking, with regard to the magnificent shot that wraps up the sequence, and which has Donoso walking slowly across the unfinished building's window of concrete that frames the city panorama in the background.

But, as Catherine Russell observes in her study of experimental cinema, even in the most self-reflexive and constructivist films 'the social is never completely banished; even the withdrawal from "the social" is a social practice. Within the work of film language and filmic principles and axioms, the desire to see is never entirely eradicated.'[109] Framed and all, the city in the background remains undeniably present, and the social emergency denounced by the teachers' strike is painfully real despite the mock-heroic commentary that accompanies the strikers' manifestations on the soundtrack. The real plight of teachers and

Figure 10 In Marcelo Donoso's Opus (2005), *a panoramic shot of the city of San Juan from the ruins of the abandoned government palace building site is at one and the same time an eloquent image of social crisis and a reference to the film's own framing devices, which problematise the documentary image's status as visual evidence.*

schoolchildren (even if not including epic walks across the desert) keeps the film from turning into a merely formal exercise – ironically enough, it is the sequence shot in the faraway mining post of La Panta, where the crew finally succeeds in filming a country school in operation, which finds favour even with the *Variety* reviewer. Yet all through *Opus*, in fact, social space remains present in its materiality and mortality (the latter exemplified in the sculptor Miguel Angel Sugo, who died before the final editing). It is not the real but its capacity to be apprehended and empathised with that has been thrown – as has society itself – into severe crisis.

It is tempting to associate this folding-in upon itself of the road movie genre, variations of which I have tracked through a number of recent films, with Fredric Jameson's well-known idea of a 'postgeneric cinema'. According to Jameson, the hyperanxious self-referentiality of contemporary genre cinema points to an impossibility to wield its conventions to an allegorical representation of the social totality (the increasing opacity of which he takes to be one of the wider characteristics of postmodernity).

Autoreferentiality, for Jameson, is the collapse of allegoresis as a form of social knowledge and its triumph as an expression of the commodification of culture, which is being 'acted out' in the way films (and other aesthetic products) obsessively point to themselves and other films *as fetishised goods* stripped of social meaning beyond their exchange value.[110] However, as I have suggested, we might also think of the films discussed here as 'postgeneric' in a more traditional, Bazinian sense, regarding the way in which they critically exhaust the allegorical repertoire of the road movie and, more generally, the tradition of the filmic journey into the interior, allowing instead for the latter's idiosyncrasies of place to emerge and conquer our attention as objects of observation and curiosity.

Small worlds: violence, cruelty, innocence

Idiosyncrasies of place are also paramount for a different group of films set in marginal locations, where instead of the road movie's epic movement outward towards the horizon there is an inward movement into the depths of seemingly banal and inconspicuous places – a tendency Gonzalo Aguilar, no doubt inspired by Walter Benjamin's classic distinction between the narratorial archetypes of seaman and peasant,[111] has described as the 'sedentary' mode. Yet as Aguilar cautions, the nomadic and the sedentary are but two complementary figurations of the present, centring on different effects of crisis: 'Whereas nomadism is the absence of home, the lack of powerful ties of belonging [...] and a permanent and unpredictable mobility, the sedentary depicts the decomposition of homes and families, the inefficiency of traditional as well as modern forms of association, and the paralysis of those insisting on perpetuating the present order.'[112]

The home – as well as, more widely speaking, the village or small-town world as its most immediate setting – is indeed the focal centre of many recent films returning to the rural interior of the costumbristic tradition. In marked contrast with the natural sublime of Trapero's road movies, in Celina Murga's *Ana y los otros* (*Ana and the Others*, 2003) and in Santiago Palavecino's *Otra vuelta* (Another Return, 2004) the twenty-something protagonists return from Buenos Aires to their unspectacular provincial hometowns, looking to reconnect with the places and friendships of their youth. Yet in both films, they come to discover that years of absence have created a barrier in space and time, turning the once familiar strange and even somewhat ominous, as faces and places from the past stubbornly refuse to coincide with their memories: friends have grown up and moved on, shops opened and closed, gardens become overgrown. A feeling of traumatic loss underlies the images of unremarkable, somewhat decadent and trivial small-town locales, shot in quiet, unhurried long takes: in Palavecino's film, the young protagonist Sebastián's (José Ignacio Marsiletti) return to his hometown Chacabuco in the interior of Buenos Aires province, initially in order to prepare a film shooting based on a story by Haroldo Conti (a major writer of the 1960s, assassinated by the dictatorship, who also grew up in Chacabuco), turns into a more immediate confrontation with Sebastián's own past as he attempts to investigate, and come to terms with, the suicide of a childhood friend. In Murga's film, Ana's (Camila Toker) return to her hometown Paraná after an eight-year absence, initially to complete the sale of her childhood home and attend a school reunion, gradually turns into a more obsessive quest to recompose a past which, to all appearances, is slipping away from her – finally driving her to venture even further afield and track down her high school sweetheart Mariano, who has moved to a small village upriver. Where Palavecino's film, shot in sharply contrasted black-and-white that underscores the bleakness of its locations, slips into the pretentiousness, Murga's pastel-coloured travelogue is an exercise in delicateness. The film's final sequences of Ana's long wait for Mariano's return from work, hanging out in the empty streets and squares of the village at siesta hour, in the company of a small boy, sum up the film's exquisite balance between boredom and longing, inconspicuousness and intensity – a balance Murga maintains right to the end, by narrating Ana's and Mariano's re-encounter only elliptically, through a long shot of the sunlit facade of his house and the empty street.

What these young adults look back on, only to find it to be irretrievably lost, is of course the world of childhood, promising a form of anchorage and a point of reference – an origin, in an updated version of the way classic cinema's rural melodrama had counterpoised countryside to city as a space of innocence and simplicity in the face of a modernity harbouring decadence and perversion.

But, as Owain Jones has argued in relation to British film, the idyll as the dominant mode of articulating rurality and childhood is but a surface image beneath which neo-ruralist films encounter 'issues of poverty, but also oppression through patriarchal power, and other harsher realities of children's lives', in an exploration of what he calls 'the otherness of childhood'.[113] The observant, lingering gaze uncovering this 'reality beneath the surface' is not without its affinities to the perspective of the child itself, credited by Deleuze with a raised sense of audio-visual awareness due to 'a certain motor helplessness' that prevents it from realising action-cinema's reconversion of optical and sound situations into movement. If for Deleuze the child is therefore a privileged bearer of the time-image – 'a pure optical-sound image, the whole image without metaphor, [which] brings out the thing in itself, literally, in its excess of horror or beauty, in its radical or unjustifiable character, because it no longer has to be "justified" for better or worse'[114] – the 'nature of things' this gaze uncovers is always the one underlying the patriarchal order of home and family.

In Pablo José Meza's *Buenos Aires 100 km* (2004), a coming-of-age story of five boys on the verge of adolescence, the camera charts the goings-on in the title-giving provincial town a short bus ride away from the capital, from a perspective of anxious curiosity – proper to an emergent social and sexual awareness as yet unable to intervene in a world it nonetheless already begins to understand. It is from this intrusively curious point of view – not quite the ingenuous gaze of the child anymore, but one that already suspects what it will find – that we uncover the adults' secrets, unleashed by the boys' stalking of Alejo's (Emiliano Fernández) mother Raquel (Sandra Ballesteros) during one of her secret tête-à-têtes with a lorry driver. Between these small discoveries, the more or less direct aggression suffered from parents and older youths and the episodes of violence and reconciliation between the boys themselves, the film's rhythm is dominated by lacunae of inactivity and boredom – shot in long takes of streets, patios, the village green – during which time simply passes; small-town space providing an image of growing up as a time-in-waiting, as yet without the means of interfering in the world.

Whereas Palavecino's, Murga's and Meza's films, then, represent each in their own way a wider movement of cinematic returns to the *patria chica*, the small-town world of costumbristic rural comedy – now reflexively updated and folded upon itself through the perspective of children and young adults – a more disturbing vision of countryside, infancy and domesticity emerges in another group of films more akin to what Michael Leyshon and Catherine Brace call 'dark ruralities': a discourse on the non-urban as primal and regressive rather than redemptive and transparent, using 'rusticity to foreground the primitiveness of rural life'.[115] *La ciénaga* (The Swamp, 2001), Lucrecia Martel's feature debut,[116] is set almost entirely on the decadent family estate in the subtropical *yunga* wetlands of northwestern Salta, where Mecha (Graciela

Borges) and Gregorio (Martín Adjemian) live with their children and servants, and occasionally in the nearby town of La Ciénaga, home to her cousin Tali (Mercedes Morán), who comes visiting with her family after Mecha suffers an alcohol-fuelled accident during an agonic pool-party. From the film's opening images – a bottom-up shot of treetops in front of mist-shrouded mountains, followed by one of red peppers drying on the terrace – the determining presence of the spatial setting is clearly established (literally speaking: the pepper *latifundio* is what sustains the family's well-being and social rank). Also from the outset, it is clear that the film's two generations entertain radically different relations with the location; the adults languishing in the confined space of house and garden (with the putrid swimming pool at its centre), the children and adolescents opening up lines of flight towards the natural surroundings (the *monte*, the nearby reservoir) and the social exterior of the town, which is in the midst of carnival celebrations (a permanent offscreen presence, occasionally invading the film's domestic interior as in the costumes and make-up worn by the little girls at Tali's house, or in the TV transmitting a parade, unnoticed by her husband Rafael (Daniel Valenzuela)). If the town represents a space of adolescence, nature is associated with the children. As Emilio Bernini and Domin Choi have suggested, in *La ciénaga* 'wild nature is associated with childhood as irresistibly ominous, as if in the children's activities up in the hills the powers underwriting life in the house below, the pool, the bedrooms, were revealing themselves'.[117] Martel's own synopsis of her film underscores this primacy of the setting over the action:

> February in the Argentine Northwest. A sun that makes the earth crack, tropical rainfalls. In the woods, some of the soil turns into swamps. These swamps are deadly traps for the larger animals. For the happy vermin, on the contrary, they are hotbeds. This story is not about swamps, though, but about the town of La Ciénaga and its surroundings. 90 kilometres from there is the village of Rey Muerto, and close from there the estate La Mandrágora, The Mandrake. The mandrake is a plant that was used as a sedative, before ether and morphine were discovered, when someone's pain had to be soothed during an amputation. In this story, it's the name of a farm where red peppers are being harvested, and where Mecha lives, a fifty-something woman with four kids and a husband who dyes his hair. But that's something you can forget about after a few drinks. Although, as Tali says, the booze enters through one door and doesn't leave through the other. Tali is Mecha's cousin. She also has four children, a husband who loves hunting, his house, and his children. She lives at La Ciénaga, in a house without a pool. Two accidents bring these two families together in the countryside, trying to survive a devilish summer.[118]

Figure 11 The opening shots of Lucrecia Martel's La ciénaga *(The Swamp, 2001) establish the relations between estate and surroundings in the image of red peppers drying on the verandah – also anticipating, in terms of colour, the red wine and blood of the following sequence narrating Mecha's accident.*

David Oubiña and Ana Amado have both analysed in great detail the difference in rhythm, velocity and duration by which the relation between bodies and surrounding space in *La ciénaga* choreographs the film as a crossroads of heterogeneous temporalities; sometimes intersecting and at others falling apart. Time is inscribed in the body (as in the scars, wrinkles and other marks of violence and decay carried by numerous characters) but it is also, more importantly, the body's mode of occupying and arranging its spatial surroundings through motion and stillness, verticality and horizontality, which determines narrative progression or stagnation. This minute attention given to bodies and their engagement with space, Oubiña claims, in *La ciénaga* as in many other recent Argentine films represents a form of social history: 'Indirectly, the film shows what has become of Argentina after the military dictatorship of the Seventies and the socio-economic meltdown of the Eighties and Nineties. If Martel fixes her gaze on bodies, it is to observe in these the nervous system of the social. What does a body know? It is here that what voices keep silent or dissimulate is being spoken.'[119]

The corporeal temporalities of adults, adolescents and children are endowed in *La ciénaga* with 'a capacity for constructing the shot [...], corporeal presence affecting narrative itself, rather than merely the visual.'[120] As Bernini and Choi propose (and as I will explore in more detail in chapter 6), Martel maintains a relation of auteurial exteriority with respect to the action, but this exteriority is not achieved here through a detached camera perspective – instead, the latter remains always loosely attached to the perception of one or several characters, especially that of Mecha's daughter Momi (Sofía Bertolotto) – but through the discontinuous editing, which re-establishes narratorial sovereignty and autonomy. This editing foregrounds an alternation of bodily rhythms, in which – as Amado calls it – a 'principle of gravity' or 'precipitation' associated with adulthood and decay, as well as, more generally, with reclining, horizontal postures such as the ones all characters assume during their endless siestas, clashes with and ultimately triumphs over the 'trajectories' of children and adolescents, whose explosive movements interconnect and 'abruptly interrupt the lethargic motion with the unforeseen speed and violence of their tumultuous movements, their races and persecutions'.[121] This unbound, life-affirming movement, with its attitude of curiosity and experimentation, is placed under appeal right from the beginning of the film, not just through the continual foreshadowing of little Luciano's (Sebastián Montagna) fatal accident at the end but also, more generally, by the morbid and destructive pulsation running beneath the children's own playfulness, as in their fascination with the agony of a cow caught in a mud swamp or in the horror stories of 'African rats' the older girls tell the younger children. This darkness is embodied most clearly in the disfigured, violent and prejudiced Joaquín (Diego Baenas), who appears most of the time shooting game, abusing lower-class boys and pummelling dogs in the wood, an 'animalisation' further underscored by the low, hand-held camera following him in his ramblings through the undergrowth.

The challenge of youthful movement and flight to adult immobility, then, is always already contained by the pull of gravity, which organises the diegesis as an immobile, literally *swamped*, time of sameness caught in between two accidents: without any initiative of their own (even Mecha's and Tali's projected trip across the border to Bolivia to buy school stationery is forever postponed), the entire cast are in thrall to accidents and miracles as the sole agents of change, befalling them out of nowhere and without them being able or willing to do anything to induce or prevent these. Space, both 'domestic' and 'natural' – the two complementary faces of a rural patriarchate – makes its presence felt in *La ciénaga* in the absence of temporal becoming: it assumes a determinant and fatal role, not of itself but as the effect of people's loss of insight into, and control over, their own lives (Oubiña's 'social nervous system' produced by the dictatorship and subsequent neo-liberal raids). Yet this tangible, discomfiting presence of space is not that of a 'setting' commanded by a sovereign *gaze* – there are no establishing shots in *La ciénaga* nor any spatial continuity between the different locales of action, from the rooms in the *finca* to the wider geography of estate, town and mountains – but a mobile and uncertain web of permeable enclosures opened up by fleeting *glances* – the mode of perception, according to Norman Bryson, closer to the affective ambiguities and limitations of embodied beholders. For Bryson, 'against the Gaze, the Glance proposes desire, proposes the body, in the *durée* of its practical activity: in the freezing of syntagmatic motion, desire and the body, the desire of the body, are exactly the terms which the tradition seeks to suppress'.[122] Moreover, it is in this peculiar engagement with space that 'the narrative appears to mimetize a mode of perception proper to children',[123] one that subverts the primacy of visual over aural space which, as cultural geographer Yi-Fu Tuan has suggested, originates the perceptual hierarchy by which adult (and, implicitly, male) unidirectional vision is enshrined above the omni- or even non-directional senses of hearing, smell, taste and touch that predominate in the child.[124]

Take for example the brilliant first sequence transcurring at Tali's house, starting with a shallow-focus shot down the corridor, the scarce depth of field centred on the observing Agustina (Noelia Bravo Herrera) in the middle distance, with both ends of the action – her brother Martín entering the hallway at the bottom of the frame, her mother talking on the phone in the extreme foreground – barely visible. Tali's presence, rather, is signalled *acousmatically* (in Michel Chion's expression)[125] before it is rendered visually (following a close-up shot of a pressure cooker near boiling point). Even then, her attention to – the inaudible – Mecha on the telephone situates her in a position of spatial detachment and distraction towards the multiple movements and activities of her children, spliced between close-ups of her face, in short fragmentary shots that fail to surround her in any coherent spatial envelope. Even her aural centrality within the sequence is subsequently challenged by another acousmêtre, the dog barking from the neighbouring patio, as well as, appearing out of nowhere, the two chattering little girls in carnival dresses. As they squabble with Tali and Agustina over who makes themselves heard, Martel cuts away again to images of Luciano at the kitchen sink, trying to clean his bloodied leg – an accident neither we nor any of his relatives have witnessed. Next, Tali is seen taking the cooker onto the patio (where a tortoise is slowly crossing), the silence suddenly interrupted by strange voices reciting a nursery rhyme – only the following shot shows them to be the girls chanting through a moving fan.

Throughout *La ciénaga*, Martel systematically fractures the cohesion of image and sound into a single, audio-visual screen space – a constitutive perceptual and ideological operation of sound film, as Mary Ann Doane has pointed out, where sound is employed to complete the screen's imaginary self-containedness rather than attempting to provide a 'realistic', true-to-life sonic experience.[126] In Martel's film, by contrast, the non-convergence between visual and auditive cognition gives rise to a naturalist aesthetics of place, in which adult visual sovereignty and control is surrendered to the more fluid, non-linear and anti-causal perceptual experience of children and adolescents. Gustavo Constantini has called attention to the rigorous, even musical, composition of the soundtrack in *La ciénaga*, which often de-naturalises the take by including sounds of uncertain origin alongside others that do have an equivalent inside the visual field.[127] Martel herself has linked this form of composition to the oral mode of storytelling: 'For me, orality is the origin of the narrative. Not in the sense of someone sitting down and starting to tell a story but as the situation in which something is being narrated. When your grand-mother comes to tell you a story (you're with your brothers and sisters, all squatting in bed together) perhaps you don't have a shot of her speaking; you've got one of your siblings playing but the sound of the story invades and orientates your look. It's the sound that guides you. The image is a way of avoiding something you want to hear, not see.'[128]

This association between oral storytelling, rural or provincial space and a certain uncanny feeling or mystery manifesting itself in the landscape is a common thread in the films discussed in this section, together composing a kind of resurgent rural regionalism in Argentine cinema. Two recent works in particular, Santiago Otheguy's *La León* (2006) and Albertina Carri's *La rabia* (*Anger*, 2008), tackle the countryside's association with childhood, innocence and free-spirited, 'natural' sexuality unburdened with the prejudices and inhibitions of urban society. Instead of an Edenic retreat untouched by capitalist alienation (as in the nostalgic ruralism which, as Raymond Williams has shown, runs from romanticism to sci-fi, projecting the countryside as an antidote to the crises of the industrial city),[129] here we are confronted with a 'counter-pastoral' of faceless, brutalised worlds where capitalist hyper-exploitation has long hollowed out the last remnants of local identities and traditions. This is the countryside characterised by Gilles Deleuze as the landscape of filmic naturalism: 'an immense rubbish-dump or swamp' where all the impulses converge 'in a great death-impulse', uncovering an 'originary world' that is 'both radical beginning and absolute end […] It is thus a world of a very special kind of violence (in certain respects, it is the radical evil); but it has the merit of causing an originary image of time to rise, with the beginning, the end, and the slope, all the cruelty of Chronos.'[130]

In an interview with the film journal *La Fuga*, Albertina Carri mentions the children's tale as a guiding narrative principle for *La rabia* – the threatening 'moral story' such as the one Poldo (Víctor Hugo Carrizo) tells his autistic daughter Nati (Nazarena Duarte) to stop her from undressing in public. She also refers to John Berger's description of the peasantry as the survivors of capitalist modernity, deprived of any form of political agency, which leaves them with only the regressive option 'to cling to their customs, to the primal'.[131] Although her film is not explicitly set in the present – in many ways its images of a dark, violent countryside echo the cruelty and anguish in nineteenth-century naturalist writer Eugenio Cambaceres' novels – *La rabia* also engages in a critical dialogue with the left-wing, utopian ruralism of the New Latin American Cinema of the 1960s *and* with the post-2001 resurgence of a right-wing *ruralista* lobby in Argentina.

The film follows two children – mute, mentally disturbed Nati, living with her parents Poldo and Alejandra (Analía Couceyro), and the slightly older, lame Ladeado (Gonzalo Pérez), living on the neighbouring farm with his father Pichón (Javier Lorenzo). When they witness Alejandra having brutal, clandestine sex with Pichón (filmed in matter-of-fact, disturbingly explicit sequences), relations between the two families become increasingly strained, the two fathers channelling their anger and humiliation towards their children until conflicts explode in a violent, terminal climax. This atmosphere of increasing bestiality manifests itself, on the one hand, in a chain of on-camera killings of, and between, animals (Ladeado kills a pack of weasels, which have massacred Pichón's chickens; Ladeado's dogs hunt down and kill a rabbit and one of Poldo's sheep; Poldo shoots one of Ladeado's dogs; a pig is slaughtered, skinned and eviscerated). On the other hand, there are short sequences of cartoon animation (by graphic artist Manuel Baremboim) that link up with the ink drawings of monsters (and, following the traumatic discovery of her mother's sexuality, of an aroused Pichón) Nati fabricates intradiegetically. Together with an expressive, both hyperreal and non-naturalist soundtrack by Rufino Basabilbaso, dominated by animal noises and a frequent presence of bodily sounds – breathing, groans, footsteps – even when there are no actors onscreen, these sequences impregnate diegetic space with a latent ominousness and brutality always on the verge of exploding into the open; yet one which, from the children's point of view to which Alejo Moguillansky's masterful editing approximates our own, appears perfectly ordinary. In Enrique Aguilar's words, 'the images of *La rabia* contain a natural violence, something that is proper to the world where the story is located, and its grandeur derives from the way it suggests something which permeates each and every shot: we do not always see the violence but it is always there.'[132]

Otheguy's beautifully shot film likewise takes place in a self-enclosed, literally insular space: the amphibian world of the Paraná delta, where Álvaro (Jorge Román) makes a meagre living harvesting reeds, fishing and working shifts at the local sawmill, as well as caring for the old islander Iribarren (Jorge Muñoz II, a real-life inhabitant of the delta). A gay man with scarce opportunities for sexual release in the closed, patriarchal milieu of the rural poor, Álvaro also has to endure aggressive bullying from El Turu (Daniel Valenzuela in a bravura performance), the bigoted, embittered local football coach and boatsman of the ferry line 'El León' – the community's sole connection to the mainland. Although much slower-paced than *La rabia* – its intense, forward-floating shots moving with the rhythm of canoes drifting with the stream –

Otheguy's film likewise builds up gradually towards its final escalation of sexuality and violence, involving both protagonists as well as a family of nomadic migrants from the north encamped on the island, who El Turu has previously tried to drive out by setting fire to their camp.

In both films, the landscape shot in long, *temps-morts* sequences set to dense, orchestral soundscapes of animal and forest noises (occasionally superimposed in *La León* to a somewhat mannered jazz score by Vincent Artaud) tends towards the sublime: a painterly kind of Pampean gothic, in Sol Lopatin's cinematography for *La rabia*; an (especially French) filmic and photographic tradition in Paula Grandío's black-and-white HD compositions for *La León*, harking back to Henri Cartier-Bresson's pictures of the misty Seine or to the way Jean Vigo's classic *L'Atalante* (1934) associated the river's mobile, liquid and reflexive yet opaque surface to that of celluloid itself. Rather than, as in *La ciénaga*, as a presence hardly ever seen but implied in the way movements and gazes cross the screen – a space invoked and invested with verisimilitude rather than shown – the rural landscape in Otheguy and Carri envelops the characters in a dimension of threatening strangeness, putting them at a distance. Rather than one of closeness, even empathy, here the relation between the camera and the space of the diegesis is one of exteriority – the marginal world is inexorably *other*, yet the existence of dramatic conflict, delivered in both films through superb ensemble performances, also re-conducts and contains the excess of this otherness within the boundaries of narrative cinema. It is only when narrative is radically stripped down to its minimal elements – a solitary body in its spatio-temporal milieu – that the political nature of this otherness and exteriority fully comes to the fore, as the radical estrangement neo-liberal capitalism inscribes between centre and margin, the gaze and its object. This politics of

Figure 12 Shots of the island landscape floating forward with the stream in La León (Santiago Otheguy, 2006) at once introduce a doomed temporality, channelled slowly yet inevitably towards its violent denouement, and associate the aquatic, light-reflecting surface of the stream with cinema itself.

the look, its possibilities for exposing – and potentially, of surmounting – the radical inequalities of contemporary society, is the subject of the cinema of Lisandro Alonso, the most uncompromising among Argentina's neo-naturalist film-makers.

Alonso's ghosts: nature, crisis and the pulsation-image

In their extreme reduction of the diegesis, the almost complete absence of language, and the denial to provide much biographical or social context for their solitary protagonists' actions, Alonso's films *La Libertad* (*Freedom*, 2001), *Los muertos* (*The Dead*, 2004) and *Liverpool* (2008) constitute, in Maria Delgado's words, 'one of the most notable trilogies in contemporary film' where, 'as with every great director, a question about the world becomes a question about the cinema'.[133] Alonso is also one of the few young directors in Argentina to have publicly reflected on the implications of his work – characteristically, however, not in the medium of writing, as radical film-makers of the 1960s and 1970s were prone to do, but through another film, the essay-manifesto *Fantasma* (*Ghost*, 2006), which functions as a displaced, reflexive commentary on the trilogy and its place vis-à-vis the national and universal tradition and circulation of cinema, including self-quotations, irony and direct, performative involvement of the spectator. All this Alonso achieves, however, without stepping outside the boundaries of his own formal asceticism, as if – against film criticism's persistent calls to 'move on' and 'develop' his oeuvre – he was to force the elementary procedures of his cinema constantly against their own limits, taking them through the folds and margins of Argentine social space and into ever wider reaches of narrative complexity.

Precisely in its radical exclusion of any direct reference to politics and history, I would argue, Alonso's cinema captures the contemporary crisis of Argentina in the naturalistic pulsation-image – as a trace of violence, hardship and resistance in bodies and things encountered at the margins of the social.[134] Deleuze distinguishes the pulsation-image from the classical, expressive action-image of realism, on the one hand, and from the affect-image of European avant-gardes, on the other, as it restores the psychological subject and its historical milieu to their original, natural moorings. The pulsation-image is therefore not 'beyond history' but describes a peculiar form of immanence: as incision, rupture, radical beginning and inevitable end. Associated with liminal moments of the human, in which the latter both collapses and constitutes itself – birth and death, sexuality and violence – the pulsation-image is not a style-giving form that spans the entire course of action but rather appears as a *caesura*, a break in the continuity of action and affect; often manifesting itself as symptom or as fetish (taking hold of the body or of the object-world). For

Deleuze, then, naturalism in film is first and foremost an expression of crisis: internally, as crisis of the narrative logics of action and affect; and externally, as that of the historical milieu portrayed by the narrative, which is revealed by the pulsation-image in its true, torn and violent, state.

In Alonso, the very contemporariness of film – and indeed of the profilmic – is from the outset simultaneously marked and called into question. *La libertad* narrates in long, quiet shots, the labour day of a woodcutter, from choosing and preparing the trees, cutting and scraping them of leaves and branches, and transporting the trunks to the sawmill, to the purchase of provisions at a roadside gas station, the return to the wood, the chase, killing and roasting of an armadillo, and finally the evening meal by the campfire, illuminated by the lightning of an approaching storm. Alonso does not specify the spatial or temporal setting of this minimal plot; even the protagonist's full name (or rather, that of the actor playing him(self): Misael Saavedra) is only disclosed in the production credits at the end, following a sharp cut against a shot of Misael eating by the fire. Only at the start of the credits, Alonso dates and locates the action – or rather, its construction as a cinematographic artefact: 'Argentina, 2001'. Just as the film's title, however, which appears to suggest the opposite, this inscription of the diegetic chronotope into the present of the nation has a propositional rather than affirmative character, inviting viewers to reflect on the ways in which Misael's existence on the outer borders of society – in 'open nature' – might still participate in, or rather break free from, the plight of the nation. Is his 'exodus among the trees' really an example of 'liberation' from the constraints of modern life under late capitalism, an image of bliss through ascesis, as Gonzalo Aguilar has suggested?[135] Or does Alonso's film, as Christian Gundermann counters, rather 'narrate the history of the country's privatization and its effects on the subjects that inhabit it [...] the story of those deprived by privatization'?[136]

La libertad refuses to give an unequivocal answer to these questions, thus leaving them in a state of radical indetermination. Both Aguilar's romanticising and Gundermann's historicising reading project upon the film an 'out-of-field' – a context – which *La libertad* in fact radically suppresses. Moreover, this radical exteriority between the filmic process and its subject is also emphasised by the harsh contrast between the techno score underlying the production credits and the lush, textured soundscape of the crepuscular forest preceding it (both, incidentally, the work of Catriel Vildasola, perhaps the most talented among a crop of extraordinarily gifted Argentine sound engineers). If the film *La libertad* thus identifies itself as the outcome of a contemporary, urban process of production, made in the Argentina of 2001 – at the cusp of socio-economic crisis – it is much less clear whether the same spatio-temporal coordinates also apply to the diegesis.

The question is both of an ethical and political nature – or, to quote Bill Nichols' term, it is one of *axiographics*: 'the question of how [...] an ethics of representation comes to be known and experienced in relation to space'.[137] What form of commonality, of contemporariness, asks Alonso, would today include both urban film-maker and cinema-goers and the woodcutter whose labour they witness onscreen? Representation itself seems to be his answer, as he inscribes the 'documentary' footage of Misael's workmanship into a fictionalised, narrative order (including a script which, among other things, changes some aspects of Misael's real-life persona, such as his employment status). Misael's working day is itself narrated in the form of a journey – ethnographic cinema's most important scheme of action ever since Robert Flaherty's classic *Nanook of the North* (1922). In its movement from the wood to the sawmill and the gas station – from 'nature' to 'the market' – and back, Misael's travelling is simultaneously one from 'documentary' to 'fiction', the indetermination of which also imposes on the film, as Domin Choi and Silvina Rival suggest, a vaguely threatening atmosphere.[138] The pulsation-image, interrupting the flow from action into affect, is here the effect of an oscillation between the observation and the staging of a 'naked life' on the margins, which exposes its own performance.

However, between the long first section of the film, which accompanies Misael's labour in the wood, to his business at sawmill and gas station and finally the chase and preparation of the campfire on his return, Alonso subtly twists the balance. The entire first 30 minutes of *La libertad* consists of a mute dialogue between, on the one hand, Misael and the trees, and between his manual labour and Alonso's camerawork, on the other, always looking for the right – the adequate or even equivalent – shot to the task at hand. Thus, we get a series of mobile takes from the medium distance (allowing to show Misael as well as the tree on which he works with axe, spade and electric saw), where frame, depth of field and duration are almost entirely subordinate to the rhythms of Misael's woodwork. With the appearance of the voice in the second part, by contrast, performance and fiction come to the fore, at just the moment, moreover, in which the exchange value of Misael's labour is at stake: the fiction of equivalence, of money. "No me sirve esto – this is of no use for me", the sawmill owner refers to Misael's day work, to justify a payment which, as we see in the following sequence, barely buys some bread and cigarettes at the station store.

If the film's middle section thus approaches (albeit in a laconic and minimal fashion) a more classical action-cinema, complete with shot-reverse-shot sequences showing bodies in dialogue and conflict, the final part tends more towards a cinema of affect, for the first time interrupting the medium distance for close-ups of the agonising armadillo and of Misael's face while eating. Misael's furtive look at the camera towards the end, however, briskly cuts off any empathetic affective investment, re-conducting attention to the documentary terrain of the opening section. Camera, voice and look – elementary forms of cinematic composition – in *La libertad* maintain a precarious balance between reality and fiction, the same in which the film shows labour and nature to be always already subjected to exchange value and the market. Just as its protagonist, however, Alonso's film forces from this tension moments of autonomy: echoing the reduction of Misael's existence to its minimal necessities, Alonso posits the possibility of a radical minimalism in order to liberate the observational powers caught up in cinema's commodity form. This strive for autonomy becomes manifest most strikingly in the oniric sequence closing the first part, in which the camera (while Misael goes to sleep the siesta) takes to the wood on its own, in a strange dance or flight through trees and undergrowth, as if it were another animal in the community of the forest: a gaze-being on the hunt for images.

Los muertos revisits this literally 'spectacular' shot right at the beginning, as well as adding to it a new element, which radically changes its meaning and function. Here, apart from the thicket of subtropical rainforest, this disembodied, meandering gaze encounters as if by accident the bloodied corpses of several children and, recoiling into the distance, a hand brandishing a dagger. The shot ends with a fade-to-green, followed by a static medium-length shot of Argentino Vargas (again, played by a local man of the same name), a prison inmate, as he wakes up and gets out of bed. *Los muertos* follows Argentino's release from prison and his return journey to the family home deep in the island maze of the Paraná river, with a similarly detached curiosity as Misael in *La libertad*. Thus the temptation to reinsert the initial sequences into the narrative, as a nightmare or flashback of the protagonist himself, is left unsatisfied by Alonso, who denies us any response as to the nature of Argentino's crime and its association with the bloody opening shot: the genre expectations of the prison drama and its obsession with guilt, penitence and vengeance are only being called on here in order to be systematically disappointed.

Yet even if left in suspension, this genre quotation infuses the film with a climate of tense expectation absent from *La libertad*, as Alonso's camera observes Argentino's gradual re-immersion into nature: short, monosyllabic conversations with the islanders, his dexterity in collecting wild honey or in slaughtering and disembowelling a stray goat. But as in *La libertad*, nature is never outside politics, and it likewise attains this political dimension here in its ambiguous status as object of documentary observation and as fictional setting. Rather than to a question about the nature of relations between marginality and the market, as in Alonso's previous film, here this ambiguity leads to an inquiry into the State's hold over a 'bare life' (to use Agamben's expression), in a milieu where the former is present merely as an ominous instance of punishment without investing the penal subject with any form of right or entitlement.[139] Argentino's release from prison thus also marks the limit of the State's pastoral responsibility: having served his sentence, he is literally shut out from the social bond (represented, paradoxically, by the prison community with its workshop, football match, and conversations over maté with fellow inmates) and released once more into the solitude of the forest – filmed in a magnificent travelling shot from the back of the police lorry, which drops him off at a bus stop before losing him, literally speaking, in the distance.

Whereas, in La libertad, the movement from documentary observation to narrative and performance had paralleled the one from 'nature' to 'the market', here the sequence is inverted. Now, it is the natural setting itself, which charges the documentary image with a fictional surplus or excess, as the origin of an ominous, enigmatic and latent violence, that overshadows the entire film. Thus, a static shot of the nightly forest moving in and out of focus, cut against one of Argentino sleeping in a prison inmate's hut (whose family he visits on his way home) not merely signals the passing of time but it also invokes a vague sense of menace in echoing the opening shot: not only for the memory of slain innocence it calls up, but for the way it introduces a gaze with no relation to the diegesis, a gaze somehow as external to human affairs as the natural forms it beholds.[140]

Whereas the predominant camera position, just as in La libertad, maintains a respectful medium distance allowing both a proximity towards Argentino and the observation of the surroundings, social and fluvial, with which he engages on his journey, the forest shot's immediate address of nature devoid of narrative function inscribes the action in the temporality of the pulsation-image. This 'pre-historic' time of an originary world (in Deleuze's expression) remains

Figure 13 Shot in a single take from the back of a police pick-up truck, the prison release sequence of Argentino Vargas in Lisandro Alonso's Los muertos (The Dead, 2004) stages the abandonment of the marginal, as 'bare life', on behalf of the State. Here nature is the violent founding site of the political, the place of absence of citizenship and the law except in the form of punishment.

radically political, its 'primitivity' being that of a marginal world held in a state of abandonment by the State (a relation where, as Agamben puts it, abandonment becomes the active engagement between the suspension of rights and the 'bare life' to which it lays claim). In *Los muertos*, this passing of the threshold of the *polis* and into 'nature' is beautifully staged in the way Argentino – having previously been groomed and ironed for his release into civic life – gradually strips down again to near-nakedness.

Nature, then, becomes stage-like in *Los muertos* because it is still inscribed in the political as the scene of an originary exclusion: its secrecy and ominousness are those of a question about the origins of power and their relation to justice and violence. Incidentally, it is at the moment of leaving polite society behind and returning to the wilderness – his arrival at the waterside to board a canoe – when Argentino is challenged by an old fisherman to unravel the mystery ("So they say you've killed your brothers?"), only to claim oblivion and switch from Spanish to Guaraní (from the language of the State to that of the margins) before rowing off into the distance, all in a single panning shot. Its secret unresolved, nature in *Los muertos* becomes the origin of fiction. As in Otheguy's *La León*, the figure of *the drift* is key here, providing not only a rhythm of spatio-temporal movement that eventually becomes one with the narrative chronotope itself, but also as the form in which Argentino's story is constantly referred back to this mysteriously charged natural setting – as when, in one of the film's most beautiful shots, a lateral view of Argentino resting aboard his canoe while floating downriver, the camera drifting alongside finally parts ways with the actor, drifting off into a separate current to deliver an autonomous image of river and forest. Similarly, at the end of the film, the camera drifts off from observing Argentino and his grandson entering the family hut, panning slowly downward until it re-encounters in the dust the toy Argentino had fingered just before: a small plastic football player wearing the national dress, next to the remains of a miniature cycle. This long pan, I would argue, in the logic of the film does not so much represent an allegory (of the nation, of childhood, of poverty), although this dimension remains undeniably present. Rather, its relation to the diegesis is the same as that of the previous, digressive images of the natural landscape, but now extending the latter's ominous, enigmatic power to the little object, investing it with a fetishistic or talismanic quality. Moreover, this shot also signals a change in point of view, a camera staying on after the protagonist has left the frame, which becomes fully manifest in *Liverpool*.

Liverpool, in this sense, concludes and radicalises the paradoxical journey towards narrative and, simultaneously, towards the real, which Alonso had begun in *Los muertos*. This change is not just one of environments – although the move from the lush, buzzing woodlands of *La libertad* and *Los muertos* to the frozen solitude of Tierra del Fuego has a profound impact on the film, in particular the soundtrack, featuring instead of a densely layered tapestry of noises a forbidding, almost tangible silence. Again, as in *Los muertos*, the story sets out as that of an enigmatic, taciturn character's solitary journey: the sailor Farrel (Juan Fernández) who, as his ship docks at Ushuaia, asks for a few days' leave to visit his mother who, if alive, might still dwell on the island. On arrival at the hamlet, Farrel spends the night squatting outside the village canteen and almost freezes to death before being reluctantly rescued by an elder who has taken Farrel's bedridden mother and learning disabled daughter into his care and tells him to piss off – which Farrel promptly does, following a half-hearted attempt to reconnect with his mother (who does not recognise him) and exchange a few sentences with his daughter. Alonso's camera, in a characteristic long take, watches him walk off across a snow-covered clearing, before cutting back to the family home, the sawmill, the forest where the old man and the girl go to check their fox traps; that is, it returns to the common, everyday reality Alonso had left behind in *La libertad*, but which is now re-encountered as a *social* rather than solitary (and exclusively male) everyday, one the film effectively chooses over its protagonist. This is an ethical as much as an aesthetic choice, as the final sequences taking place at the backwoods community make it clear, hinting at complex, intricate relationships of tenderness, anguish and misery: just what Farrel may have been running away from. Alonso's decision to stay with the villagers, then, is almost akin to an act of betrayal, of switching sides: it signals a point of arrival, a different response to the question about cinema's relation with and responsibility towards its object, which has driven all of his oeuvre.

In *Fantasma*, the experimental film-essay he made in little more than a week in 2006, Alonso had already anticipated this move away from the formal exclusivity which, in his first two films, had locked actor and *auteur* in a kind of mystical duel and quest for truth beyond – or better, for truth *in* representation. Bringing together Misael Saavedra and Argentino Vargas on occasion of a – fictional – Alonso cycle at the Teatro San Martín, Buenos Aires' municipal cultural centre, the film follows their wanderings through a space both foreign and fascinating to them: the very space of the arthouse viewers' gaze which had previously entertained a similar relation with Misael's and Argentino's 'native environments'.[141] Incidentally, *Fantasma* was only released in a single cinema in Argentina, the San Martín's own Sala Lugones – the very same auditorium where, in Alonso's film, Argentino Vargas witnesses a screening of *Los muertos*. Thus, *Fantasma* also transforms film-watching into a performative act, which becomes uncomfortably conscious of itself as the intradiegetic ambient noise (sounds from the street and from other parts of the theatre perforating the showroom) turns indistinguishable from the one entering the (same) showroom during projections. Moreover, the 'action' transcurring onscreen – Argentino representing 'himself' as spectator, watching his own acting –

mirrors our own spectatorship, but with a difference: he is, after all, still an actor, watching an actor's (his own) performance, while we are watching, as spectators, a performance of spectatorship.

Fantasma, then, returns us to certain fundamental questions about the nature of cinema, its relation to the photographic index and to spectatorship (in other words, about mortality, desire, the body and the apparatus) and it does so through the disarmingly simple device of the shot-reverse-shot sequence. A shot of Argentino in the theatre, the cone of light streaming from the projector above his shoulder, is followed by one of the spools rotating in the projection cabin, and finally one of the screen (where Argentino's canoe is drifting down the river). On the soundtrack, this visual self-reflexivity has previously been both anticipated and counterpointed through the use of electric feedbacks. From the film's first shot of Argentino looking pensively outward through a large glass window (a shot which, from the outset, also brings the – both transparent and opaque – materiality of the screen into view) Alonso cuts to a black screen, leaving the image suspended for another three minutes while improvisations from a distorted guitar and drums fill the dark auditorium. These reverberations between instrument and amplifier anticipate aurally the configuration of a self-observing gaze the film forces upon us once the image-sequence has recommenced. Indeed, the feedback loop might also be a figure of thought to understand Alonso's cinema more generally, as an experimental production of reverberations between material acts and recording devices in order to provoke real performances, ones that solicit an active viewing, and thus become capable of transforming the dark cinema showroom once more into a space of coevalness and moral education.

Chapter Four

Perforated Presence
The Documentary Between the Self and the Scene

In the previous chapters, I have somewhat indiscriminately discussed documentary films alongside fictional ones. The possibility of such a reading across generic boundaries also testifies to two interesting aspects of present-day film culture, none of them for sure restricted to Argentina alone. Firstly, the process Michael Chanan describes as 'the return of documentary to the big screen in the times of digital video', thanks to the spread of cheap, accessible and lightweight digital recording and editing technology and, on the level of distribution, the installation of video projection facilities in a rising number of arthouse cinemas, making it possible to eschew the obstacle of expensive 35mm prints.[142] An increasing number of documentary DVD releases are also now available through the more select video-rental stores. As Chanan points out, the number of documentaries commercially released in the United States alone has increased more than fivefold between 2000 and 2005, now representing roughly 10 per cent of the overall total. In Argentina, the share of documentaries in the national production total is even higher, a recent official survey of the industry estimating that as many as 40 per cent of feature-length films made per year now fall into the documentary category.[143] In addition, independent documentary-makers have also created alternative distribution channels through screenings at libraries, schools and universities as well as in collaboration with social movements (including the Madres de la Plaza de Mayo, the piqueteros, and organisations of sexual minorities and indigenous communities).[144] DocBsAs, an annual showcase of Latin American documentary production, including pitching and editing workshops for work-in-progress, is now in its tenth year, with around 100 participants each year. In recent years state television, now under the aegis of film-maker Tristán Bauer, has also started to actively support and co-produce documentaries through themed cycles and prime-time broadcasts.

Secondly, if documentaries today compete almost on a par with fiction films, this has also contributed to a further blurring of the traditionally imprecise boundaries between the two. Whereas directors such as Alonso, Poliak and Trapero incorporate in their films elements of an unstaged real, in Burak's *Bar 'El Chino'* or in Liliana Paolinelli's *Por sus propios ojos* (*Proper Eyes*, 2008) the shooting and editing of social documentaries, and the challenges and dilemmas to which these expose both the film-makers and their subjects, become the very substance of fictional narrative – including, in both films, sequences of the protagonists' computer screens while editing their real-life footage. As we have seen above, a documentary such as Donoso's *Opus* resorts to very similar forms of playful self-reflexivity, introducing into the narrative his own, auteurial subjectivity in the process of selecting and organising content and, in the case of his producer Jerry, even including fictional characters in the process. If, as Stella Bruzzi has argued, documentaries are always 'a negotiation between filmmaker and reality and, at heart, a performance',[145] in films such as *Opus* these performative aspects of the relation between their subject are no longer disavowed but actively brought to bear on the construction of narrative itself. Documentary film-maker and producer Carmen Guarini has suggested the category of 'creative documentary' for this new wave of films in which, she asserts, a narrative or story provides the enunciatory structure, including the proper shooting process and thus actively implying the film-makers in its construction and performance. The vision of local reality is explicitly marked here as subjectively mediated, leaving viewers to draw their own conclusions. Rather than a finished product with a 'message', 'these films present themselves as open processes, the novelty being that time is now being included as yet another narrative element'.[146]

As in the case of fiction film, these changes in the protocols and preoccupations of documentary are increasingly global in nature. Indeed, the resurge of documentary across the world in order to become a veritable counter-information circuit to the news media (themselves more and more globally operating and increasingly intertwined with corporate interests), has been paralleled by a formal, epistemological and political process of self-revision that has resulted in the demise of the classic, Griersonian principles of objectivity, transparency and civic pedagogy, which still held sway in 1960s *cinéma-vérité* and Direct Cinema. Emilio Bernini has argued that, whereas the documentary avantgardes of the 1960s and 1970s (including Latin American *Tercer Cine*) had redirected the attention of spectators from the presumed ontology of classical modernism's images of the social or ethnic 'other' to the filmic apparatus as the locus of ideological production – which had to be ex- and re-appropriated for the cause of popular struggle – the present mode of 'performative documentary' (Bruzzi) completes the 180-degree turn of the camera, as it were, in order to focus attention on the auteurial subject that had been silently operating it all along.[147] In Michael Chanan's words, this has brought about 'a crucial shift in the documentary idiom, almost an epistemological break, in which the old idea of objectivity is seen as naive and outmoded, and is revoked by asserting the subjective identity of the film-maker within the body (or "text") of the film'.[148] As Michael Renov has suggested, in the 'post-vérité age' the documentary form has thus increasingly turned into a medium of self-representation and self-performance, 'in which the representation of the historical world is inextricably bound up with self-inscription'.[149] He associates this process with the shattering of classical-modern documentary's epistemological framework drawn from the social sciences, and based on a belief in the transparency and capacity of optical devices to capture and render 'the other' in an objective, unbiased and self-contained fashion. This 'epistophilic' will-to-knowledge (in Bill Nichols' terms) was challenged from the 1970s onward by second-wave feminist politics, encouraging the interrogation of the play of power in the private sphere, the body, and more generally the construction of identity and subjectivity as multiply interpellated performances.

In Argentina, this global process of resurgence and refashioning of the documentary form coincided with an exceptional and peculiar 'explosion of the real': the sudden revelation, in the 2001 crisis, of social emergency and the more or less ad hoc improvisation of practices of solidarity and resistance – including roadblocks (*piquetes*), pot-banging marches (*cacerolazos*) and street parliaments (*asambleas*), as well as barter clubs (*clubes de trueque*) and the takeover of defunct factories by workers' cooperatives. Thousands of families of suburban poor, meanwhile, roamed the streets of Buenos Aires and other cities every night searching through the rubbish for recyclable materials – the legions of *cartoneros* eventually becoming so massive that special trains (without seats, to make room for their trolleys) were being scheduled between the city centre and the impoverished periphery. The infamous 'white trains', lacking even the most basic comfort and security, quickly became a metaphor of social segregation in the country and also the subject of a documentary by Sheila Pérez Giménez. Nahuel and Ramiro García, *El tren blanco* (The White Train, 2003). Banks all over the country barricaded their glass facades behind improvised metal vaults and shields to protect them from angry customers reclaiming their deposits, in the process creating an eloquent image of corporate plunder. This sudden burst of the speculative bubble of the 1990s called on documentary (and on the arts in general)[150] as a mode of social chronicle, reviving the predicaments of a combative and participant *cine-guerrilla* put forth in the 1960s and 1970s. One of the video-collectives active during the crisis, *Cine Insurgente*, for instance, issued a manifesto insisting on the need to reconnect with 'the cinematographic experiences abruptly interrupted by the dictatorship of 1976'.[151]

In an attempt to recover the 'counter-informational' practices of film collectives during the 1960s and 1970s such as Fernando E. Solanas' and Octavio Getino's *Cine Liberación* and Raymundo Gleyzer's *Cine de la Base*, video-collectives such as *Adoquín Video*, *Boedo Films* and *Contraimagen* had begun to emerge from the end of the 1980s, often in close contact with social and political movements such as the *piqueteros*, on the one hand, and with audio-visual education institutions, on the other. In January 2002, under the immediate impact of the December 2001 events, a number of these collectives formed the association *Argentina Arde* (Argentina is Burning), dedicated to the creation of counter-informational circuits, which would centre on social and political issues neglected by the mainstream media. Among film professionals, the uprising resulted in the creation of *Adoc (Asociación de Documentalistas)*, an organisation of more than a hundred directors, producers and film-educators committed to collective productions in solidarity with social movements. Adoc also created alternative circuits for the distribution and exhibition of documentary material. Edited by Fernando Krichmar and Myriam Angueira, in 2002 Adoc released a compilation of footage on the December events from its members, titled *Por un nuevo cine un nuevo país* (For a new cinema, a new country, 2002).[152]

Whereas some groups of documentarists reassert the figure of the activist film-making collective, participating in the struggle and turning the video-image into a form of political militancy rather than merely a mode of representation, others take a less interventionist approach more akin to the fly-on-the-wall observation of Direct Cinema: a contrast which can be observed, for example, in two films about the squatted and co-operativised Brukman textile factory, *Brukman confecciones* (Brukman Tayloring, 2002) by the group *Alavío*, and *Obreras sin patrón* (Workers Without Bosses, 2003) by *Boedo Films*. Both of these grant an important status to workers' discussions about the form and legal framework of cooperative control, but whereas *Alavío* observes these as yet another element of collective experience without taking sides or marking the camera's presence, *Boedo* defends a particular model – state ownership – both through the video crew's intrafilmic intervention in the debate and through an editing sequence that supports their faction's point of view.[153]

Although video-activism has petered out in recent years, just as the forms of struggle and social mobilisation it supported, it has nonetheless sparked a huge interest among Argentine documentarists more generally in exploring the nation's social margins and the multiple struggles of unemployed workers, ethnic and sexual minorities: from feature-length chronicles of factory collectivisation such as *FASINPAT – Fábricas sin patrón* (Factories Without Bosses; Daniele Incalaterra, 2004) and *Corazón de fábrica* (*Heart of the Factory*; Ernesto Ardito and Vilma Molina, 2008) to films about the plight of indigenous communities and their attempts to recover land rights and cultural identity such as *Las Palmas, Chaco* (Alejandro Fernández Mouján, 2002) or *Mbya, tierra en rojo* (Mbya, Red Earth; Philip Cox and Valeria Mapelman, 2004), or on the gay-lesbian and travesti communities in their daily encounters with discrimination and violence and their attempts to assert an alternative sexual and gender identity, as in *Lesbianas de Buenos Aires* (Santiago García, 2002) and *Hotel Gondolín* (Fernando López Escriva, 2005). What these films share with the more interventionist and militant video-activist shorts is an attempt to step outside the spaces and temporalities of the commercial news media, attempting to wrest the complexity and historical density of social experience from the reified instantaneousness of the latter. A vast number of films have also revisited the country's social and political history, from particular episodes such as the repression of rural peasants and high school pupils during the dictatorship – as in Pablo Milstein and Norberto Ludin's *Sol de noche* (Night Sun, 2003) or Pablo Osores, Roberto Testa and Nicolás Wainszelbaum's *Flores de septiembre* (Flowers in September, 2003) – the Malvinas war – as in Jesús Mora's *Operación Algeciras* (2003) – or the violent overthrow of Peronism in the 1950s – as in Fernando Musante's *Maten a Perón* (Kill Perón, 2005) and Cecilia Miljiker's *Los fusiladitos* (The Executed, 2003) to biographies, in particular those of figures associated with left-wing struggle such as trade unionist Agustín Tosco – in *Tosco, grito de piedra* (Tosco, a Cry of Stone; Adrián Jaime and Daniel Ribetti, 1998) – poet Francisco 'Paco' Urondo – in *Paco Urondo, la palabra justa* (Paco Urondo, the Word of Justice; Daniel Desaloms, 2004) – and film-maker Raymundo Gleyzer – in *Raymundo* (Ernesto Ardito and Vilma Molina, 2002).

Many of these films revert to more classical – 'expository' in Nichols' categories – modes of documentary storytelling,[154] and it would not be wrong to say that the exceptional degree of social and political mobilisation in post-2001 Argentina has to some extent countered or delayed the 'subjective turn' noticed by Bruzzi, Chanan and Renov in contemporary, global documentary film. However, films such as José Luis García's *Cándido López, los campos de batalla* (Cándido López – the Battlefields, 2005) or Ulises de la Orden's *Río arriba* (Upriver, 2004) also approach their historical subjects – the Triple Alliance War of 1865–70, in which almost the entire male population of Paraguay perished, in the first, and the forced labour of Toba and Kolla Indians in the cane fields of Tucumán during the first half of the twentieth century, in the second – in ways that entangle textbook history inextricably with individual obsession, family memory and the cinema itself as a form of visualisation and (re)staging. In García's film, the traumatic memory of the war is investigated in a personal journey up the Paraná river, visiting each of the four countries involved. The narration is punctuated by the director's attempts to reconstruct with a panoramic camera the oniric, 'widescreen' battle paintings created from memory by the nineteenth-century painter and war invalid Cándido López. In the film we never see García's photographs, just his complicated preparations for the shooting, including discussions with locals and historians about the 'right' location and angle (during which the memory of war gradually resurfaces as a question of representation). In *Río arriba*, the film-maker narrator identifies himself as the grandson of the homonymous sugarmill owner whose brutal dealings with the indigenous seasonal labourers destroyed their millenial terrace agriculture and, with it, the regional ecosystem. Here, discussions between de la Orden and his family alternate with archive footage and a – re-enacted – journey to the indigenous village, where the director had his eye-opening encounter with a 'native informant' (an indigenous musician, intellectual and activist who, playing himself, subtly takes over the reins of the narrative). In these films, then, as in a number of other contemporary documentaries, the foregrounded auteurial subject is both a target of ethical, epistemological and political self-reflexivity *and* an instrument of social enquiry. What is held together through this highly self-conscious subject, at least in the most accomplished works, are the three main thematic strands of contemporary documentary in Argentina: the social present, the history of Argentine modernity (especially the 1976 dictatorship and the revolutionary struggle that preceded it), and artistic practice itself (music, painting and cinema) in the way it responds to as well as reasserts its autonomy from the determinations of past and present.

Revisiting the margins: documentarists and the new poverty

If a film such as *Opus* self-consciously asserts the performative, 'inherently fluid and unstable' nature of the director's encounter with the crisis of his home province, to the effect that 'the very notion of a complete, finite documentary is continually challenged and reassessed',[155] Fernando 'Pino' Solanas' *Memoria del saqueo* (internationally released as *Social Genocide*, 2003) does just the opposite. Returning to the documentary form a quarter of a century after his and Octavio Getino's seminal film-pamphlet *La hora de los hornos* (*The Hour of the Furnaces*, 1968), which in its Eisensteinian montage of attractions scanded with *nouvelle-vague*-style intertitles famously proposed not just to chronicle four centuries of colonial oppression and resistance but also to propel its audience into revolutionary action, *Memoria* claims nothing less than the ongoing validity of its precursor following the 'popular insurrection' (Solanas) of 2001. Whereas *Opus* shows the film-maker adrift in a reality whose precipitation into crisis forbids narrative closure, Solanas' essayistic tour de force through the nation's recent history firmly re-establishes narratorial authority both through his own voice-of-God commentary and through the intertitles which, just as in *La hora de los hornos*, emerge in bold white lettering from the depths of a black screen. Arguably, however, the changes imposed on the original model both by the sequel's archival content (essentially, footage from 1990s TV newsreels and talk shows) and shooting equipment (digital *handicam* instead of 35mm film camera), as well as in terms of editing decisions and verbal discourse, in fact also reveal a profound change in Solanas' aesthetics and politics, which his film disavows.

Suffice to compare the opening moments of *Memoria* with the famous first sequence of *La hora de los hornos*: in the 1968 film, an increasingly frantic percussion solo on the soundtrack accompanied short, discontinuous 'flashes' of acts of political struggle – a torch, a manifestation, a marcher throwing a Molotov cocktail – and of brutal repression, alternating with black screens and titles quoting slogans and passages from, among others, Aimé Césaire, Fidel Castro, Perón, Josué de Castro and Frantz Fanon. As the drumming and singing reached its peak and faded out, the voice of Solanas assumed the narrative: 'Latin America is a continent at war. For the dominant classes, war of oppression. For the oppressed people, war of liberation…' Next, an intertitle announced the beginning of the first chapter, 'La Historia' – 'History'. *Memoria del saqueo* starts with a similar 'prologue', this time set to an elegiac string score by Gerardo Gandini: a slow, circular pan around the high-rise towers in Buenos Aires' commercial district shot from below, followed by a match cut to a dirty, rag-clothed child shot in close-up from above, leading into an alternating rhythm of similar visions of palatial architecture – in medium-range, distance-imposing tracking shots – and of the poor in close-up: street kids, rubbish collectors, an old man eating soup in a shantytown hut (referencing a famous nineteenth-century painting, 'The Soup of the Poor', by Reynaldo Giúdici). Eventually, this alternating rhythm is interrupted by a panoramic long shot of downtown Buenos Aires (taken from atop an office tower), with storm clouds gathering on the horizon, to which is superimposed an intertitle locating us in time and space: Argentina, the end of 2001, the government has just lost the mid-term election but refuses to change course. A series of intertitles appear between TV footage of Presidents Menem and De la Rúa and treasury secretary Cavallo: 'millions of poor and unemployed'; 'massive capital flight'; 'December 19' before Solanas cuts to footage of the *caceroleros* marching towards Plaza de Mayo. Eventually, his camera singles out among the multitude a man carrying his small son, shouting "Argentina, Argentina!" It is at this point that, just as in *La hora*, Solanas' own voice takes over, as if speaking on behalf of the multitude of the 'disinherited' – although this time, in a notably more personal and affective intonation than in *La hora*: "After many years", he begins, thus relating not just this 'uprising of the nobodies' but also his own activist film-making back to their 1960s predecessors, to eventually pose the question his film sets out to answer: "What had happened in Argentina?" Once again, the film answers with a history lesson, beginning with "Chapter 1: the Eternal Debt".

But if, then, the formal similarities are many and deliberate, the differences are no less pronounced. As Emilio Bernini has argued, whereas in *La hora de los hornos*, the staccato-paced montage of attractions and use of found footage and quotations aimed at dissolving the auteurial gaze of 'second cinema' in a collective, revolutionary vision – countering bourgeois cinema's techniques of identification and affect through a radical fragmentation of the scene – in *Memoria* both author and scene are reinstated through the redemptive figure of Solanas himself. As well as being the implicit confidante of anguished protesters telling their stories straight to Solanas' camera, the film-maker also appears onscreen, in archive footage of an interview he gave after having suffered an armed assault for denouncing state corruption under Menem. As Bernini asserts: 'in *Memoria del saqueo*, it is the author who forges all the images, and the single or ultimate source of meaning, even that of the speeches made by others, in spite of the film's proposition, through its structure and partly through its montage, to be the continuation of that earlier, clandestine film which had based its truth precisely on the negation of the author.'[156]

But thus, the short, slogan-like images of social misery and oppression, which in *La hora* had been part of an attempt to change the documentary itself from an instrument of representation into one of transformation of society, in *Memoria del saqueo* threaten to relapse into well-meaning clichés. Reducing the worlds of misery and opulence he shoots to mere evidence of the truth-claims asserted in the voice-over, without exploring them in their singularity or even so much as naming his interlocutors (only he himself, 'Pino', is addressed by name), Solanas' film ends up becoming the very mirror-image of the shallow and superficial news coverage he claims to be denouncing. Of course, Solanas – just as Michael Moore against criticisms of his similarly self-centred *Fahrenheit 9/11* (USA, 2004) – would claim to be fighting the enemy with its own weapons. But the way *Memorias* and its more recent sequels – *La dignidad de los nadies* (*The Dignity of the Nobodies*, 2005), *Argentina latente* (Latent Argentina, 2006) and *La próxima estación* (Next Stop, 2008) – edit their images of social hardship and mobilisation into mere audio-visual background material for Solanas' own redemptive, truth-speaking voice, in fact transforms these images into extended election spots for the political party he now leads (*Proyecto Sur*, named after a previous Solanas movie): *Memorias del saqueo* ends, tellingly, with a long panning shot of Solanas' subjective camera entering the presidential palace, to the cheers of a triumphant crowd on the soundtrack: "El pueblo no se va": "the people won't go away".[157]

Arguably, however, the return of veterans such as Solanas and Leonardo Favio (whose six-hour docu-epic *Perón, sinfonía del sentimiento* – Perón, Symphony of Emotion, 1999, was only released on DVD) is part of a wider, and generally more innovative, documentary wave in Argentine cinema, in which the global 'performative turn' diagnosed by Renov and Bruzzi is producing more open and negotiated representations of social experience in a time of crisis. Two films in particular – *Bonanza* (2001) by Ulises Rosell and *Estrellas* (Stars, 2007) by Federico León and Marcos Martínez – stand out for provocatively challenging the tradition of the politically 'committed' documentary about social marginality, the exhaustion of which Solanas' recent work exemplifies.

Bonanza – subtitled '*En vías de extinción*', under threat of extinction, in an ironic reference to the Darwinist rhetoric of natural history and colonial ethnography – chronicles the daily routine of towering, white-bearded family patriarch 'Bonanza' Muchinsci and his children and protégés somewhere on the suburban, post-industrial periphery between Buenos Aires and La Plata. A one-time bank robber (hence the nickname), Bonanza now lives off a multi-faceted family business on the outer edges of the 'informal market' and the law – including an overgrown scrapyard, odd jobs for local political fixers, and the hunting and sale of riverside wildlife: birds, snakes, fish, hares, foxes. Rosell's portrait of Bonanza calls on the rhetorics of a long tradition of ethnographic and social documentary, in particular the self-effacing, fly-on-the-wall shooting style of Frederick Wiseman or the Maysles brothers. Fragments of their daily routine alternate with testimonies by Muchinsci and (to a lesser degree) his children delivered straight to camera, acknowledging its presence and the interaction between 'actors' and crew (in spite of the latter remaining rigorously out of frame). Other scenes – such as a sequence of Bonanza's eldest son Norberto arriving at the scrapyard on his motorbike, the camera already expecting him – are more openly staged, with the effect of constructing an implicit, third-person narratorial instance closer to fiction than to the omniscient narrator of classic expository documentary. The non-chronological editing, highlighting certain themes and rhythms of the family's everyday life – the 'recycling' of car wrecks and other leftovers, the hunting and raising of animals, moments of play, conversation and reminiscing – further reinforces this hybrid, 'impure' form, also accentuated by the inclusion of extradiegetic sound (instrumental tracks from Anglo-Argentine songwriter Kevin Johansen's cumbia and chamamé-based fusion folk) and of animated, handwritten lettering superimposed on the image to introduce the main characters (always by family nickname rather than civic register).

Together, the Direct Cinema-inspired techniques of forging authenticity and those of affective investment and identification, rather than straightforwardly satisfying viewers' epistophilic desire for real-life 'otherness', stage the exotic in a much more subtle and self-reflexive fashion. True, Rosell's camera promises an ethnographic, participant-observation glimpse of Bonanza's and his children's routines, deliberately avoiding an establishing shot of their labyrinthine, ramshackle cabin to suggest closeness; and the old charmer obligingly delivers one charismatic performance after another, telling anecdotes, kissing poisonous snakes or simply reflecting about life and survival. Gonzalo Aguilar, drawing on Claude Grignon and Jean-Claude Passeron's critique of sociological populism, has accused Rosell of airbrushing poverty by highlighting the intensity and adventure of his subjects' lives, which the film's bricolage editing – he claims –

seeks to mimetise in its own formal make-up. For Aguilar, *Bonanza* therefore offers 'an *imaginary escape*, when what is really at stake is [...] a life of misery, which can only be romanticized thanks to the editing and its omissions'.[158]

But does such a straightforward reading really do the film justice? I would argue, instead, that by enlisting Direct Cinema's and the ethnographic documentary's rhetorics of authenticity in the service of its main character's charismatic performance, *Bonanza* also shifts the question from whether or not the 'reality of misery' is faithfully represented. Rather, the film becomes a study about the ways in which subject and film-maker anticipate, and satisfy or challenge, each other's and their viewers' expectations, drawing attention to the construction and performance of 'authenticity' itself. In one sequence, for instance, the camera accompanies Bonanza through the heap of rusty and derelict car parts in his back yard, while he points to especially valuable pieces – "That one's unaffordable, you don't find that anymore. Ask what you want for it, six, seven grand…" As he goes on enumerating his scrap treasures, the contrast between his verbal discourse and the visual image of dilapidated and overgrown wreckage generates a comic effect: we 'know' there is nothing of real value here, only 'a life of misery' from which Bonanza's ramblings and the camera's unchallenging, observant gaze offer 'an imaginary escape'. But can we really take Bonanza's over-the-top performance at face value? Or is he in fact fully conscious of the camera's and of spectatorial epistophilia, and responding with a performance that both satisfies *and* subverts these expectations? And could this camera-smartness of Bonanza and his children – the way they seem to know how to negotiate someone else's gaze and turn it to their own advantage – not be the real lesson of Rosell's film, rather than their evidence-value as documents of social misery?

Bonanza, I would argue, takes on board the performative documentary's challenge to our demand for an 'objective', detached representation capable of delivering a 'true' image of otherness, with the foregone conclusion that otherness equals misery. The film does not simply make the opposite claim but, rather, shifts the grounds on which such claims could possibly be made. It is among a number of recent films that shift attention from the 'objective' description of social space and process to the performance of subjectivities, in the awareness of the camera's capacity to act, as Jean Rouch once put it, as 'a kind of psychoanalytic stimulant which lets people do things they wouldn't otherwise do'.[159] Stella Bruzzi has defined as 'performative documentaries' films that are actively and emphatically constructed around the interactive, negotiated relationship between film-maker and subject routinely disavowed in observational documentary's self-effacing, fly-on-the-wall style.[160] Performative documentaries, she claims, approach realness in a new and different way, shifting the emphasis – as Fredric Jameson puts it – from 'the suppression of the formal properties of the realistic "text" [to] an intensified awareness of the technical means or representational artifice of the work itself'.¹⁶¹ For Bruzzi, this can either be achieved through featuring a (self-avowedly) performative subject or through the film-maker's own intrusive presence inside the image she or he manufactures.

Whereas the second mode of performance is being employed more in films working through the 'postmemory' of the dictatorship and its legacy, which I discuss in the next section of this chapter, another example of the first type, perhaps more radical than *Bonanza*, is Federico León's and Marcos Martínez's *Estrellas*. Made collaboratively by León, an off-mainstream theatre director and film-maker, and Martínez, a journalist and video-activist, the documentary revolves around the charismatic figure of Julio Arrieta, a shantytown dweller and former low-level political fixer who, after the 2001 crisis and sensing the business opportunity presented by a rising number of 'neo-realist' cinema and TV productions, set up his own casting and location-support agency. As well as running acting workshops inside the Villa 21 shantytown, Arrieta has put together a database of film extras and locations, as well as offering on-site technical support, catering and security to producers looking for convincingly marginal settings. To date, members of Arrieta's project have participated in music videos, TV series such as Israel Adrián Caetano's *Tumberos* (América TV, 2002) and in films including María Victoria Menis' *El cielito* (*Little Sky*, 2003) and Eliseo Subiela's *El resultado del amor* (*The Effect of Love*, 2007). Arrieta has also protagonised – as himself, saving the nation and indeed planet Earth – the feature-length sci-fi drama *El nexo* (*Nexus*, Sebastián Antico, 2007), about malignant Martians invading Villa 21, the making of which (including the fabrication of a home-made cardboard spaceship) is featured in *Estrellas*.

León and Martínez's film is structured around Arrieta's declarations to camera, downplaying the crew's own presence (only Antico's during the shooting of *El nexo* is acknowledged in *Estrellas*). Spliced in between Arrieta's speeches are clips from films, videos and TV ads featuring shantytown dwellers (edited into a sequence of the Arrieta-organised, open-air 'First Shantytown Film Festival', screening these same clippings) and of Arrieta and participants of his workshop visiting TV talk shows where, with varying degrees of emotion and emphasis, he delivers essentially the same lines as to León and Martínez's camera: "Why do you have to cast blondes as blacks, if we blacks can do it better?" Or, as he puts it more crudely to León/Martínez, a near-toothless smile on his face: "I can get you better ones, I can do it quicker, safer, and I give you a blowjob as well!" Thus, *Estrellas* appears at first sight to cater to the same sensationalist and voyeuristic fascination as the TV shows with a marginal 'other' who is granted his five minutes of fame thanks to his eccentric, charismatic exoticism, and invited to speak (as during his previous stunt in clientelist politics) on behalf of his community, as a 'shantytown ambassador'.¹⁶² But in fact, by allowing us to see and compare, as performances, the ways in which

Arrieta (just as Muchinsci in *Bonanza*) expertly delivers the right 'character display' for both the TV shows' three-minute-interview *and* for the *vérité* doc's gritty realism, the film also plays with this self-avowedly performative element as 'an alienating, distancing device, not one which actively promotes identification and a straightforward response to a film's content'.[163] Rather, I would argue, the film self-critically re-inspects the 'neo-realist' protocols of a certain, 'socially themed' strand in contemporary Argentine cinema.

This cinema's claim to authenticity appears on first impressions to be vindicated, for instance, in a sequence filmed during the ceremony for the national television awards, where film-maker Caetano (of *Pizza, birra, faso, Un oso rojo* and *Bolivia*) stood down in favour of Arrieta to collect the prize for the TV series *Tumberos*. Cutting Arrieta's televised speech against their own footage of the event, León and Martínez enjoy themselves spotting celebrities and starlets among the audience as they struggle to contain their irritation under a mask of relaxed indifference. Yet the opposition between showbiz and reality this sequence appears to suggest – and which Arrieta's speech reinforces – is playfully complicated in *Estrellas* by focusing on the way Arrieta and his shantytown actors expertly satisfy the demands of a middle-class gaze, at the same time as extolling an agency of their own from this performance. The division, it soon becomes clear, is thus not one between simulation and the unmediated presence of the real itself: in one of the most wonderful shots from *Estrellas*, a group of extras from Arrieta's workshop set out to prove the latter's claim that he and his boys can put together a shantytown film set in less than an hour. In front of a static camera – a time counter running at the bottom of the image – we witness the unhurried construction of a wood-and-metal shack, complete with 'typical shantytown family' having *maté* (played by Arrieta, his wife and child) in an impressive 3 minutes 26 seconds. Filmed in real time, the shot nevertheless is about a performance – and a highly self-conscious one at that, being about nothing less than the construction of an image of the real. Indeed, this 'typical' scene undoubtedly references one of the most famous pieces of performance art from the 1960s, Oscar Bony's *Familia obrera* (Working-Class Family, 1968), during which a worker, his wife and child sat on a pedestal in an art gallery for several hours, a label explaining that their hourly pay as models far exceeded the father's wages at the factory.[164]

In another sequence, Caetano reappears for an on-camera discussion with members of the national actors' union, filmed at the latter's art deco headquarters. Led by veteran thespian Jean-Pierre Reguerraz, they challenge Caetano's use of non-professionals instead of real actors – who, Reguerraz insists with dramatic aplomb, know how to play marginals as good or better than real-life ones. Caetano, meanwhile, insists that he can only get the authentic diction of the streets from those who live on them. But in fact, as the long establishing shot indicates, panning along the mansion's crumbling stucco and emphasising the

Figure 14 The construction of a shantytown film set in Federico León and Marcos Martínez's Estrellas *(Stars, 2007), shot in real time, is at once an ironic critique of social-realist representations of poverty and proposes a new, alternative articulation between realism and performance.*

theatrical, stage-like character of the location, the discussion is itself a duel of performances, which unsurprisingly ends in a draw: both parties play their parts expertly, Caetano the mumbling, unshaved and streetwise non-actor; Reguerraz and his colleagues the mannered, over-emphatic theatre divas. Returning to Jean Rouch's ideas about the community of laughter and gentle mockery making possible the ethnographic encounter,[165] Martínez and León resort to self-ironisation and parody as means of forging empathy and intelligibility across class boundaries. Thus, the professional actors' self-mocking interview performance is counterpointed in *Estrellas* by the website of Arrieta's casting agency (in a sequence which transforms the cinema's big screen into a virtual computer monitor). In its playful incorporation of class, gender and ethnic stereotyping, the site includes a photo gallery offering 'stock characters provided' – such as 'hooligan', 'thief', 'maid', 'policeman', 'Paraguayan worker' or 'bodyguard' – and of 'shantytown locations available' – from a 'dead end for fight scenes' to a 'kidnapper's house', a 'dirt street for chase scenes', a 'classic shanty house' and a 'drug dealer's den'.

More radically than *Bonanza*, then, *Estrellas* moves the question of documentary truth away from the authenticity of the images of otherness (which, in Solanas's documentaries, still underwrite the moral authority of verbal discourse) and towards the performative relationship in which not only the documentary-makers and their subjects but society in general is found to be caught up. Performativity, in *Estrellas* and *Bonanza*, is thus employed as a prism through which to interrogate not only the always already staged, constructed nature of 'reality' but also the political forces and material conditions determining these constructions, and the ways in which they can be challenged by oppositional tactics.

Elective affinities: memory and the politics of the self

Issues of performativity have always been of crucial importance for the artistic and social responses to dictatorial violence in Argentina, first as a way of challenging terror, repression and censorship themselves (as in the symbolically powerful silent marches of the *Madres de la Plaza de Mayo*) and subsequently as a therapeutic and politicised acting-out of the wounds inflicted by state terrorism (as in the *siluetazos* and *escraches* of the 1980s and 1990s), dragging into public view the absence of justice and reparation. The *Madres'* silent marches every Thursday around the Independence pyramid on Plaza de Mayo to claim for their 'disappeared' children began in April 1977, a year after the military coup of 24 March 1976. The first *siluetazo* took place on 21 September 1983, inspired by visual artists Julio Flores, Guillermo Kexel and Rodolfo Agueberry, with thousands of people covering the centre of Buenos Aires with white silhouettes, either made with paper and cardboad or painted on streets and sidewalks with white chalk. An *escrache* (from the slang term for mugshot) is a type of street action developed by the organisation HIJOS (*Hijos por la Identidad y la Justicia contra el Olvido y el Silencio*), of children of 'disappeared' parents, in which former members of the dictatorship's repressive forces are 'outed' in their neighbourhoods through flyers, posters and door-to-door conversations, eventually culminating in a street parade.[166] Perhaps more than in any other area of contemporary Argentine cinema, questions of staging, re-enactment and representational self-reflexivity are also of key importance for the numerous films – fictional as well as documentary – dealing with the recent past of leftist revolutionary struggle and dictatorial terror. This abundance of material concerned with questions of remembrance (not limited, moreover, as in the cases of *Cándido López* and *Río arriba*, to the dictatorship and guerilla struggle alone) appears at first sight to contradict claims about new Argentine cinema's 'absolute contemporaneity' (Wolf), its 'opening towards the present' (Aguilar), revealing 'a world that has grown apart from its own past to the point of making it incomprehensible or ridiculous, without being able to imagine a future' (Aprea).[167] Rather than, as Aprea argues, pointing to an impossibility of constructing narratives of memory in the idiom of contemporary cinematic fiction, compensated by a proliferation of documentary reconstructions, I would argue that – from fiction films such as Marco Bechis' *Garage Olimpo* (1999) or Julia Solomonoff's *Hermanas* (*Sisters*, 2004) to documentaries such as Laura Bondarevski's *Panzas* (*Wombs*, 2001) and Alejandra

Almirón's *El tiempo y la sangre* (Time and Blood, 2004) – a shift in representations has occurred from the establishing of (juridical, political) truth to its implications in and for the present; that is, a displacement from *historical reconstruction* to the *act of remembrance*, however entangled the one still remains with the other.

Within this filmic corpus, it is possible to distinguish three major strands: firstly, fictional narratives, which coincide from moving away from the allegorical figuration prevalent in postdictatorship cinema and towards a more realist, descriptive enactment of dictatorial violence as in Adrián Caetano's *Crónica de una fuga* (internationally released as *Buenos Aires 1977*, 2006) or Lucía Cedrón's *Cordero de Dios* (*Lamb of God*, 2008). Secondly, starting with David Blaustein's path-breaking *Cazadores de utopías* (*Hunters of Utopia*, 1996), the experience of revolutionary struggle in the 1960s and 1970s has been recovered in a number of testimonial documentaries from the perspective of the survivors' generation. Thirdly and not least, following the lead of María Inés Roqué's *Papá Iván* (2000) and Andrés Habegger's *(h)istorias cotidianas* (Common Stories, 2000), the generation of children of the 'disappeared', now in their late 20s and 30s, have started making their own 'family pictures' – autobiographical or 'autofictional' docu-essays about orphaned selves inquiring about their own identities and those of their abducted parents and relatives. Among these, Albertina Carri's *Los rubios* (*The Blondes*, 2003) stands out as probably the single most controversial Argentine film in years, if not decades. According to film critic Diego Lerer, *Los rubios* 'opened up the discursive field of political cinema in Argentina in ways no other film has done since *The Hour of the Furnaces*'.[168]

If there is an opposition between contemporary cinema's attitudes towards the past of struggle and dictatorship, then, it is not one between fiction and documentary (and even less between present-centred oblivion and the exercise of archival memory). Rather, a radical break has appeared between the 'survivors' tales' of the generation of 1960s and 1970s political activists and the 'secondary witnessing' or 'postmemory' of their children who, at the time of their parents' exile, abduction and assassination, were still in their early infancy and childhood. Postmemory, in Marianne Hirsch's influential formulation, is by no means a state of oblivion 'after' or 'beyond' memory. Rather, it is particular in that its relation with the object of commemoration – here, the struggles of the 1970s and their violent repression – 'is mediated not through recollection but through an imaginative investment and creation'.[169] Neither first- nor second-generation memory can thus be understood as a homogeneous block without ignoring the singularity of each individual's aesthetic and political choices; yet both formations share a common condition of possibility rooted in the very idea of generation, 'as – in Ana Amado's words – a narrative and temporal (and also biological) construction of genealogy, as a form of resisting inheritance and, finally, as the formal operation of anachrony'.[170]

Among fiction films, a similar counterposition as among documentaries can be traced between, on the one hand, films such as *Garage Olimpo* and *Crónica de una fuga*, which critically revisit the testimonial realism of 1980s postdictatorship cinema, but now from a perspective decidedly identified with the victims and their political choices, and, on the other hand, films such as *Hermanas* or *Cordero de Dios*, which focus on the conflicts of second-generation descendants trying to come to terms with absence and loss without being immobilised in melancholy. The latter are films, then, about the *work* of mourning as a politics in and for the present – a work in which the former, testimonial re-enactments of the 1960s and 1970s (a still recent past which now seems remote and near-incomprehensible to the second-generation protagonists of *Hermanas* and *Cordero*) are certainly involved as well. But whereas *Garage Olimpo* and *Crónica de una fuga* focus on the *object* of commemoration (and its 'truthful' representation, in a constant and productive tension between an ethics of the image and a realist narrative poetics), the fictions of postmemory turn the *act* of remembrance itself into the critical core of their narratives.

In the field of documentary, Carlos Echeverría's *Juan, como si nada hubiera sucedido* (Juan – As if Nothing had Happened, 1987), about the kidnapping and disappearance of a young student in the sleepy Patagonian resort of Bariloche, had set an early benchmark, anticipating several of the narrative and symbolic procedures of subsequent decades. Like contemporary cinematic reflections on the Holocaust such as Claude Lanzmann's *Shoah* (1985), Echeverría's film – a graduation piece for the Munich Academy for Film and Television – chose the form of the journey or quest ('a pervasive documentary impulse', according to Stella Bruzzi, allowing films to 'contain both a sense of a grand narrative they are intent on pursuing and a realisation that this narrative's specific conclusion cannot, at the outset of filming, be known'[171]). Here, the journey form allows both to accommodate multiple voices and testimonies in a single narrative structure *and* to reinforce the absence at its heart, which the movement between Bariloche and Buenos Aires (presumably repeating the final journey of Juan Marcos Herman, the 'disappeared' student, himself) can only stage but never unmake. Remarkably, too, Echeverría's film introduces a detective figure –in fact anticipating Marcel Ophüls's self-performance in *Hôtel Terminus* (1988) – in local journalist Esteban Buch (today a renowned musicologist) who plays himself as a kind of *alter ego* of Echeverría, yet also of Juan himself, who just as Buch at the time of filming was just 22 years old when he was kidnapped and murdered. In various sequences, Buch and sometimes other members of the crew are seen watching and working through previously recorded footage, fast-forwarding or rewinding to particularly important moments of interviews. Like Lanzmann in *Shoah*, Echeverría also resorts to a hidden camera, in particular during a visit to ESMA – the Naval Mechanics School at Buenos Aires, the most important clandestine torture centre under the dictatorship, then still under military control – where he directly confronts one of Juan's presumed kidnappers. Continuity between staged and *vérité* elements is established by landscape shots (sometimes from the buses and planes on which Buch – and the unseen crew – travel), the music of Mercedes Sosa, and a diary-style, reflexive voice-over (written by historian Osvaldo Bayer), in which Buch reflects on the social and political wounds inflicted by dictatorial terror. As Gonzalo Aguilar suggests, *Juan* condensed 'all the motifs of the [...] postdictatorial era: the journalistic inquiry, the need to create an innocent victim (Juan hadn't been a particularly active militant), the attempt to make the military talk (an objective which is frustrated except for a lapsus or for the general clumsiness of the interviewees), the association between repression and socio-economic decay and, above all, the need for justice.'[172]

This choral structure of multiple testimonial voices piecing together a past in ruins would be adopted by almost all the documentaries of the following decades, as would, to a different degree, the narrative form of the journey as a spatial figure of memory itself. However, there are also important aspects in which survivor and second-generation memory before and after 2000 depart from the postdictatorship cinema of the 1980s, and part ways with one another. *Cazadores de utopías* by David Blaustein, a documentary about the left-Peronist *Montoneros* guerilla, set the tone for the way in which the recovery of 1960s and 1970s revolutionary militancy now moved beyond the denunciation of the dictatorship's homicidal violence, which had prevailed during the 1980s in an attempt to establish consensus on the essential difference between leftist armed struggle and state terrorism. If the critical reassessment of the revolutionary Left itself had proved difficult in those years, films such as *Cazadores* as well as Mariana Arruti's *Trelew* (2002) – on a group of political prisoners' escape from the Trelew high-security prison – or Gabriel Corvi and Gustavo de Jesus' *Errepé* (2004) – on the Guevarist ERP guerilla – propose a vindication, if not necessarily of the means of revolutionary violence, then certainly of its ethical motivations, which they contrast with the apathy and cynicism of the neo-liberal present. As *Errepé* asks, quoting Roland Barthes: "In the name of which present do we have the right to criticize our past?"

Yet in upholding the validity of the past's revolutionary ideals, these films also risk getting caught up in a melancholic confirmation of irreversible defeat, of which the shift in the title of Blaustein's film from 'revolution' (indicating a political goal and a strategy for the future conquest of power) to the more abstract, even sentimental, 'utopia' (implicitly confirming its unattainability) is symptomatic. As Carlos Altamirano asserts in a review of *Cazadores*, the film 'is not, nor does it attempt to be, an instrument for reflection. It is a film of mourning, made by ex-*Montoneros* for other ex-*Montoneros*.'[173] I would argue, however, that *Cazadores* and other 'survivors' tales' also allow for a somewhat different reading: as staging, in their cinematic form itself, the aporias of re-validating an experience to whose catastrophic failure the very faces and bodies of the survivors at the same time testify, bearing the traces and wounds of their brutalisation at the hands of State repression – not to mention the vast majority of comrades on whose behalf (in whose absence) they are compelled to speak. As Hugo Vezzetti writes, 'the surviving activists have confronted the difficulties stemming from the almost untenable position of the *aparecido* ["appeared"], charged with suspicion and faced with contradictory demands [...] They testify for the others, those who didn't come back, embodying the living evidence of an abandonment and a disprotection that point back to a society incapable, to say the least, of sparing them such a destiny.'[174]

Cazadores is structured as three large 'chapters', chronicling the emergence, apogee and defeat of left-Peronism from its post-1955 beginnings in the underground resistance to the emergence of a Peronist student left and of various urban and rural guerillas in the late 1960s, eventually provoking Perón's return in 1973 and the rupture with the leader the year after, and, finally, the movement's return to the underground and its crushing defeat by the military, followed by the bestial and systematic assassination of leftists and sympathisers in the dictatorship's concentration camps. Each section is narrated by several witnesses – introduced through subtitles indicating their political affiliations during the period – one of whom appears as the leading voice, with other, secondary characters providing additional detail: Envar El Kadri, a historic participant of the Peronist resistance and of the first, rural-based Taco Ralo guerilla, is in charge of the first part, Juan Manuel Abal Medina – a leader of the Peronist Youth, whose brother Fernando participated in the kidnapping and killing of General Pedro Aramburu, one of the leaders of the 1955 putsch – of the second, and Graciela Iturraspe and Graciela Daleo, low-level members of the organisation during the 'Dirty War' and concentration camp survivors, of the third. Their testimonies straight to camera, apparently without any interference from Blaustein and his scriptwriter, Ernesto Jauretche (both also ex-members of the organisation), and often set in symbolically charged locations – a dockyard during El Kadri's statements, a derelict basement (a prison cell?) during Daleo's – are edited together in a kind of discursive match cut, sometimes interspersed with archive footage to smoothen transitions from one statement to the next, giving the impression of a single, homogeneous discourse without contradictions. With only minor modifications, the same formula is also adopted by *Trelew* and *Errepé*. In *Cazadores*, this main narrative is preceded by a prologue of archive footage, most of it in slow motion, of Evita and Perón addressing jubilant masses, and of the military bombardment of Plaza de Mayo in 1955, while on the soundtrack atmospheric music by Litto Nebbia alternates with famous speeches from the two leaders (including Perón's statement that "to violence you have to respond with an even greater violence").

Some of this footage is of course familiar from Solanas and Getino's *La hora de los hornos*, and it is precisely the tradition of 1960s agitation cinema's montage of a multiplicity of fragments into a single, overwhelming political statement which, Emilio Bernini argues, these films homage through their choral structure: 'The omnipresent voice-over of the elders' documentary cinema is transformed here into a multiplicity of internal voices, yet which nevertheless, thanks precisely to a remarkably precise editing work, converge in a single voice. [...] All the testimonies agree on one and the same version of the process [...], not because they use similar arguments nor necessarily because they share the same vision, but because their discourses are cut up and pieced back together in a way that makes each of them become part of the unified discourse constructed by the film.'[175]

From the very beginning of *Cazadores*, then, it becomes clear that the history of Montoneros will be passed on to us *as part of a Montonero history* of the nation and of Peronism in particular, the validity of which is confirmed precisely as it proves capable of narrating its own defeat. This is the melancholic triumph to which Blaustein's film aspires: to reassert the past moment of passion and intensity, even at the price of withdrawing from a present that (despite the – unmentioned – ongoing political activism of some of the interviewees) is merely the mournful place of talking heads filmed in static takes, reminiscing about a past which the archive footage glorifies as one of bodies-in-motion, in their youthful grace and beauty and still without the scars of torture, exile and defeat. More than a history, *Cazadores* presents us with a eulogy to the 1970s.

But in order to re-introduce defeat into a unitary group discourse, the editing has to make some radical omissions, first and foremost of the leadership of Montoneros, none but one of whom is so much as mentioned by name. Gonzalo Aguilar has shown in detail *whose* memory the film privileges – that of medium-rank activists belonging, in their majority, to the organisation's northern column, historically in dissent with the central leadership's political and military strategy.[176] But the significance of Blaustein's and Jauretche's historical and cinematographic choices becomes fully clear only when contrasting them to another film of the same period, Andrés Di Tella's *Montoneros, una historia* (Montoneros, a Story, 1994), which – even though some of the interviewees are the same – tells a rather different story, and it tells it in a different way that points forward to the following generation's performative documentaries of secondary witnessing. (Di Tella, who was 18 at the time of the 1976 coup, spent most of the dictatorship studying in England, where he and his parents had already been exiled during the previous military regime of 1964–73.) Here, the leading voice is that of Ana Testa, a former low-rank militant, whose personal story from her entry into student politics to her kidnapping and survival of ESMA (thanks to her having been picked out for a perverse brainwashing – or

Figure 15 An epic past of revolutionary struggle is invoked in David Blaustein's Cazadores de utopías (*Hunters of Utopia*, 1996) through the choral narrative of ex-activists identified by their political affiliations in the 1970s, their statements to camera being shot in locations affectively associated with workers' struggle, clandestinity and repression.

'recovery' – experiment carried out by the Navy) provides the film's main thread. Unlike the interviewees in *Cazadores*, Ana becomes a virtual co-author in *Montoneros*, as she and Di Tella (who remains invisible but whose voice is frequently heard from behind the camera) embark on a journey across Argentina to former places of study, underground shelters and meeting places, including her hometown CineClub where watching Gillo Pontecorvo's *Battle of Algiers* (1966) had been a formative political experience. Fragments of Pontecorvo's film, depicting counter-insurgency operations of the French and the torture of FLN prisoners, are also subsequently spliced into the narrative, standing in for the absent images of military repression in Argentina.

Ana's personal quest, rather than the collective re-assertion of group identity, provides the film's main focus. Her research had been prompted, she explains (to the film's opening shot of a car windshield being cleaned at a filling station) by her 16-year-old daughter Paula asking her "What happened in the seventies?". This allows Di Tella not only to provide a more harrowing, close-up account of the day-to-day reality of undercover activism (told with a remarkable lack of sentimentality) but also to include its more intimate dimensions, such as the instant crush Ana admits to have felt for Paula's father Juan when seeing him speak, moustachioed and long-haired, at a protest march (the

Communists, she says, were all neat and pimply). Di Tella counterpoints her narrative, indicating his own presence not just through his stark editing decisions – as when an explanation by Ana about the 'recovery process' to which she was submitted at ESMA is cut to a panning shot of grazing cows on the side of the motorway – but also by carrying out his own, independent research, and visiting other witnesses. Unlike in *Cazadores*, here these are not merely supporting voices confirming the story of the lead character. On the contrary, their sometimes violent clashes bring out the tragic, irreconcilable dimension of history, as in the statements by Roberto Perdía, an ex-commander (who defends the leadership's commitment and strategy), and by Jorge Rulli, co-founder of the Peronist Youth, who accuses Perdía and other Montonero leaders such as Mario Firmenich and Roberto Galimberti of cynically wasting the lives of thousands of 'surface activists'. Di Tella does not hesitate to explicate his sympathies by editing into the sequence TV footage of an interview with Firmenich (made after President Menem's amnesty decrees liberated detained guerilla leaders as well as army personnel accused of crimes against humanity) to which he superimposes a subtitle indicating the payment Firmenich received for appearing on the show. In another chilling fragment, a former mid-rank activist confirms – and justifies – the 'revolutionary trials' and executions of fellow activists accused of treason. The film ends with Ana's account of how, on her release from ESMA in the early 1980s, Juan – then still living underground, prior to his own disappearance – refused to even see her, arguing (as she would later find out through another ex-militant) that, having been released, she must have become a traitor to the cause.

Di Tella's film, then, refuses to provide the narrative closure which, by way of omission, allows Blaustein to recompose the group, if only as a community of mourners. In fact, both films could be understood as 'acts of melancholy', in Christian Gundermann's formulation. For Gundermann, in the context of the postdictatorial remembrance of left-wing revolutionary struggle in Argentina, melancholy equals the 'Antigonesque' attitude of 're-invention of political strategies from the standpoint of a subjectivity in a state of absolute disprotection and disarray'.[177] Yet whereas, for Blaustein, the past literally has to be re-invented through mytho-poetic suture, for Di Tella the work of mourning demands on the contrary an anamnestic staging of the wound which both constitutes and forecloses Argentine identity in the present. In this – and in its transposition into a camera style constantly on the move, often without any 'investigative' motivation but rather incorporating into the image itself a state of uprootedness – *Montoneros, una historia* also looks forward to the testimonial films which, only a few years later, the generation of sons and daughters would make. Here, the act of film-making itself would become a spectral echo of the political activism of their parents some 20 or 30 years earlier *when they were the same age as their children are now*.[178]

Andrés Habegger's *(h)istorias cotidianas* (Common Stories, 2000) offers just like *Montoneros* an interesting, transitional link between first and second-generation memory. The film is dedicated to the memory of Habegger's own disappeared father but told in the third person, following six other sons and daughters in their daily dealings with the absence overshadowing their lives. Habegger's film draws out the singularity of each individual's pain precisely in searching for common experiences and gestures: dreams about the parents' return, the treasuring of photographs and personal objects, the private and political rituals of homage in the absence of a grave. Some interviewees reflect on the ways in which grandparents, relatives and friends see their absent parents in their own physical features and everyday gestures, and on the problems of forging an identity of their own while being interpellated as living memorials. Others, in particularly impacting sequences, take their family pictures and memories out to the streets, enacting in front of camera a revisiting of places where their parents had stood a quarter of a century before ("Here was the last time I saw my dad," says one, pointing to a school entrance). Through this gaze in a state of memory, the city becomes re-signified, long black-and-white shots of empty streets, squares and bridges and of the interviewees criss-crossing Buenos Aires on trains, buses and subways being intercalated between the interview sequences, as time-images of 'disappearance', of a temporality forever held in suspension.

These images of space recorded by a camera on the move, on a journey without any particular destination, are a recurrent feature in the films of the second generation, figuring the work of mourning as a refusal to acquiesce in the face of the enduring non-event of disappearance (designed by the dictatorship to present an ongoing and irreversible threat to all forms of social mobilisation).[179] Yet at the same time, and once more following the lead of Echeverría's *Juan*, the postmemory documentaries thereby also participate in new Argentine cinema's 'cognitive mapping' of the social geographies of the present, the journeys through neo-liberalism's unequal city and into the desolate interior being a way of reflecting on the dictatorship's lasting impact. All three first-person narrators in María Inés Roqué's *Papá Iván* (2000), Albertina Carri's *Los rubios* (2003) and Nicolás Prividera's M (2007) are almost constantly on the move, travelling shots from moving buses (*Papá Iván*), the film crew's minivan (*Los rubios*) or from a hand-held camera carried while walking (M) syncopating the films' rhythm. To this movement across space – figuring the uprooted, adrift yet also active, combative subject of enunciation – corresponds a split or crisis of narrative agency: 'a first person which can and will not occlude, in its performance, the impossibility of constituting a self-sufficient communicative instance.'[180]

In *(h)istorias*, this incompleteness or lack of a subject forced to speak itself in the absence of the parental gaze – inscribed by the bracketing in the film's title, of the very initial for *hijo* (son), *herencia* (inheritance), *historia* and, of course, Habegger, the family name – unleashes a multiplication of narrative instances whose own incompleteness mirrors that of the director. In *Papá Iván*, the autobiographical subject is present only as a voice, whose Mexican accent carries the indexical trace of an enforced exile, but only appears once, furtively, at the corner of a panning shot over the city, as if confirming in this half-presence to camera her own voice-over: "What I miss the most is his look. Your parents' gaze confirms you, makes you, constructs you. And this – it's almost like growing up in the dark." In *Los rubios*, the actress Analía Couceyro appears at the beginning of the film explaining that she is an actress who will play Albertina Carri, the film-maker and subject of the film – who also appears, as herself, directing Analía and the crew, the distinction between the 'true' and the 'fictional' Albertina through the use of black-and-white and colour footage becoming quickly blurred. As Gabriela Nouzeilles points out, in *Los rubios* 'there are at least three "Albertina Carri": Albertina, the author behind the frame; Albertina, the *auteur* inside the film, who appears holding the camera, giving instructions and discussing the movie with the crew; and Albertina, the daughter in a state of memory [played by Couceyro], who stands before the camera delivering a rehearsed testimony.'[181]

Finally, in M, Nicolás Prividera self-consciously *acts out* a variety of role models of investigative narratorship already inscribed in the growing canon of (post)memory documentary, including those of Echeverría, Carri, Ophüls and Lanzmann (and beyond these, of cinema itself, starting with the title-giving reference to Fritz Lang's classic M *for Murder* [1931] – the initial, too, of 'mother', 'Marta', 'memory', and so forth). In all these cases, Gonzalo Aguilar suggests, the question 'rather than about staging, or *mise-en-scène*, is about embodiment, or *mise-en-corps*, and rather than about first-person documentaries, about documentaries on the difficulties of arriving at the enunciation of the person (the first, second, and third). […] Embodiment in these documentaries produces a *vicarious* "I" reflecting on the possibility of memory and of politics.'[182]

This crisis of the subject of enunciation, both interpellated by and incapable of returning the address to the absent parent, but also of fully reconstituting her or him as a historical object of research, also has consequences for the documentary form itself, no longer able to offer viewers 'access not to *a* world but *the* world', as Bill Nichols still confidently asserts in his classic *Representing Reality*.[183] The postmemory documentary perhaps more than any other stages this constitutive aporia of enunciation – for example, in the way in which, in *Papá Iván*, the narrative begins by María Inés Roqué reading (giving voice to) the farewell letter her father left behind for his children at the moment of going underground, explaining his revolutionary choices (by drawing, incidentally, on his own childhood memories of social injustice, which are thus grafted onto those of his children). These readings are set to the slow panning over of old family photographs, taken by her father and showing little María Inés with her mother and brother – thus replicating the absent presence of Juan Julio ('Iván') Roqué frozen in a gaze captured through a camera and in the letters printed on a page by a typewriter. As Roqué herself asserts, acknowledging the impossibility to close the gap: "I wanted this film to be a grave ... but no, it didn't work out."

Nicolás Prividera, in M, takes the opposite path (and clearly there is a fascinating dimension of gendered archives and memory here) in drawing profusely on photographic and Super-8 footage of his disappeared mother Marta Sierra, her youthful grace and beauty recorded by what is clearly a lover's gaze. But Prividera the son/film-maker appropriates the photographs' point of view, by editing them into his own footage, and even at one point juxtaposing his own face to that of his mother from a rear-projected slide; the image becoming the performative site of encounter in an abyssal temporality and of politicised Oedipal desire. In Albertina Carri's *Los rubios*, a pan similar to Roqué's across family photographs laid out on a table only captures the faces of the children, those of the adults – including her parents Roberto Carri and Ana María Caruso – covered as if by accident under other photographs and papers. The film denies us an image, but it also keeps its disjointed and contradictory fragments and tokens of remembrance from cohering into an apprehensible 'idea' of her parents. As Carri asserts: 'I tried to avoid the diverse elements such as testimonies, photos and letters from leaving this reassuring sensation, this "okay, fine, now I know Roberto and Ana María, let's go home". What I suggest is precisely that we're not going to know them, that no reconstruction is possible. They're inapprehensible because they aren't here.'[184]

Instead of the reassuring certainties of the archival image, *Los rubios* opts for the discomfiting restaging of Albertina's own childhood imagination, such as when – in one of the most radical and controversial choices of the film – the kidnapping of her parents is narrated in a stop-motion animation with Playmobil figures, abducted by a flying saucer while driving along on a motorway. In a review of *Los rubios*, published in the journal *Punto de Vista*, writer and critic Martín Kohan accused Carri of depoliticising dictatorial terror: 'She suppressed a reality, that of political violence, and not only in her toy-play but also in *Los rubios* as a whole, just as earlier on in the film she had suppressed the past, or the exercise of memory, or the possible ties of a possible identity.'[185] Apart from misconstructing the scene, as Gustavo Noriega has noted – Kohan wrongly claims that one of the parents is flashing a gun at the start of the stop-motion sequence, to sustain his claim for an active disavowal of revolutionary struggle[186] – he also takes it out of context, since in the film the sequence is framed by another – and itself partial – memory of the kidnapping, that of the family's former neighbour who proudly confesses to having betrayed them to

THE DOCUMENTARY BETWEEN THE SELF AND THE SCENE

Figures 16 and 17   *A pan across family photographs in María Inés Roqué's* Papá Iván *(2000) to a voice-over of the director reading from her father's farewell letter to his children performs the aporia of postmemory in the materiality of the image itself, as an originary absence that cannot be restored either through re-shooting the photographs or through filial voicing of the father's last words. Nicolás Prividera's* M *(2007) likewise makes the gap, and the impossibility of its unmaking through film, present in a shot of the director himself appearing 'next to' his mother, whose face he projects onto a screen from a slide.*

Figure 18 The abduction of her parents – subsequently retold, firstly, through her sister's recollections voiced by the actress Analía Couceyro, and secondly through those of the neighbour who betrayed them to the police – is restaged in Albertina Carri's Los rubios (*The Blondes*, 2003) as a stop-motion animation using Playmobil figures, 'documenting' not the act in itself but the director's memory of herself as a child, trying to make sense of it.

the kidnapping squad, and from whose testimony about Carri, her sisters and her parents being "all blondes" the film takes nothing less than its title. Far from suppressing history and politics, Carri's film reinscribes them but in a way that strips them of the certainties of discursive convention. The Playmobil sequences are toy-play, yet these are not just any kind of toys but they reinscribe, from a child's perspective, the dictatorship era as one of imposed social uniformisation and economic surrender to transnational imports (the Playmobil brand started to be distributed worldwide in 1975, a year before the military coup). Meanwhile, the – false – assertion of blondness on the part of the (furiously black-dyed) neighbour leads Carri and her crew to reflect on the politics of the 1970s and her parents' faith in 'the people' as a revolutionary agent, cruelly disproven by the neighbour's betrayal of 'the blondes' next door to the forces of repression. As Analía Couceyro – playing Carri – asserts about the film crew's own experience in the neighbourhood (a rundown suburb where Carri's parents had moved to carry out 'base activism' tasks): "it was clear that we weren't from there. It must have been similar to what happened with my parents."

The film's own politics are then certainly more complex than merely an infantilist refusal; 'indifference, or even hostility, towards the world of her parents', as Beatriz Sarlo believes.[187] Couceyro is wearing a blonde wig when she makes the observation quoted above, and the film closes with a long shot of the crew walking down a country path together, backs turned to the camera and wearing blonde wigs, to a Charly García pop-song called 'Influencia' – 'Influence': a performative reassertion of the parents even, and especially, through the very sign that marks in the body the failure and defeat of their political ideal. The song is actually itself a 'copy', the transformation and embodiment of a legacy, being the hispanicized cover-version of a Todd Rundgren track. It is worth quoting some of the lyrics: 'I can see and speak and feel myself asleep under your influence / Your influence / A part of me says stop, you went too far / I can't contain it / I try to resist, I try to resist, but in the end it's no problem / What a pleasure this pain / If I were another, I couldn't understand it, but it's so difficult to see that something controls the way I am / I can see and feel and speak my life asleep, it'll be for your influence / This strange influence."[188] The sequence is filmed in the countryside – the space of Carri's orphaned childhood and also, in Los rubios, a space of transforming the child's ludic imagination into the formal experimentation and play of the film-maker: a space of flight, opposed to the city (the place of work and adulthood) and the barrio (the 'other' place of history and the people, from where Albertina's parents were abducted).[189] The closing shot of Carri and her crew in the countryside, re-embodying the lost ones in the self-chosen, prosthetic family and its queer politics of – or beyond – identity, is then also a reassertion of radical aesthetic and political experimentalism as the best way to be truthful to the parental legacy without becoming trapped in melancholy.

Ironically, while accusing Carri of having put the intimacy of the family before the historical comprehension of the politics of the 1970s, a critique such as Kohan's and Sarlo's aims to re-impose on the memory of militancy and dictatorship a politics of the family. Firstly, the values they reassert are none other than those of filial modesty – as when Sarlo opposes the bad daughter Carri to 'those more humble kids' interviewed by Carmen Guarini in *H.I.J.O.S., el alma en dos*, whose political militancy 'has allowed them to think that they have managed to understand their parents and the ideas motivating their activism'.[190] And, secondly, they demand respect for the elders, instead of the 'catalogue of rash attitudes' (Kohan), which Carri displays towards her witnesses by transmitting testimonies through the mediation of a staged scene or even replacing the testimonial first person entirely with her 'own' (or Analía Couceyro's) voice. Contrasting with the immediacy, even reverence, with which the survivors' testimonial account is made available in films such as *Errepé* and *Cazadores*, in *Los rubios* their talking heads appear doubly enframed on the TV screen in Albertina/Analía's editing room, sometimes barely audible or cut short in mid-sentence. Likewise, in M, Prividera retells an encounter with an ex-comrade of his mother, in a mirror-shot of himself addressing his younger brother, but denying us direct access to his original interlocutor. It is worth quoting Prividera's version of the discussion, which explicates his and

Carri's *political* critique of the survivor generation, while staging in the refracted composition of the shot their impossibility of constructing a stable place of enunciation:

> ... he used this discourse they always do, of, well, we fucked up a couple of things. But when one wants to dig deeper, about what exactly these things were, he says, no, this isn't the moment for self-critique, we mustn't play into the hands of the right. There, I told him: I think the ones playing into the hands of the right were you in the Seventies. Being on the Left is to be self-critical. If you're not self-critical, if you're not critical, you are on the Right. And the guy says, look, I can understand you, you're looking for someone to blame, you're very subjective in your search. Well, I'm looking for those responsible. Someone who takes responsibility at least assumes their role...

In very different ways, then, and more than willing to risk the charge of self-righteousness, Carri and Prividera's films insist on the political nature of their own, contradictory feelings of reverence and scorn, admiration and abandonment, which they translate into a documentary form that, by refusing to provide closure and putting under suspicion the self-sufficiency and presence of the image, remains true to the tenets of radical film-making in the 1970s but questions and challenges its political assumptions. Both films are also remarkably aware of the charges of subjectivity and irreverence that will be laid against them, but they counter-attack by exposing – through ways of framing, in *Los rubios*, or through an aggressive, confrontational interview style, in M – the generational abyss motivating these charges. In a remarkable sequence midway through the film, the crew of *Los rubios* discusses the fax in which the National Film Institute refuses to fund the project on the grounds of 'insufficient documentary rigour', adverting that 'pain can cloud the interpretation of excruciating facts'. Instead of 'fictionalizing her own experience', the Commission exhorts Carri 'to undertake a more exigent search of proper testimonies, to be completed through the participation of her parents' comrades, with their affinities and discrepancies. Roberto Carri and Ana María Caruso were two committed intellectuals of the Seventies, whose tragic destiny demands this work to be carried out.' In a remarkably measured, intelligent analysis the crew decides to use the verdict to its advantage, clarifying its own project *in counterposition* to the Commission's suggestions, and explicating the disagreement by including the sequence in the film: "This is the film they need as a generation", Carri herself comments during the debate, "and I can understand this; the point is that this is a film they have to make, not I. They need this film and I can see why they need it. But I'm not in a place to make it."

Prividera, in an essay published in the journal *El Ojo Mocho* prior to the release of M, goes further in his critique of first-generation memory, reclaiming for his own generation's critique of testimonial discourse the task of recovering historical experience: 'The testimonies accumulate – he writes – without helping us to understand better. For some time now, they have ceased to be cathartic [...] Their multiplication (outside the juridical field) has generated an effect of saturation: a meaningless thicket of experiences of suffering.' There are too many memories but a lack of history, he asserts, in the sense of imposing meaning through the construction of critical distance towards the immediacy of experience. This, he concludes, is the ongoing task of his own generation, suspended in a no-man's-land of time as heirs to a defeated revolution, 'the rearguard of a vanguard which turned into a lost platoon':

> How can we write the rest of H/history? How act without repeating? How speak of the absent without speaking for the absent? How trust one's proper memory when there is no proper memory? How fix in words a memory closer to the clamour of an eternal battlefield than to the quietness of an arms museum? Reflecting (without memorializing). Fabulating (without lying). Re-creating (without concluding). Restoring to (historical) experience its (political) meaning.[191]

Intermedial counterpoints

Although in less agonal and tragic fashion, questions of personhood and enunciation, subjectivity and performance, and of cinema's relation with other media and their modes of indexicality and self-inscription also occupy a number of recent documentaries dealing with the experience of modernity through the prism of *another* – or an other's – performance, thus turning documentary cinema into an exercise of citation. In these films, the documentary encounter stages a confrontation between cinema and other artistic and mass-medial forms: television in Andrés Di Tella's *La televisión y yo* (TV and me, 2003), painting in Alejandro Fernández Mouján's *Pulqui* (2007), contemporary music in Rafael Filipelli's *Esas cuatro notas* (These Four Notes, 2004) and Gastón Solnicki's *süden* (2008), and tango in Cristian Pauls' *Por la vuelta* (Around the Corner, 2002) and Sergio Wolf and Lorena Muñoz's *Yo no sé qué me han hecho tus ojos* (I Don't Know What Your Eyes Have Done to Me, 2003).[192] Filipelli's film about the composer, pianist and conductor Gerardo Gandini, Solnicki's about Mauricio Kagel's last performance in Argentina, shortly before the German-Argentine composer's death, and Pauls' about the bandoneonist Leopoldo Federico, are highly original meditations about the problem of rendering musical experience in a medium that subordinates aural perception to the visual coherence of the shot. Here, however, I will discuss the ways in which Di Tella, Fernández Mouján, and Wolf/Muñoz's films set up both an intersubjective performance – a dialogue and sometimes a duel – between the film-makers and their subjects *and* derive from it a reflection on cinema's particular place in modernity.

Only at first sight, these films are less 'political' than those studied in the previous section. In fact, as Andrés Di Tella has argued, the melancholy and obsession of his first-person narratives and those of some of his peers with truncated, failed or ruined stories also reflects the historical experience of a 'lost generation' of younger brothers and sisters, born too late to have participated in the struggles of the 1970s and too early to partake in the *Nachträglichkeit* and performatic self-assertion of the generation of sons and daughters: 'The failure of the Montoneros generation overshadowed us, those who are in their mid-forties now. We are also a failed generation, but for different reasons [...] we never had the protagonism, nor the ability which, in Argentine cinema, the younger ones have, those who are now in their thirties. We always had it much more difficult, for thousands of reasons, subjective as well as objective ones.'[193] This particular, in-between point of view appears, for example, in the way Di Tella, Wolf/Muñoz and Mouján's films are all concerned with ways of quoting popular and mass culture and its political correlate – Peronism – but without falling into the mythical hagiography of Solanas or Blaustein nor coinciding entirely with the scepticism of Carri and Prividera. Indeed, shifting the focus from politics to the mass-medial and cultural expressions of 'the people' in Argentine modernity is a deliberate attempt to allow for more ambiguous and fluid narratives of history to emerge in the suspension of political judgements.

Di Tella's *La televisión y yo* returns to the counterpoint between archival and individual memory already explored in *Montoneros* but now in more radically essayistic and performative fashion, subsequently developed and further radicalised in his next film *Fotografías* (2007). Taken together, the two form a kind of 'family saga', in which Di Tella chronicles Argentina's insertion into cosmopolitan modernity and into global capitalist exchange over the twentieth century through, in *La televisión*, the story of the SIAM-Di Tella manufacturing empire founded by his Italian immigrant grandfather, which floundered in the 1980s, and, in *Fotografías*, that of his Indian mother, an artist and intellectual who cut all ties with her family in India on moving first to England and then to Argentina with Andrés' father. Yet both films also constantly oscillate between the private and confessional – including home videos featuring Andrés' own family and his little son Rocco, who shoots his own monster movies using his dad's camera and a toy dinosaur – and the public and archival: in *Fotografías*, Di Tella's own physical and spiritual journey to India and into Oriental philosophy brings into view the cultural moment of decolonisation and of political and artistic radicalism in the 1960s, channelled in Argentina through the Di Tella art institute (organised by Andrés' father and uncle). But he also traces the forgotten influences and exchanges with Eastern spirituality at the outset of Argentine modernity, even tracking down in remote Patagonia the Indian adoptive son of modernist writer Ricardo Güiraldes' widow, and foregrounding the Buddhist roots of the latter's classic gaucho novel, Don Segundo Sombra (1926). In La televisión, it is on the contrary the documentary *sujet* – television – which prompts the 'autobiographical turn', as Di Tella, while researching the story of Jaime Yankelevich, Argentina's first radio and television entrepreneur and himself a (Jewish) immigrant, is drawn to the parallels between their two families' stories (not least since SIAM-Di Tella also fabricated the first national television receivers). As Di Tella reflects in La televisión: "The story of Yankelevich, like that of my grandfather, is also the story of a project for the country that failed. And these contraptions are something like its ruins."

The impossibility to divide public from private, personal memory from official history, is of course also the signature of the televisual age, which Di Tella's film seeks to bring once more under the mastery of cinema by performatively enacting it through the montage of TV and personal footage (including, as in Donoso's *Opus*, that home-movie classic, the wedding video). From the outset, La televisión y yo cleverly establishes its narrative and material entanglement of memory and history, the personal and the collective: as a voice-over from Di Tella announces his first memory of television, at age seven, a black-and-white screen shows the high-modernist, jazz-scored jingle of the Telenoche news magazine, all jump cuts and city lights, before Di Tella cuts to other archival footage of a uniform-clad gathering, his voice-over explaining: "I remember perfectly being in front of a black-and-white TV, SIAM-Di Tella of course. And I remember seeing the image of the General Onganía. It was a military coup and he had seized power. That day they didn't let me go to school, because they said the tanks had been brought." Next, while Di Tella tells of his father's resignation from his university post and the family's exile for the next seven years, 8mm footage of little Andrés and his brother on holiday in a northern pine forest fills the screen, literally taking the place of the TV image, while Di Tella comments: "I lost seven years of television, half the collective memories of my generation." The experience of the coup, its political and cultural as well as biographical consequences, are masterfully invoked through the contrasted editing of archival fragments, the found footage becoming allusive and polysemic through its re-inscription in the documentary text. By purloining found footage from their respective places in the historical and the familial archive and editing them together in an ambiguous, intermediate zone between history and memory, Di Tella's films create a filmic discourse of 'double voicing', to use Mikhail Bakhtin's phrase, in which images appear as if between quotation marks. As Michael Chanan has commented, La televisión y yo, 'with a few deft steps […] stakes out an autobiographical position in the historical world which jumps back and forth in time, like private memory, and vaults across the globe and back, and this fluidity is somehow indicated by his thinking about television, which of course does something very similar'.[194]

Di Tella himself has defended the 'centrifugal' nature of his films as central to the documentary enterprise itself, the main challenge of which 'is not to let myself be swallowed up by "themes" and rather to defend the singularity of the story I am telling. To remain confident that the story will speak in its singularity about these things but indirectly so. All the art of documentary narrative is contained in this "indirect speech".'[195] Di Tella's definition of documentary's indirect, refracted approach to the general through the singular also fits Alejandro Fernández Mouján's *Pulqui – un instante en la patria de la felicidad* (Pulqui – an Instant in the Fatherland of Bliss, 2007), which, just as Mouján's previous film *Espejo para cuando me pruebe el smoking* (see chapter 1) uses not a first but a third-person narrator as mediating instance between the camera and its subject. Just as, in *Espejo*, Ricardo Longhini's artwork had provided a reflexive screen for the events of December 2001, here the small-scale reconstruction by visual artist Daniel Santoro of the 'Pulqui' – a fighter plane designed and manufactured in Argentina in the 1950s – opens up a performative space of reflection on, and re-enactment of, the memory of Peronism. The latter functions as a mythical counter-history to subsequent waves of economic liberalisation laying waste to Argentina's dreams of industrialisation and prosperity after World War II. As Santoro writes in his notes on the project (also quoted in the film): 'The project Pulqui JFO (Justicialist Flying Object) attempts to reconstruct a lost epic, to conjure by way of an evocative ritual the furtive passage of a plane escaping into time as if in a dream.'[196]

But if *Pulqui* thus returns to the formula already tried out in Mouján's previous film, of approaching the history of the present not directly but through the medium of art (of which the film becomes a 'critique' in the most literal sense by carefully registering the stages and procedures of the artwork's construction), here this formula is also substantially complicated: first and foremost, through the presence of not one but two protagonists – Santoro, the painter-designer of the object, and Miguel Biancuzo, a veteran carpenter and stage decorator in whose workshop the replica aeroplane is being assembled. The movement between Santoro's downtown atelier (where we see him at work painting his allegorical variations on Peronist iconography) and Biancuzo's workshop on the outskirts, alive with drilling, hammering and welding noises, provides Mouján with a narrative rhythm and an argument. The crossings by car of the bridge over the Riachuelo which limits the city from Greater Buenos Aires offer a stark visual contrast to the mythical past invoked by Santoro and Biancuzo, with the sudden presence everywhere of *cartoneros*, homeless and shantytown dwellers. Yet it is at the same time a re-immersion into what remains of this same past's industrial landscape. Finally, the technical discussions between Santoro and Biancuzo and the collective assemblage of the Pulqui, eventually culminating in the model plane's 'launch' on the toy airstrip of the 'Children's Republic' (an amusement park from the 1950s), performatively re-enact a mythical vision of the Peronist Golden Age, as one of solidary cooperation between intellectuals, engineers, workers and industrialists. This is an epic of labour, which the filmic register teases out in its character as a memory performance, most notably when a shot sequence of Miguel welding and adjusting joints is accompanied intradiegetically by the words of Virgilio and Homero Exposito's tango 'Naranjo en flor' (Orange Blossoms, 1944) on the radio: 'What does it matter what comes afterwards / All my life is yesterday's / forever keeping me in the past...'

But Mouján's film also does something else – and something more – than merely to register and 'document' Santoro's and Biancuzi's work (even if, thanks to the presence of his camera, this work is self-consciously turned into a performance, *which becomes part of the object of memory* and vice versa). In addition to shots related to the construction of the Pulqui and to slide-shows of Santoro's dreamlike paintings intercalated in-between, Mouján edits archival footage from period newsreels and propaganda films covering not just the launch of the Pulqui I and II prototypes (in 1947 and 1951, respectively) but also the Peronist 'Fatherland of Bliss' more generally: a radiant, smiling Evita waving from a train, schoolgirls in white coats playing at a youth hostel, smoking factory chimneys and sunlit workers' holiday camps. Just as Santoro himself (who at one point is seen flicking through illustrated magazines of the Peronist era), Mouján is interested not in the historical value but the mythical density of these iconic visual memories, which he compresses and diverts – in a filmic homage to Santoro's oeuvre – into a mythical image of his own: a white-clad schoolgirl and an aureoled Evita sitting in a light-flooded clearing, in the midst of a fairy tale wood alive with birdsong, whispering to one another. The sequence is a composite of several Santoro paintings featuring Evita and 'Juanito's mum as a schoolgirl' (in allusion to a shanty boy character from the paintings of Antonio Berni in the 1960s) in the woods of the Children's Republic. Yet this sequence is also, Ana Amado suggests, evocative of the way Mouján's film lets itself be inhabited at the same time as appropriating, and imposing its own rules of composition on, Santoro's image-world. Thus, she concludes, the film both duplicates and exposes, the mechanism by which Santoro himself takes hold of Peronism's iconography and, 'in this way, [Mouján] ends up narrating, in parallel to the replica of the Justicialist aeroplane being constructed and through a metonymic movement occurring almost naturally, the trajectory of the documentary itself, with its subsequent alternatives of enthusiasm, failure and recovery with regard to the utopia of "making it fly".'[197] Whether or not the little plane has actually taken to the air at the Children's Republic remains, to the end, a matter of contention between

Santoro and Biancuzo – but in Mouján's film, by way of superimposition, a Pulqui as painted by Santoro does eventually cross the sky over the Riachuelo, to the sound of the Peronist anthem played slowly on a piano.

In Mouján's as in Di Tella's films, the use and intervention of archive footage becomes self-consciously performatic, an 'act of memory' at the close of the age of (physio-chemical) indexicality, which, as Laura Mulvey has argued, brings into view 'the relation between [cinema's] material base and its poetics' in the very instant of its crisis, while other relations, 'intertextual and cross-media, begin to emerge'.[198] Sergio Wolf and Lorena Muñoz's *Yo no sé qué me han hecho tus ojos* (*I Don't Know What Your Eyes Have Done to Me*, 2002) connects this crisis and critical self-reassessment of cinema with the demise of the national-popular moment in which cinema as a mass-cultural form had flourished. Ostensibly an investigative quest for the legendary 1930s actress and tango singer Ada Falcón, who mysteriously retired from the entertainment industry after a tormented romance with bandleader Francisco Canaro, *Yo no sé* is in fact an exercise of mourning and imaginary suture. It is a film which interweaves, at the same time as it embodies the discontinuity between, three cultural moments: the present of enunciation just after 2000, the period between 1920 and 1930 with its studio-based star system and national entertainment industry founded on the twin pillars of tango and cinema, and, finally, the 1960s and 1970s. Here these are remembered not as a period of political struggle but rather as one of film and mass-cultural connoisseurship – the time of cinematic modernism, or *cinéphilie* – alluded to and parodied in the Bogartian performance of the trench-coated Wolf as narrator-detective, but also evoked through the experts and collectors he meets and, more generally, through a host of allusions and quotations only accessible to fellow initiates. As Emilio Bernini points out, Wolf's melancholic odyssey through the city to once-glamorous street corners and dance-halls, only to find them replaced by anonymous food outlets and pharmacy chains, is itself a quote of Edgardo Cozarinsky's film *Boulevards du crépuscule* (*Sunset Boulevards*, 1992) – an already meta-cinematic film, of course, from the title-giving reference to Billy Wilder's 1950 melodrama, and whose historical subject (the exiled French actress María Falconetti) also bears an uncanny phonetic resemblance to that of Wolf/Muñoz, Ada Falcón.[199]

But it is through Alejandra Almirón's vertiginous cross-editing of archival and video footage, more than anything else, that Wolf and Muñoz's film stages a resistance against the mutual estrangement of present and past. Paradoxically – or not – the film-makers, in order to recover a decaying archive, use the very techniques of digitalisation, which have spelled the end of the analogical index (the devices of which are by contrast mournfully recalled in appreciative takes of collectors' items such as vinyl records, film spools, photographs, radio receivers and microphones). Wolf and Muñoz, through editing wizardries such as match cuts between their investigative journey and archive sequences from the Golden Age of national studio cinema, recompose a texture of imaginary wholeness. Often the effect is reinforced through the aural presence of radios and telephones preceding, or continuing beyond the end of, the archival shot edited into the sequence, thus literally resonating through time. But however hard it tries, of course the documentary cannot but expose, in its own materiality, the impact of a radical disjuncture – one that remains unsutured even as the film finally 'tracks down' the nonagenarian Ada Falcón in a remote monastery, only for the old lady to refuse any offer of reconciliation with, or even acknowledgement of, her past self, as the film-makers play a record of her greatest success to her: 'Yo no sé qué me han hecho tus ojos' – 'I Don't Know What Your Eyes Have Done to Me'. Even the real colour of Ada's eyes, never revealed by the black-and-white archive footage, remains, to the end, a mystery. But thus, without ever mentioning politics, the film also stages *in the medium of cinema* the temporality of trauma in its radical discontinuity and irrepressible return, an experience of time that is at the heart both of the modern experience in general and of Argentina's political struggles of the twentieth century in particular. It exposes the present – of the image and of documentary enunciation – as incomplete and perforated by a past of which it cannot get hold. In this *performance of discontinuity*, Wolf and Muñoz's film is also one of the most subtle reflections on a temporality that is out of joint, and turning this temporality into a dimension of the documentary image itself.

Figure 19   A photograph of Ada Falcón in Sergio Wolf and Lorena Muñoz's Yo no sé qué me han hecho tus ojos *(I Don't Know What Your Eyes Have Done to Me, 2002) that connects a crisis and critical self-reassessment of cinema with the demise of the national-popular moment in which cinema as a mass-cultural form had flourished.*

Chapter Five

Embodiments
Genre and Performance

In order to understand how Argentine cinema has changed over the last 15 years, as well as beyond the fiction film, we need to look beyond auteurial styles and explore the importance of casting choices and new forms of screen acting, as well as of narrative genres and their reconfiguration. Remarkably, cinema critics in the country, even as they acknowledge the shifts in film practice since the mid-1990s – especially the replacement of *cineclubismo* by academic professionalisation as the main point of entry to a cinema career[200] – have been reluctant to let go of a modernist notion of the director-author – one that has been fundamental to the institution of criticism itself ever since its inception in the 1950s. But arguably, the film-*auteur* now less than ever describes a collaborative production process in which the majority of professionals shift between roles: directors such as Lisandro Alonso or Enrique Bellande are also accomplished sound engineers working for Pablo Trapero and Adrián Caetano, among others; editors such as Verónica Chen and Alejo Moguillansky have directed outstanding films such as *Agua* (*Water*, 2006) and *Castro* (2009); actors including Marcelo Zanelli, Martina Guzmán or Federico Esquerro also regularly work as assistant directors, producers, sound engineers, and so forth. Indeed, a film such as *Los rubios* is remarkable also as a performative discourse on film-making today, as the collaborative, negotiated production of audiovisual events and their collective *and* individual subject of enunciation.

Genre criticism, star studies and the analysis of actoral performance have traditionally provided critical alternatives to auteur theory, shifting the focus away from the work-immanent analysis of film stylistics and towards the social meanings and ideological implications of the rules and conventions of narrative and embodiment in the cinema, as well as their subversion and contestation in individual works and performances. Whereas the myth of the auteur has both allowed film criticism to hang on to a largely intuitive, hermeneutic mode of analysis *and* to cast contemporary film production in Argentina in a Manichean opposition between 'independent' and 'industrial' cinema imported from the United States – which, as I have argued in chapter 1, does not properly account for the fluid range of production models in the absence of a national studio system – the questions of genre and actorship allow us to understand contemporary cinema and its relation to other media such as television and theatre from an angle less implicated in the politics of the field. I shall begin this chapter by analysing some of the models of screen acting that have emerged over the last decades, including the new performances of stardom and *mises-en-scène* they call forth. Rather than these, however, I look towards the 'actor-medium' (as characterised by Deleuze), a mode of actorship more concerned with observation and ostentation than action, as the most distinctive kind of performance in new Argentine cinema. Next, I will skim through some films exemplary for their treatment of genre elements as well as for the critical debates these have sparked at home and abroad, crystallising – I attempt to show – around questions of realism and self-reflexivity allegorically read against the breakdown of economic convertibility (of currency value), of which the 'universal' formulae of genre are sometimes taken as the figuration and embodiment. Thus, I argue, genre also provides a critical location from where we can understand the conflicting demands and investments to which audiences subject Argentine cinema at home and abroad.

The other auteurs: actoral performances in new Argentine cinema

Estrellas, as we have seen, is a film about casting politics in present-day Argentine cinema, but one which complicates matters by granting voice not to film professionals but to the 'popular subject' that attempts to negotiate and exploit to his own advantage the former's quest for reality effects. Through the multifaceted, indeed theatrical character of Julio Arrieta, León and Martínez's film also exposes the limits and contradictions of a new 'neo-realism's' hold on the immediate and unstaged. As I have suggested, these contradictions are drawn out, and performatised, in the sequence pinning Adrián Caetano against representatives of the actors' union; but they are also present in the discourse of Arrieta himself who claims, on the one hand, that it is the shantytown dwellers who are better placed than 'real actors' to perform the parts of the marginalised and poor – because, he suggests and the film obligingly confirms in its 'gallery of types', their faces and bodies are indexically inscribed with experience in ways that cannot be simulated. In the same manner, film-makers such as Caetano and Trapero have been praised for casting – as Gonzalo Aguilar writes about Luis Margani's performance as El Rulo in *Mundo grúa* – 'not an actor but a *body*, because the traces of years of work and of sudden dismissal cannot be acted'.[201] But at the same time, Arrieta complains that he and his protégés are being cast in token roles only, underestimating their capacity to *act* beyond the reproduction of social stereotypes projected onto them. Thus, without so much as noticing the contradiction (or at least, *pretending* not to notice), Arrieta insists, at one and the same time, on the primacy of experience over performance *and* reasserts the capacity of performance to transcend experience.

Indeed, I shall argue here, it is precisely this fragile and always uncertain balance between experience and performance that is being sought in the casting choices and modes of actorship deployed in new Argentine cinema. Perhaps more than anything, the habit of confounding the boundaries between actor and character by way of a shared name, already noted above in the films of Lisandro Alonso and Raúl Perrone but also widespread in others (including Caetano's *Bolivia*, Luis Ortega's *Caja negra*, Gustavo Postiglione's *El asadito*, Martín Rejtman's *Sílvia Prieto* or Juan Villegas' *Sábado*), is an indicator of this deliberate ambiguity which, as we have seen in the case of Carri and Di Tella's documentaries, is also not restricted to fiction films alone. Among film scholars, Aguilar has been the most alive to this 'politics of actors', as he calls it. In many films, Aguilar argues, *the name* opens up and destabilises the closed envelope of a fictional narrative folded upon itself, while *the face* provides a blank page that is being inscribed and constructed in the course of the diegesis, and *the body* provides a dimension of experience and historicity in its singularity and diversion from the codes of beauty laid down by television and advertising. Either through the use of non-actors (as in Alonso's films or in *Pizza, birra, faso*) or through the casting of experienced professionals but with a theatre rather than film background (Daniel Valenzuela, Susana Pampín, Víctor Hugo Carrizo, Daniel Levy), and even by re-casting established film divas from the past in novel and unexpected roles (as in the case of Graciela Borges and Mercedes Morán in *La ciénaga*, or of Borges, Rita Cortese and Evangelina Salazar in Luis Ortega's *Monobloc*), in many of today's films the face is an unknown quantity rather than – as in Hollywood's star system emulated, on a more modest scale, by the Argentine cinema of the past – a fixed asset: 'The face is being constructed in the measure in which the film transcurs. We see it for the first time and, rather than an actor, we find ourselves before a person [...] To search for the connections between a face and the real (reducing the pretense of acting) could well be one of the casting principles of the new cinema.'[202] Meanwhile, the bodies of El Rulo in *Mundo grúa*, of the youths and adults in *La ciénaga*, or of Misael and Argentino in *La libertad* and *Los muertos*, are placed under intense scrutiny by the camera, just as the surfaces and textures of the locations they inhabit and the objects they manipulate, exposed to an almost 'zoological gaze' which, Joanna Page argues, makes 'many of these films read[able] as provisional forms of (auto)ethnography' at the same time as they reflexively 'deconstruct the relationship between visibility and knowledge'.[203]

As in the actors' union sequence from *Estrellas*, already commented on in the previous chapter, this deliberate production of ambiguity between experience and performance is often achieved by casting non-actors alongside professionals. As Pablo Trapero explains, describing the shooting of *El bonaerense* (2002), his anti-procedural about the provincial police of Greater Buenos Aires: 'The force of the performances is a mixture of things, an experienced actor alongside one with less films to his name. [...] *El bonaerense* was a real stew: some characters were retired policemen, some were in active service, and the majority were actors. [...] The result was a sensation that we had entered the police force and made something like a documentary.'[204] Incorporating some of the most innovative experiences from contemporary theatre practice such as Vivi Tellas' *Biodramas* series – in which different theatre directors research and stage experiences of real people – film-makers such as Trapero, Caetano, Martel and Postiglione maintain the delicate balance between the real and the staged by exploiting both the professionals' capacity to contain and 'fictionalise' the non-actors' performances through their more accomplished and self-aware movement across the set *and* the dose of indexical realism inserted into the scene by the non-actors' spontaneity and presence.

There is more to the politics of casting in new Argentine cinema, however, than merely the introduction of non-professional actors in order to heighten the films' reality effect. If indeed on one end of the spectrum there are the real-life performers of Lisandro Alonso's films – at first sight, pure experience at the null point of performativity, only for Alonso's camera to tease out a dimension of the theatrical almost indistinguishable from experience and always on the verge of collapsing into it once more – on the other end we are also witnessing a renovation of the national star system in the cinema of Fabián Bielinsky, Daniel Burman, Juan José Campanella, Lucía Puenzo or Juan Taratuto. The most important figure here is undoubtedly Ricardo Darín, who after a long career in television and regular appearances in supporting roles in film ever since the late 1970s has turned into Argentine cinema's main asset after his performance as the small crook Marcos in Bielinsky's *Nueve reinas* (*Nine Queens*, 2000). Yet his rise to the stellar heights of becoming 'the Latin De Niro', as the Sunday magazine *.dom* recently titled, came thanks to his collaborations with Campanella, now in their fourth edition with the Academy Award-winning *El secreto de sus ojos* (*The Secret in Their Eyes*, 2009). In these, Darín developed a screen persona somehow both in tune with his own edgy, seductive and vulnerable beauty *and* the projections and identificatory desires of audiences, male as well as female, looking for imaginary releases from the effects of a crisis threatening their social position, personal and gendered identities and self-esteem.[205] As I have argued in chapter 2 in respect of Campanella's *El hijo de la novia* and *Luna de Avellaneda*, Darín's performances revolve around a vulnerability that is constantly warded off until it explodes into full-blown, yet also purifying and revivifying, crisis: the grace and elegance with which his face and body occupy and move across the screen are often punctuated by moments of exhaustion or a wry squirm appearing on the edges of a smile. In this exhibition of insecurities and cracks in the armour of male self-assurance, often diegetically related to moral ambiguities in his characters, Darín's performances distinguish themselves from the more straightforwardly masculine and tough characters impersonated by male leads from the 1980s such as Federico Luppi or Miguel Angel Solá (who he supported in Eduardo Mignona's *La fuga – The Escape*, 2001). As Axel Kuschevatzky, producer of *El secreto de sus ojos*, puts it: 'Like James Stewart, Darín is the personification of the common guy who, if one has a closer look, hides behind those eyes something much more profound, much more complex.'[206] In fact, we could say that the effectiveness of Darín's performance stems from his ability to invoke the dimension of (potentially painful and displeasing) experience – something akin to Aguilar's and Arrieta's 'years of work inscribed in the body' – while at the same time being able to re-channel it once more into the pleasurable and performative release of cinematic fiction. More recently, Darín has explored the darker side of this screen persona – without entirely veering away from it – in his role as the murky insurance lawyer Sosa in Trapero's neo-noir *Carancho* (Hawk, 2010), an interesting and thrilling-to-watch attempt to test the boundaries between commercial action and independent 'quality cinema' from which both Trapero and Darín emerge unscathed and enhanced in their possibilities.[207]

Between the performances of non-professionals – including vocational actors from a popular background such as Héctor Anglada, 'El Cordobés' from Caetano and Stagnaro's *Pizza, birra, faso*, who tragically died in a traffic accident in 2002, but also occasional actors such as rock musicians Rosario Bléfari, Gabriel 'Vicentico' Fernández Capello or Iván Noble, cast in the films of Martín Rejtman and Raúl Perrone – and the star performers appearing in the films of Campanella, Marcelo Piñeyro or Juan Taratuto (apart from Darín, we could mention Pablo Echarri, Soledad Villamil, Natalia Oreiro, Leonardo Sbaraglia or Diego Peretti), a different kind of actorship is flourishing in non-mainstream cinema, often through actors with a background in theatre rather than, as in the case of the commercial star performers, in television. Gustavo Aprea has argued that the break with 'the different styles of "realist" acting as defined by the televisual protocols of credibility', and incorporating 'many of the dramatic innovations taking place on the theatre scene',[208] constitutes one of the defining features of new Argentine cinema. This new mode of actorship has some affinities with the 'new type of actor' that Gilles Deleuze saw emerging in Italian, French and Japanese post-war cinema: 'not simply the non-professional actors that neo-realism had revived at the beginning, but what might be called professional non-actors, or, better, actor-mediums, capable of seeing and showing rather than acting, and either remaining dumb or undertaking some never-ending conversation…'[209]

Deleuze's characterisation of the actor-medium rather nicely describes the spectrum of performances between, say, Valeria Bertuccelli, Marcelo Zanelli and Fabián Arenillas' verbosity in Rejtman's *Sílvia Prieto* and *Los guantes mágicos*, and Julio Chávez's near-speechless, outwardly numbed yet intense presence in Santiago Loza's *Extraño* (*Strange*, 2003) and Rodrigo Moreno's *El custodio* (*The Bodyguard*, 2005). More importantly, Deleuze also calls attention to the way in which the 'professional non-actor', through the way she or he 'shows and sees', calls attention to as well as accommodates within the context of film performance the presence of non-professional actors and real locations. Through their capacity for holding a moment in suspense (either through a quiet intensity or through an excessive, nonsensical outburst of speech), these actor-mediums can jam or break the sensory-motor schemata by which, according to Deleuze, action cinema's movement-image solicits a desensitised, brutalised gaze oblivious to a violence it has learned to digest as mere cliché and re-assimilate it into its system of actions and reactions. By contrast, the actor-medium's capacity to show and see prompts a different, pure optical-sound image to appear – an image of the real torn from cliché – that Deleuze calls the time-image.

From a different perspective, Andrew Klevan has signalled the suspended moment as the cusp of performative mastery in the cinema – the ability to assert, and maintain in the balance, the complexity and openness of a situation before a choice (moral, political, pragmatic) is made in favour of one of the options for resolving it: 'This suspended moment prevents us fixing our interpretations and it opens up possibilities. The performer resists asserting a single emotional response, and allows us to wonder at the different stories available to this character.'[210] In this way, Klevan argues, the suspended moment becomes the litmus test for actoral intricacy: the capacity for simultaneously revealing and withholding aspects of a character's sensibility. A remarkable study in this kind of intricacy is Julio Chávez's performance as the title-giving bodyguard Rubén in Rodrigo Moreno's *El custodio*. Appointed as a government minister's (Omar Núñez) personal shadow, Rubén's job is, quite literally, to follow in the minister's footsteps day in, day out, in order to be on hand for throwing his bulky, heavily armoured and buffeted body in the line of fire in case of an (unlikely) emergency. The film never tells us much about the minister's political opinions or even about his brief, as – like Rubén – the camera stays outside the meeting rooms and broadcasting studios where 'politics are made'. Instead, it focuses on the bland, day-to-day routine of escorting the important man from his home to his office and to cabinet meetings, in a minutely choreographed movement of bodies and vehicles. Bárbara Alvarez and Catriel Vildasola's camera and sound work emphasise the mechanical nature of this horology of power, the camera often shooting from some undefined, fixed point in the back of the car, across the shoulders of Rubén and his driver (Marcelo D'Andrea), as if it were in fact part of the vehicle – a sensation reinforced by the prominence of engine, indicator and wiper noises on the soundtrack. Another recurrent image is an extreme top-down shot of the ministry's courtyard, observing the precise, rehearsed positions of the minister's car and those of his security escort on arrival and departure, the actors' bodies transformed into chess figures performing their strategic and highly formalised moves.

Chávez's performance of this professionally self-effacing character is extremely subtle, in dialogue with a camera that often suddenly 'finds' him inside a frame he has been quietly sharing all along, but in which we only notice his presence once the minister and his entourage have abandoned him on entering some office or meeting room. A man who, for professional reasons, can never be at ease in any given situation, but must be forever on the lookout for potential intrusions, Rubén is a loner excluded from interpersonal relations, which he is nonetheless made to witness in intimate detail, as when he has to escort the minister to a tête-à-tête with a mistress or when he is exposed to the sexual provocations of his protégé's pubescent daughter. We gradually come to share a sense of humiliation when witnessing the remarkably uninhibited display of intimacy Rubén is made party to by the minister, his family and entourage, and the way in which these naturalise the deeply unequal, debasing relationship they cultivate with their subalterns. Chávez's quietly brooding, almost self-effacing yet ominously intense performance, combined with Moreno and editor Nicolás Goldbart's composition of a detached perspective close to but never entirely coinciding with Rubén's, draw our gaze towards this naturalised, everyday relation of abuse in which all participants are complicit. A moment of culmination of this system of debasement occurs during a barbecue the minister hosts at his country mansion for some eminent French visitors, during which he turns one of the few qualities marking Rubén out as a person rather than merely an anonymous, minor wheel in the machinery of power – his passion for drawing – into a private joke to entertain his guests.

What little the film reveals about Rubén's private life – his clumsily caring relationship with his mentally ill sister, punctuated by bouts of nervous aggression, his sorry attempt to find sexual release with a prostitute, contrasting with the almost tender care he dedicates to the collection of guns and rifles at his stale, solitary apartment, the collection of drawings (female portraits and act studies) he keeps hidden in his desk – suggests a man damaged by his self-denying profession, and labouring under an intense, brooding anger. Only towards the end, immediately before the film's violent denouement, are we given so much as a hint about the character's past, when Rubén is addressed by a colleague as someone 'who deserved to be higher up' for the merits assembled during an earlier spell in the military. Whether or not this might be an ominous hint at his participation in dictatorial repression is never made clear, since Rubén brusquely evades, as usual, the colleague's invitation to reminisce about old times. Chávez is again masterful here in simultaneously revealing and withholding the character's moral and emotional depths; a suspended reaction that both defers and foreshadows a propulsion towards violence.

Earlier in the film, in a remarkable sequence just after he has been made the subject of ridicule at the barbecue, Rubén, having cross-checked the locks of the country house, stumbles upon the minister asleep in his armchair in front of the television. The sequence starts with a shot of the sleeping minister from Rubén's point of view, the large glass window behind the armchair reflecting both the television screen and Rubén's own silhouette as he approaches the scene. A reverse shot on Chávez's face and upper body follows, silently, intensely watching the sleeping minister, then turning his head slowly towards the TV screen, as implied by the subsequent shot of the TV, where a pianist plays a solo concerto. In fact, the TV image also refers back to the mirror shot at the beginning of the sequence: a close-up of the pianist's face appears superimposed to a medium-range shot of him at the piano – thus also referring back to the 'superimposed' relationship (and its similar consequences for the composition of the image) between the minister and his shadow, Rubén. This relationship comes to the fore again in the following shots, but its normal constellation is now being complicated, or even reversed, by the minister's unawareness of Rubén's gaze: from the TV screen, Moreno cuts once more to Chávez's face and body in bottom-up shot, now performing the opposite movement – his look slowly turning back from the screen and onto the minister – followed by a medium-length, top-down shot of the minister's face, inadvertently

Figure 20   Julio Chávez's look in Rodrigo Moreno's El custodio (The Bodyguard, 2005) is a fascinating example of performative intricacy, holding the balance between his character's vigilant, protective attitude and the violent impulses that might be hiding beneath it.

at his subaltern's mercy (whose long, scrutinising gaze the shot in fact replicates). Another shot of Chávez follows, now slowly moving forward, an inscrutable look on his face that could just as well be contempt, pity or professional indifference. Chávez bends down, towards the minister who is out-of-frame, roughly in the position from which the shot is taken, his hands quietly manipulating something we cannot see until, in a medium-distance shot which closes the sequence and resolves the moment of tension, it is revealed as the remote control he has gently taken out of the minister's hands to switch off the TV.

The sequence, then, is an exercise in ambiguity, a moment, to quote Klevan again, which 'exemplifies the performer's ability to keep alive the various options which have emerged from the world that the film has established'.[211] Chávez's smooth, near-expressionless face remains enigmatic about the character's feelings and intentions towards his superior, but there is an ever so slight, almost intractable hardening of his features, just prior to the sequence's remarkably tender resolution, that makes us suspect a conflict of contrary emotions. It is this very ambiguity which, enhanced by the extended duration of the sequence, also produces a vaguely but increasingly threatening sensation as the bodyguard gets closer to his master, for once stepping across the barrier of respectful distance. What the sequence draws out, then, is *the potential of the look*, its complex and unpredictable relationship to the action once the automatism of sensory-motor responses has been broken (an automatism which, as *El custodio* shows, is cinema's equivalent to the smooth, mechanical functioning of the gaze and body in the relations of power in which Rubén and the minister are both inscribed). At the same time, the sequence draws attention to the way in which the film as a whole is structured around the actor-medium's *performance of showing and seeing*, which grants us access to the *acting* of the minister and his entourage. This second framing the action internal to the diegesis, through the look of Chávez's character, is also emphasised through frequent mirror shots or shots through half-open doors and windows, refracting as well as locating our gaze at the margins of the scene. Thus, we ourselves are made to observe in a fashion that is close to the dire, humiliating daily routine of vigilance – watching Rubén's showing-and-seeing performance as well as seeing through it.

This tangible performance of the act of witnessing, as a suspended action that simultaneously protects and threatens the object of the gaze and propels the narrative towards its resolution, in a 'breach of distance' that can lead to either violence or tenderness, is also central to another film starring Chávez in the lead role, Santiago Loza's *Extraño* (*Strange*, 2003). Once more, the look and its affective implications are of central importance, as the long opening shot – an extreme close-up of an eye – anticipates. Chávez plays former surgeon Axel who, having left his profession and, apparently, decided to refrain henceforth from any kind of interference, physical or emotional, with the lives of others, nevertheless strikes a relationship with Érica (Valeria

Bertuccelli), a pregnant woman who lives similarly withdrawn following the suicide of her friend and housemate Ana, with whom she had set up a small video enterprise shooting family events and ceremonies. The film follows the two as they build up a fragile, delicate and non-committal relationship, their distance and restraint allowing each other room for their personal sorrows yet also keeping them from fully opening up to one another. Counterpointing each other's performances, Chávez and Bertuccelli maintain an ambiguous state of indetermination, here not primarily (as in *El custodio*) to postpone the explosion of a contained violence but as warding off the despair each character is struggling with, gradually turning into a nurturing of the life to which Érica will, after all, give birth at the end of the film. The protective character of the gaze becomes evident here as we see Axel's face through a textured glass pane at the obstetric ward, followed by a long, intense series of close-ups of Érica's sweating, pain-ridden face as she is having her baby.

Throughout Loza's film, this protective gaze – holding the other in the balance, giving each character space to face their ghosts – is incorporated in the composition of the shot through one of the characters appearing, out of focus, in the extreme foreground of the image, with the other occupying the focal centre in the medium distance. Rather than with a reverse shot, these shots of a performance made room for by the gaze of another character are often spliced together with close-ups of nearby objects or with long shots of empty landscapes, at times indicating the 'lost' gaze of the character who is being looked at and allowed to reminisce or drift off, or simply producing a 'direct time-image' of the kind Deleuze defines as a crystal.[212] Importantly for my argument, this accommodating gaze (present in the image itself as suspended action) also allows both Moreno and Loza to include and re-signify in their films a different kind of actoral performance as embodied, for instance, by Cristina Villamor and Raquel Albéniz as Chávez's older sister – a remarkably similar character in both films, to the point of physically confounding the two actresses, who counterpoint Chávez's taciturn silence with their endless, hysterical conversation.

Even more interesting is the appearance, midway through *Extraño*, of Chunchuna Villafañe as the mother of Érica's dead housemate Ana, who Axel visits to return some of the latter's belongings. Villafañe, known to international audiences for her role in Luis Puenzo's *La historia oficial* (*The Official Story*, 1985) as the former political prisoner and torture victim Ana, gives an intensely melodramatic performance during a conversation with Axel/Chávez, during which, Christian Gundermann writes, she 'showcases the entire theatrical repertoire […] at her disposal, from sobbing to suppressed tears (which turn out to be uncontainable), to the seductive look, all the way to the sarcastic smile of the punished mother who does not comprehend why she has been condemned to suffering'.[213] However, her uninterrupted monologue on the

Figure 21   Julio Chávez and Valeria Bertuccelli in Santiago Loza's Extraño *(Stranger, 2003). The composition of the shot, in shallow focus and with one of the two actors half out of frame, replicates the relation of a mutual, silent empathy building up between them, one character showing and seeing the other's performance.*

soundtrack about the conflicting relationship with her daughter is fragmented on the level of the image by several cuts to Chávez's inscrutable face as he listens, as well as to long close-ups of the cup of tea Villafañe has forced upon Chávez as an excuse to engage him in conversation. Gundermann reads these shots as distancing devices that displace attention from the actress soliciting an emotive response to the act of detached listening performed by Chávez, to the effect that Villafañe's melodramatic performance and, with it, a particular mode of actorship in Argentine cinema, is being actively undone: 'Chunchuna is the paradigmatic manifestation of the dictatorship as melodrama and, in my reading, this role resurfaces in the sequence in Extraño as a foreign object, as a piece of rubbish from the waste bin of film history.'[214] He then proceeds to claim this active undoing of a previous mode of acting and *mise-en-scène* as a move characteristic of new Argentine cinema, as exemplified by a sequence in Martel's *La ciénaga*, where – according to Gundermann – the diva-esque performances of veteran actresses Graciela Borges and Mercedes Morán are similarly denaturalised and exposed as out-of-place through their contrast with those of the child actors surrounding them.

Gundermann is of course right to notice a de-naturalising and even objectifying effect on actoral performance by the intradiegetic presence of a gaze observing it as such. Yet, far from reducing it therefore to 'sheer ridiculousness', I would argue that on the contrary this introduction of the actor-medium and his or her active-passive attitude of spectatorship – of showing and seeing – has the effect of re-accommodating and re-discovering from a different angle the performances of veterans such as Villafañe and Borges. (In fact, the performance of Sofía Bertolotto in the role of the adolescent Momi in *La ciénaga* shares many of the characteristics of Chávez's 'visionary' characters, in the way her gaze mediates and accommodates the actions of others; only that instead of male repression or restraint, her mode of non-interference is that of a female teenager still discovering her place in life.) Both in *Extraño* and in *La ciénaga*, furthermore, the 'diva-esque' performances of Villafañe and Borges, far from breaking up and introducing a grotesque element into diegetic coherence, remain perfectly motivated by the characters they play: Borges the decadent, embittered and delusional family matriarch and Villafañe the repressed upper-class housewife as unable to confront her sorrow as she had been in relating to her daughter. In the visual grammar of *Extraño*, finally, the tea cup close-ups, far from an alienating device, function as an objectified image of the situation's awkwardness, much in the same way as the shots of objects and landscapes spliced into the conversations between Axel and Érica work to punctuate and condense personal states of self-absorption and adriftness.

The actor-medium, playing a character who is partially withdrawn from the situation he or she can therefore contemplate in a way that does not reconduct into action, brings forth a more complex, multilayered image, which viewers are urged to actively explore and analyse – a 'readable and thinking image', in Deleuze's terms, which calls on 'a camera-consciousness' instead of the movement-image's automated sensory-motor reactions.[215] My hypothesis is that this never entirely reliable observer – a character her or himself torn by complex emotions, which the performance reveals only in withholding them, and which therefore become a further, enigmatic dimension of the image rendered through the character's both highly alert and self-absorbed perception – replaces in contemporary Argentine cinema the figure of the testimonial witness frequent in the cinema of the 1980s and early 1990s. As already pointed out in chapter 1, this figure (usually a minor intellectual – a journalist, medic or schoolteacher – who stands for a liberal-bourgeois consciousness in crisis: a 'social detective', in Fredric Jameson's lexicon)[216] provided the cinema of postdictatorship with an intradiegetic point of view and identification. But rather than breaking up visual cliché, making 'our sensory-motor schemata jam or break', this ethical narrator-witness on the contrary functioned as a safeguard against the irruption of 'the whole image without metaphor', in Deleuze's formulation, 'the thing in itself, literally, in its excess of horror or beauty, in its radical or unjustifiable character'.[217] Rather than allowing to break open the allegorical surface, the introduction of the social detective on the contrary facilitated the evasion of the 'real image' of the dictatorship through allegorical figuration, thus holding recent history at a safe distance and allowing to reintroduce it into the generic structures of the family melodrama (*La historia oficial*), the psychological thriller (*Hay unos tipos abajo*) or the hospital drama (*Darse cuenta*). Whereas the testimonial witness, then, functioned as a guarantor of narrative continuity, the actor-medium interrupts the flow of the story by sowing epistemological and ethical uncertainty: his reliability as an observer can never be taken for granted, yet his performance as bearer of the look also contaminates and ultimately cancels out the possibility of an impartial and omniscient point of view. Where the 'consciousness' of the social detective of the 1980s distracted the image from the real to its figuration, the distraction or unreliability of the actor-medium brings figuration to a halt and forces upon us a real image, to be 'read' in its singularity rather than 'decoded' in its conventionality.

Albeit in very different ways, the actor-medium, whose performance of showing and seeing complicates diegetic progression and opens up a visual space for thought, can be found in numerous performances and films of new Argentine cinema: María Onetto in Lucrecia Martel's *La mujer sin cabeza* (*The Headless Woman*, 2007) or in Natalia Smirnoff's *Rompecabezas* (*Puzzle*, 2009), Jorge Román in Trapero's *El bonaerense* or in Otheguy's *La León*, Camila Toker in Murga's *Ana y los otros*, Rosario Bléfari in Rejtman's *Sílvia Prieto*, Ana Celentano in Gugliotta's *Las vidas posibles*, or Daniel Hendler in Burman's *El abrazo partido* and in Gabriel Medina's *Los paranoicos* (The Paranoids, 2008). An interesting variation on this refractory gaze is the actual presence of an intradiegetic camera, a form of visual *mise en Abîme* explored most audaciously by Gustavo Postiglione in *El asadito* (The Barbecue, 2000) and *El cumple* (The Birthday, 2002) as well as – in a rather less accomplished fashion – in *La peli* (The Movie, 2006) and, in a return to form, his most recent *Días de mayo* (*Days of May*, 2009). Shot locally in his native Rosario, Postiglione's films draw on a relatively stable core of actors (Tito Gómez, Carlos Resta, Raúl Calandra, Gerardo Dayub) performing semi-improvised group scenes in front of hand-held cameras of various kinds (digital video, HD, 8mm), the presence of which is justified – partially – by the already ceremonial, or theatrical, diegetic context providing a kind of bass line or platform on which the actors improvise their performative riffs.

El asadito, for instance, chronicles an all-male group of friends gathering on the terrace of Tito's (Tito Gómez) video-rental for the last barbecue of the millennium. Shot in a 20-hour marathon on 30 and 31 December 1999, with real-time indications given at the start of each sequence, the trivial conversations of the friends on topics including cars, women, football, politics, money and the sex lives of celebrities are interspersed with video-interview sequences filmed by a younger, film-student invitee – but mostly shot with another, handheld 35mm camera without explicit anchorage inside the diegesis. In *El cumple*, the rather more opulent birthday party of veteran heartbreaker and film lecturer Pablo (Raúl Calandra) is being recorded by his student Paola (Natalia Depetris), including 8mm and split-screen sequences of behind-the-scenes interviews with friends, his ex-wife and other old flames; all the while Pablo is trying without success to conquer Paola's favours in scenes that may or may not have been shot by cameras under her command. Both films – *El asadito* more than *El cumple* – rarely break through the shallowness and triviality of middle-class small talk and male banter, but the camera's presence introduces into the diegesis itself a dimension of theatricality, which subtly intensifies (together with the various stimulants consumed by the guests) the conflicts and frustrations simmering beneath the surface, and draws out confessional performances that slowly increase in intensity until they culminate in a violent climax, before once again fizzling out into banality just as the parties themselves. Actoral performance in this mode of improvisational role-play becomes a form of social enquiry, in which the encounters of a bunch of thirty- or forty-somethings inevitably turn, as Guillermo Ravaschino has noted, into a collective character-study of a defeated generation, broken and compromised by the dictatorship and its legacy of socio-economic depredation. In *El asadito*, the past 'weighs down, as *an absence*, on the first couple of courses and puddings during this long encounter at seven voices [...] It is the merit of the direction of actors (and of the scheme of free improvisations on pre-established topics) that this tension emerges and sustains itself subtly, naturally [...] taking us away from token representations and into "naturalism".'[218] By inscribing them into an at once theatrical (performative) *and* naturalistic (experiential) context, then, Postiglione endows the performances of his actors with a degree of spontaneity and intensity few other film-makers in Argentina can match; closer to the Fassbinder of *Beware of a Holy Whore* (1971) than to the more polished ensemble movies of Robert Altman. Rather than a particular character whose showing-and-seeing performance draws attention to the look, here it is the camera itself which attains a tangible presence as a generator of performances of intimacy and intensity, which it reveals as always already intended for it. Subjectivity, as Postiglione discovers (at least that of the particular section of the Argentine middle class featuring in his films), is always already cinematic.

Film genres in the corralito: global forms, national figurations

The concept of genre, Rick Altman has warned, is an amphibious customer, attempting as it does to address all stages and levels of the film process, from production structures through formal and aesthetic protocols to forms of distribution and audience response: 'At one and the same time, genre is a structure and the conduit through which material flows from producers to directors and from the industry to distributors, exhibitors, audiences and their friends.'[219] Involving questions of style and film-literacy, as well as of production ethics and audience appeal, the idea of genre and of its recovery and appropriation has become something of a programmatic battlehorse in contemporary Argentine cinema, even if relatively few genre films in the narrower sense of the term – as, say, the children's animation *El ratón Pérez* (*The Hairy Tooth Fairy* – Juan Pablo Buscarini / Andrés Schaer, 2006 / 2008) or the romantic comedy *No sos vos, soy yo* (*It's Not You, It's Me* – Juan Taratuto, 2004) – have been made. Yet from the 'neo-sitcoms' of Martín Rejtman to Adrián Caetano's 'urban western' *Un oso rojo* (*Red Bear*, 2002), Pablo Reyero's 'contemporary noir' *La cruz del sur* (*The Southern Cross*, 2002), Pablo Trapero's 'anti-procedural' *El bonaerense* (2002) or Fabián Bielinsky's 'grifter thriller' *Nueve reinas* (*Nine Queens*, 2000), key films from recent years – especially, and perhaps not altogether by chance, just before and after the political and economic crash of 2001 – have been discussed in terms of their generic affiliations. However, these have also been invested with markedly different meanings and agendas by, on the one hand, film-makers and critics in Argentina itself and, on the other, those writing on Argentine cinema from abroad, especially from inside the anglophone academia.

Given that film genres are global forms, it is hardly surprising that disputes over the meaning of particular film texts for different audiences and within different critical constellations should have crystallised around questions of genre as one of their few shared points of reference. But thus, the debate about genre in new Argentine cinema also facilitates an interesting insight into the way in which the latter – and perhaps 'national cinemas' more generally – negotiate the contradictory demands from local and global audiences. Reading contemporary film production in Argentina through the prism of genre, moreover, offers a critical alternative to the stale and ossified divisions between 'independent' and 'industrial' films or between 'realist' and 'non-realist' auteurs which, as I have argued in previous chapters, have turned from provisional attempts to classify an emergent reconfiguration of aesthetic choices and preferences into active obstacles for the understanding of contemporary film practice in the country.

Generally speaking, the two critical positions in play, whilst agreeing on their simultaneously global and national nature, differ with regard to the character and context of the intervention made through the use of genre elements. Whereas Argentine critics have mainly focused, approvingly or not, on a politics of form, reading the use of genre elements as a particular kind of auteurial intervention in the cinematic field, international scholarship has been more interested in films' reception and distribution in transnational markets and how these are self-reflexively anticipated and critiqued in the film text. In Argentina, the deployment of genre elements has been hailed as a way of escaping the trappings of the arthouse cinema of the 1980s – now deemed pretentious, unrealistic and self-exoticising – and of replacing it with a cinema that is at once popular, contemporary and formally and technically versatile. Critics working abroad, meanwhile, have focused on genre as a mode of allegorising the national and global dimensions of neo-liberal crisis, in a way that, through the self-reflexive deployment of cinematic forms and templates, also exposes cinema's own implication, as an audio-visual commodity, in the global regime of capital and symbolic flows that has laid waste to the country. At the same time, this reading claims, cinema reasserts the capacity of wresting from the subversion and re-appropriation of genre protocols – and of rules of exchange more generally – a strategy of resistance for the remaking of (national) community.

The 'national' argument harks back to a short programmatic manifesto published by Caetano in the journal *El Amante de Cine* in 1995, when he was still to release his first feature-length film. Entitled 'Agustín Tosco Propaganda' (a homage to the leftist trade union leader and symbol of the *Cordobazo* uprising of 1969, which Caetano would re-use some years later as the name of a guerilla squad in his TV serial *Tumberos*), the manifesto issued an only half-ironic call to arms 'against the so-called Argentine cinema, in favour of the people and the cinema as such'.[220] Speaking on behalf of a collective generational 'we' that both parodies and reclaims the combative language of the 1960s and 1970s, Caetano sentences: 'we prefer honesty, austerity, simplicity. We claim the heads of the pompous hypocrites and lackeys who pretend that cinema is the property of someone or of some country. Argentine cinema *for export*. Complicity with cultural imperialism.' And he concludes by urging his peers to 'defend the classical language against the nostalgic modernisms, with their double standards harmful to popular wisdom. To love horror, the western, crime, science fiction, pornography, as a counterculture against a false intellectualism imposed on us from the screen.' Caetano denounces a cinema which he claims refrains from genre formulae in the name of artistic quality, only to become entrapped in the niche market of 'world cinema', for which it produces suitably exotic as well as pseudo-documentary 'quality fare', often through the recognisably 'Latin American style' of magical realism. While Caetano's manifesto does not mention names, readers of *El Amante* would have understood the message: on the cover of the previous issue, under the title 'Argentine cinema: the bad / the new', a still from Eliseo Subiela's *No te mueras sin decirme adiós* (*Don't Die Without Telling Me You're Going*, 1995) appeared opposite another one from *Historias breves*, the first compilation of shorts from the *Universidad del Cine*, which included Caetano's own 'Cuesta abajo' (Downfall, 1995). The recovery of genre cinema, then, for Caetano and his peers presented an opportunity for shedding the false, auto-exoticist and precious nationalism of which they accused the previous generation, and for making 'national-popular' films by unabashedly applying the 'universal' language of genre to local settings, characters and plots.

However, rather than merely 'translating' genres into an Argentine context – in the way, say, a long tradition of gaucho movies sought to adapt the western to the conflicts between Creoles, Indians and Spaniards in the nineteenth century – Sílvia Schwarzböck suggests Caetano's cinematic practice actually inverts the relation between genre and nation: 'In *Un oso rojo*, [Caetano] not only does not propose to treat Argentina as the problem and the western as the solution (suggesting that it is the genre best suited to present the country's problems), but he turns the tables: the problem, in Caetano's case, is the western, Argentina its solution.'[221] Caetano, Schwarzböck argues, had already proved in *Pizza, birra, faso* and *Bolivia* that he knew how to film the contemporary city and its margins; the challenge in *Un oso rojo* was to move beyond the observational realism of the former and incorporate the classical protocols of argument, shot composition and performance in order to achieve a degree of intensity and narrative economy similar to those of the masters of the western genre: 'Every genre tells a story in which everyday life is represented in one single aspect [...] but in this way events develop with an intensity they do not have outside cinema, because the genre film stages only those elements which make the plot advance towards its resolution.'[222] By contrast, David Oubiña has attacked Caetano's use of genre formulae as merely nostalgic and ultimately reactionary, drawing on Fredric Jameson's argument about 'postmodern' cinema's incapacity to refer to anything but the history of cinema itself, thus confirming – and colluding in – the irredeemable commodification of culture. For Oubiña, 'whereas the new cinemas of the 1960s had their origin in a re-reading of film genres, the director's project is to turn backwards, attacking cinematic modernity through the re-establishment of the genres'.[223]

Do genre narratives intensify the cinematic representation of contemporary conflicts or aestheticise these by safely reintroducing their unbearable and unsettling aspects into the familiar protocols of classical action cinema? *Un oso rojo* can certainly be read both ways: it tells the story of ex-convict Rubén, alias El Oso – played in a swaggering, lone-avenger performance by Julio Chávez – who on his release from a seven-year prison spell for having killed a policeman in a botched assault finds his wife Natalia (Soledad Villamil) and daughter Alicia (Agostina Lage) living with Sergio (Luis Machín), who has lost his job and run up huge debts for betting on horses. El Oso tries to right the wrongs of his former self, coyly wooing his little daughter with attention and presents (the title-giving red teddy bear), but things have changed in his absence. The once-humble neighbourhood on the (western) outskirts of Greater Buenos Aires has turned into a derelict, crime-ridden frontier of civilisation: a 'far West', as it is ironically referred to by former local crime lord, one-armed El Turco – 'the Turk' – (René Lavand), who has relocated to a ramshackle saloon in La Boca, on the limits of the federal capital, and evades Oso's demands for his share of the loot owed to him. Strapped for cash, Oso assaults a clerk he has overheard in a call centre talking about a pay advance, gets a room in a cheap hotel and a job as minicab driver through Güemes (Enrique Liporace), a long-retired ex-criminal and friend of a former prison inmate. One day, returning from a visit to the playground with Alicia, where he is humiliatingly frisked by police officers, Oso is told by Güemes the story of a fellow cabbie, another ex-criminal, whose little granddaughter was shot by the police when they tried to arrest him. "Sometimes the best you can do for the ones you love is to stay away", he says. Oso takes Güemes' advice, but before walking off into the urban night he rescues Sergio from the betting office, beating up his creditors, and accepts El Turco's offer to participate in a supermarket assault, fully aware that the other is setting him a trap. The assault turns out to be another ill-prepared, bloody mess, but before his accomplices can finish him off, Oso kills the three of them and, after dropping the booty off to Sergio just in time to avoid the family's eviction from home, makes for El Turco's bar, where he liquidates the rest of the gang, nailing El Turco's sole hand to the counter (in a direct citation of Ford Coppola's *The Godfather*, USA 1972) and shooting his two henchmen with the single bullet remaining in the old six-shooter Güemes has lent him. Like the heroes from John Ford or Anthony Mann's late-classical lone-avenger westerns, then, and unlike 'the classical hero who *joins* the society because of his strength and their weakness', El Oso '*leaves* the society because of his strength and their weakness. [Whereas] the classical hero *enters* his fight because of the values of society, the vengeance hero *abandons* his fight because of these same values.'[224]

While generally well received for the muscular yet vulnerable performance of its gunfighter protagonist and for its unflattering portrayal of post-2001 Argentina as capitalism's new frontier – a society regressed into a primitive, all-out violence where 'the State is merely another of the gangs competing with

Figure 22 The shootout sequence in Adrián Caetano's Un oso rojo (Red Bear, 2002) openly reverences the genre of the vigilante western, perforating in its carefully choreographed violence the realism that prevails in other sections of the film.

each other for laying down the law',²²⁵ police officers are among the regulars of El Turco's canteen, and the gang lord himself is rumoured to be in business with the local mayor – Caetano's film also incurred criticisms for its quick-paced, choreographic violence and its supposed moral and political nihilism. On the one hand, for Joanna Page, 'Caetano's success lies in his creation of an antihero whose personal sense of honor leaves us all the more troubled by his cold-blooded cruelty. As in many westerns, rough justice emerges as a more credible alternative than the blunt instruments of the law. However, *Un oso rojo* diverges significantly from many of the more conventional westerns in its moral ambivalence...' Like Schwarzböck, she praises the film's capturing of a post-2001 perception of national politics and the state as parties in a criminal ploy to ransack the country, and approvingly refers to the sarcastic parallel montage in which Caetano splices images of Alicia's school celebration of the national holiday together with the build-up to the supermarket assault by Oso and El Turco's henchmen. The final verses of the national anthem sung by the children – 'and let's vow to die in glory!' – resonate over images of the gunmen opening fire on security guards and bystanders alike, Oso once again putting a bullet into a police officer who happens to be on scene. 'In a ruthless world', Page concludes, 'the crime of the individual serves only to throw into relief the greater crimes of the state and its institutions'.²²⁶

Others, meanwhile, have taken Caetano to account for the way in which his lone vigilante – unlike the classical western avenger who re-establishes community through a solitary, self-sacrificial act of justice – forsakes any social or political reparation. The dimension of Oso's actions is purely individual, and thus, James Scorer claims, 'in the light of the fragmented urban community, merely promotes a creed of survival that perpetuates the very fragmentation it sets out to confront'.²²⁷ In a context of widespread social mobilisations (the movie was shot in 2001) Caetano's celebration of lone-avenger-justice actively turns its back on the networks of solidarity and community emerging from the landscape of dereliction *Un oso rojo* so effectively portrays. Scorer approvingly quotes Oubiña's dismissal of Oso's act of justice in the name of property and family values: 'His only legitimacy is of a private order. He eliminates the evildoers because they steal *his* money, he threatens his wife's new husband because she is *his* wife and then he pays the debts because they concern *his* daughter.'²²⁸

It could be argued, however, that criticisms such as Oubiña's want to have it both ways: on the one hand, genre is pinned against realism and accused of aestheticising and ideologically deforming the crudeness of the real; yet, at the same time, excessive fidelity to genre also results in a failure to provide a morally edifying or exemplary resolution. What Oubiña finds wanting in *Un oso rojo* and other films of new Argentine cinema is what we could call the tutor-code of cinematic modernism, the way in which avant-garde cinemas of the 1960s and 1970s invoked generic formulae only to deconstruct them, making the spectator 'see through' the ideological machinations into which she had been lured. Yet could this insistence on an intrafilmic instance of critique, signposting the ideological trappings of genre and guiding viewers safely towards political consciousness, not also be charged with underestimating the film literacy of audiences today? If we take Jameson's post-genre hypothesis seriously, we may have to accept that spectators are perfectly capable now of understanding and appreciating generic devices for what they are: a play, a rhetorical game the purpose of which is not to 'represent reality' but through which contemporary reality can be alluded to in an indirect, ironic or critical fashion (either where it is found to coincide with the genre tradition or as an element that contradicts and transforms it). The auteurial signature, Emilio Bernini argues regarding *Un oso rojo*, is today no longer found in breaking open the generic code (as in modern cinephilia's discovery of the auteurs in classical studio cinema) but in its very deployment, in a moment in which the institutional supports that once made genres the canonic form of cinema have disappeared: 'In contemporary recourse to genre, the auteur rises before, and grows into more than, the image; the genre is an object of added value that benefits the auteur, its use being proof of dexterity, of the knowledge of the object and its laws, including their infringement and transformation, rather than of the functioning of these laws as such.'[229]

A similar argument for auteurial dexterity in the deployment and transformation of genre features has been advanced in favour of *El bonaerense* (2002). For Gonzalo Aguilar, Pablo Trapero's film combines elements from opposite ends of classical Hollywood cinema, such as the crook movie (a subgenre of film noir, protagonised and sometimes narrated by the villainous anti-hero, such as Raoul Walsh's 1949 hit *White Heat*, featuring James Cagney) and the police procedural (which, contrary to the noir's blurring of boundaries between crime and police work, chronicled the process of police investigations through the perspective of a virtuous officer, as in Mervyn LeRoy's 1959 classic *FBI Story* with James Stewart, or Norman Jewinson's anti-racist *In the Heat of the Night*, 1967, starring Sydney Poitier). The glue connecting these opposite ends of classical studio cinema, for Aguilar, is provided in *El bonaerense* by the literary tradition of the *Bildungsroman*, or initiation novel, as the film chronicles the education – or indeed corruption – of village locksmith Eduardo 'El Zapa' (Jorge Román) into the battle-hardened, cynical Corporal Mendoza of the Buenos Aires provincial police ('La Bonaerense'). Nevertheless, for Aguilar, 'Trapero's film gives us all the elements (there are armed battles, situations of violence, shots, corpses, crimes and criminals, defenders of the law, and so forth) and yet any attempt to refer these back to a particular genre typology is bound to fail.'[230]

For Aguilar, this failed genre inscription is simultaneously the film's success in drawing out the singular, dysfunctional nature of police work in a context of social disarray. Genre is being deployed here as a mode of experimental ethnography, a prism through which to observe and explore a self-enclosed, corporate world that makes up its own moral rules and power networks parallel to, and undermining, official 'procedure'. Relations of personal loyalty and betrayal stand in for, and contribute to, the decaying state institutions and social anomie. At the start of the film, Zapa is arrested as the scapegoat after being lured into opening a safe for his boss Polaco's (Hugo Anganuzzi) criminal business partners. His police-officer uncle Pellegrino (Luis Viscat – himself a former police investigator and author of a book-length study on corruption inside La Bonaerense, who also worked as a script advisor) calls in a favour from fellow *comisario* Molinari (Víctor Hugo Carrizo) to get Zapa out of jail and straight into police academy, in the meantime working as an apprentice in the suburban police station where Molinari's corrupt second-in-command Gallo (Darío Levy) is scheming to take over the reigns. At the academy, Zapa wins the attention of law tutor Mabel (Mimí Ardú), with whom he starts a sexual relationship that comes to an acrimonious end when he accepts the protection of the fast-ascending Gallo (whose attention he catches for his safe-cracking skills). Following the point-blank killing on New Year's Day of a drunk motorcyclist by an equally hung-over police officer, Gallo takes over from Molinari, with Zapa as his right-hand man entrusted with collecting bribes from prostitutes and restaurant owners in exchange for protection. When Polaco reappears to propose another heist, Zapa decides to take his revenge and reports the scheme to Gallo, only for the latter to collect the loot himself, killing Polaco and wounding Zapa with a gunshot to the leg to fake an armed encounter. Pressed into silence by Gallo, the invalid Zapa is ascended in rank and redeployed as commanding officer to his native village in the countryside.

Filmed from a free indirect perspective close to Zapa's own perception of events – a narrative form that is particularly efficient during a shootout sequence, in which the traditional reverse shot indicating the position of the opponents is missing, only showing us in hand-held shots the visibly shaken Zapa as he fires randomly into the distance – *El bonaerense* denies us any kind of social or political contextualisation, indeed any kind of detached viewpoint outside the corporate world of the police force from which to judge the characters' attitudes and actions. Released after a series of high-profile crimes involving members of La Bonaerense had come to light (including the assassination of journalists and political activists and even the 1994 bombing of the Jewish Mutual Association AMIA, which killed 85 people), Trapero's film received criticisms for not having adopted a more analytical stance towards its subject: 'Not a word, not an image, on the connections with political powers', Guillermo Ravaschino complained, 'and without the political connections (from Councillors to very high up) it is absolutely impossible to understand the *maldita policía*'.[231] 'Maldita policía' – the accursed police – was an expression coined by journalist Carlos Dutil in 1996, following a series of brutal killings by the provincial police whose (later processed and imprisoned) chief was defended by Governor and presidential candidate Eduardo Duhalde as 'in charge of the best police force in the world'. Months later, the tortured and burned corpse of José Luis Cabezas, the photographer contributing the images for Dutil's article, was discovered in a wrecked car. Dutil went on to write the book-length study *La Bonaerense* (1997), co-authored with Ricardo Ragendorfer, who advised on Trapero's script and appears in a cameo role in *El bonaerense*. Trapero defended his film by stating that it was not cinema's job to bring people behind bars: 'I think this idea is wrong and naïve. The kind of impact cinema has on its audience is not mechanical and linear. For me it's wrong to think that the director is a kind of Messiah who brings light to the cave by showing his poor audience the truth...'[232] Instead, by drawing on the procedural tradition, *El bonaerense* manages to narrate the sordid daily routines of low-level police work, including the naturalised acts of corruption and neglect – aspects investigative press coverage hardly ever tackles in its aim to uncover the political scandals 'higher up'. But by thus asking us through its unemphatic, observational camerawork in which the medium distance prevails, to suspend moral and political judgements, Trapero's film can uncover a deeply ingrained, corporate structure of affect guided by unofficial networks of favour and loyalty, a strange world in which the civil public, in Aguilar's formulation, 'is the out-of-field'.[233] However, writes sociologist Horacio González in a much-quoted review in the journal *El Ojo Mocho*, even if *El bonaerense* – and other 'post-generic' films such as *Un oso rojo* – thus succeed in their self-professed attempt to describe and observe rather than preach to the already convinced: 'they have to reinstate through artistic means the power that is nevertheless proper to all fiction: to discern the values that make a life in common possible'. González's verdict is ultimately favourable: 'Whereas *El bonaerense* goes to the grain of the national-popular drama, as if it were a "socialist realism" violated by the obscurity and resignation that weighs down on lives and things, *Un oso rojo* serves up a lavish baroque only to insinuate that we are faced with an unprecedented collective tragedy. Thus, we arrive at the conclusion of our itinerary: what we are watching is a "national cinema", in every sense of the term, immersed in the chronicle of national dissolution.'[234]

Gabriela Copertari agrees in her discussion of the late Fabián Bielinsky's box-office hit *Nueve reinas* (*Nine Queens*, 2000) that contemporary Argentine films are in their great majority 'narratives of disintegration', which 'articulate a social experience of loss'.[235] The appropriation and subversion of Hollywood genres, of which *Nueve reinas*, for Copertari, is the paradigmatic example, thus constitutes a kind of – problematic and contradictory – symbolic revenge against the perceived ransacking of the country on the hands of global capital: as in many other films, Joanna Page observes, 'nationalist readings are suggested' in *Nueve reinas* in the way in which 'homegrown criminals are pitted against evil institutions with global reach'.[236] The appropriation of genre cinema by the 'peripheral' artisans and storytellers of the new Argentine cinema is thus cleverly convoluted with the social banditry films such as *Un oso rojo* or *Nueve reinas* could be read as exalting. As Bielinsky himself suggested in an interview given on the release of *Nueve reinas*, 'to construct the film's plot I called on the proper structures of swindle. The fact that I can use those elements as cinematic forms also calls for a reflection about cinema, about how close it is to a swindle, to making someone believe in things that don't exist.'[237]

In a fast-paced succession of events over a single day, *Nueve reinas* tells the story of two con artists – slick, experienced Marcos (Ricardo Darín) and young newcomer Juan (Gastón Pauls) – who casually meet (or so it appears) during a failed swindle the latter attempts to pull off at a service station. After being rescued by Marcos, the two agree to partner up for one day, for the veteran grifter to show the young apprentice some of the tricks of the trade. After a few minor coups, sparring the two male leads against one another, Darín donning the unscrupulous rogue to Pauls' handsome charmer, events quickly gather speed: Marcos is called by his sister Valeria (Leticia Brédice) to the elegant, nouveau riche hotel where she works as a receptionist, in order to get one of his old accomplices off her back, veteran forger Sandler (Oscar Nuñez), who has appeared at the premises only to suffer a breakdown. Sandler, it turns out, was about to trick a shady Spanish businessman and amateur philatelist staying at the hotel, Vidal Gandolfo (Ignasi Abadal), into buying one of his forgeries, the

Figure 23   *The shootout in Pablo Trapero's* El bonaerense *(2002) exemplifies the film's elimination of visual detachment, point of view being restricted to the character's immediate surroundings. Just as Zapa (Jorge Román), we never get to see the criminals firing at the police from the darkness.*

'Nine Queens' stamp series. Unable to perform the scam himself Sandler desperately accepts Marcos' offer to step in for 90 per cent of the profits.

Valeria, who has fallen out with Marcos after the latter has tricked her and their younger brother Federico out of a 200,000-dollar family inheritance from their Italian grandparents, briskly orders him off her workplace, but with Juan's help, Marcos nonetheless manages to catch Vidal Gandolfo's attention, agree on a price and set an appointment for the sale later the same evening. On their way out, however, Marcos and Juan are mugged by motorcyclists in the street and lose the stamps; in their desperation, they decide to go through with the deal anyway by purchasing the originals from Sandler's wealthy sister (using the inheritance money Marcos has stolen from Valeria, and all of Juan's savings). When they arrive back at the hotel, Vidal Gandolfo drops in on another argument between the siblings and, taking advantage of the situation, insists that a tête-à-tête with Valeria be part of the deal. Valeria finally agrees to the arrangement, when Marcos admits his guilt to Federico, and takes the stamps to Vidal's hotel suite, emerging a few hours later with a cheque. But when Marcos and Juan arrive at the bank at opening time, they discover that it has closed its operations, the foreign mother company having confiscated all funds. Leaving a battered Marcos at the bank's gates, nearly trampled over by other angry customers, Juan walks off into the street – only to arrive at the backstage of a theatre where all the rest of the cast, including Sandler and his sister, Vidal Gandolfo and the motorcycle thieves, are already gathered together: they all turn out to be actors and con artists hired by Juan – whose name is actually Sebastián and who is Valeria's boyfriend, for whom he has organised the scam in order to recover the lost inheritance and take revenge on Marcos.

The old deceiver himself ends up as the one who has been framed, but so – the film proposes and many of its critics agree – does mainstream cinema, which is being caught at its own game and delightfully exposed and turned over to an auteurial, film-artisanal self-consciousness and reflexivity. For Diego Lerer, writing in the daily *Clarín*, 'in one of the most accomplished films Argentine cinema has given us in a long time, Fabián Bielinsky (a debuting director but a veteran of the industry) plays several games, and he wins almost all of them. If his film (just as his characters) is pure deceit, the illusion of truth nevertheless almost always triumphs. It's like a game of poker, of traps and illusions: and the spectator falls for almost all of them.'[238] Striking a solitary note of dissent, veteran documentarist and critic Raúl Beceyro accused Bielinsky's film in the journal *El Amante* of pulling off the ultimate scam, passing off as high art what is actually a classical ploy of industrial affect manipulation: 'The last swindle of *Nueve reinas* [...] is one the film perpetrates on its critics, in making them believe that [it] is simultaneously, "miraculously", an industrial product and a great film', when in fact, 'as a brutal instance of market cinema, its primary concern is to leave the spectators soothed once the screening is over'.[239] Joanna Page blows into the same horn when she accuses Bielinsky of 'aestheticizing crime', in a disregard not altogether unlike the characters' own for 'the senselessness, the desperation, or the random nature of crime in contemporary Argentina […], consistently ignor[ing] the role of economic misery in the growth of thefts and violent attacks'.[240] Against these criticisms which, just as the ones made against *Un oso rojo*, condemn genre cinema for its insufficient dose of social reality, Copertari has defended *Nueve reinas* as 'a doubly deluding film', arguing that, while it 'produces a compensatory effect and a symbolic reparation for the social experience of loss it depicts', through the revenge plot exerted on Marcos, it at the same time 'renders that effect unstable, undecidable, and ultimately states the radical impossibility of that reparation. Or, to put it in Beceyro's terms, the film *satisfies* the spectators, but leaves them uneasy by showing a collective social complicity in the process of national disintegration that is the film's historical and narrative context.'[241]

Copertari is right to insist on the performative rather than mimetic way in which the representation of the social is constructed in genre film. In Copertari's reading, *Nueve reinas* succeeds in embodying – in finding a formal solution for – the contradictory feelings of loss and complicity through which film audiences in Argentina experienced the crisis of neo-liberal economics in the late 1990s. The 'pleasure' of seeing these contradictions being imaginarily resolved within the generic form of the grifter movie (as the collective framing of the deceiver) remains, quite literally, a guilty one: as in *Un oso rojo*, there is no moral high ground left, neither inside the story nor in its self-conscious expropriation of 'industrial' forms (an important difference between Caetano and Bielinsky's films and the less reflexive, and rather more emphatically moralising, crime thrillers by Marcelo Piñeyro, *Caballos salvajes* [*Wild Horses*, 1995] and *Plata quemada* [*Burning Money*, 2000]). *Nueve reinas* has frequently been read, particularly for the sequence outside the closed bank, as a prescient anticipation of middle-class unrest following the freeze on bank accounts – ironically known as the *corralito*, or playpen – declared by the minister of economy, Domingo Cavallo, in December 2001. However, it can more properly be understood as the fullest expression of the twilight years of *menemismo*, during which it was written and shot: a background against which the film's frivolous cynicism turns into a complex, multilayered game of references, rather unlike its bland Hollywood remake (*Criminal*, Gregory Jacobs, USA, 2004) from which these contextual allusions are absent altogether. Political discourse in Argentina surrounding the ascension of President Menem's short-lived successor, Fernando De la Rúa, was all about the continuity of neo-liberal fiscal austerity – but 'without the corruption'. The idea sold to (and eagerly bought by) the electorate was that a decade of vigorous redistribution of wealth from the most vulnerable sectors of the population to transnational investors could be whitewashed into a 'good neo-liberalism' kept in check by boring but honest administrators (de la Rúa's administration turned out to be just as happy as that of his more flamboyant predecessor to bribe and blackmail its way to Congress majorities).

In this context, the audience and critical success of *Nueve reinas* was probably down to its construction of a political allegory which could be flipped both ways: we can indeed read the character of Marcos, as Copertari suggests, 'as a figuration of the representatives of the state who sold out the national heritage through the corrupt privatization of the state, the de-industrialization of the economy and the wholesale larceny of people's savings'.[242] In this account, Marcos – for whom read Menem or Cavallo – could be singled out as the traitor to the national family on whom the latter takes its revenge by letting him have some of his own medicine. But this very 'resolution' could also be taken as pointing to the continuities between one regime and the next (embodied in the duo Marcos–Juan/Sebastián), with the implication that the latter, if anything, is an even more expert schemer than its predecessor. *Nueve reinas*, then, did to the urban middle-class universe what *Un oso rojo*, a few years later, would do to the impoverished suburban periphery: it encounters in the narrative template and mannerisms of acting performance and *mise-en-scène* proper to genre cinema a figurative expression for the way capitalist globalisation is experienced from a particular location and class perspective. At the same time, these localised appropriations of global forms on behalf of a film culture far removed from the Hollywood studio system also reflect on and perform, in the peculiar twists they give to the generic template, the ways in which Argentina is inscribed, as a minor player, in global networks of exchange.

Chapter Six

Accidents and Miracles
Film and the Experience of History

In a recent book, Jacques Rancière associates the cinema with a particular, modern mode of historical experience caught in-between 'the age of theatre and that of television'.[243] Unlike the forms of staging and performing from which it took its earliest cues ('theatre', in the widest possible sense of the term) and the ones it would usher in ('television' and its digital sequels), Rancière claims, the cinema is haunted by a split, a non-identity at the core of the image, which is indexically marked by the imprint of real bodies which are at the same time being mobilised for the sake of storytelling, of fiction. Unlike television, which attempts to 'realize in its own way the panaesthetic project of a new art endowed with immediate sensible presence',[244] the cinematic fable is always thwarted by its own excess; therefore, the construction of film narrative (through editing and shot composition) also involves a critical self-awareness at the very level of the image, a non-immediacy which is unique to film.

In the introduction to this book, I claimed that cinema was more alive than any other medium to the 'return of history' in Argentina around the millennium. This was made possible, I argued, because of the way cinema's material form and modes of production made it both contemporary with the crisis of *menemismo*'s speculative economics (the impact of which it suffered more immediately than, say, poetry or painting) *and* out-of-phase with the immediacy in which television and digital media became a direct conduct for politics and economy. As a *representation of history* that was simultaneously *marked by history*, in other words, cinema was prompted to find formal solutions for its own paradoxical non-simultaneity with the national present (including, as I have argued in chapter 1, its counter-cyclic moments of crisis and recovery in relation to those of the national economy at large). It found these solutions, even more than in the allegorical figurations of genre (or in novel combinations with these), in variations on the Deleuzian time-image, drawing out the intensity of pure becoming by actively incorporating showing and seeing as key dimensions of the image itself. These, I have argued, became active presences either through the performance of an actor-medium or by calling attention to the camera's own presence as a facilitator of both performance and spectatorship. More than in the 1980s, when 'history' had been a favourite subject yet was filtered through an aesthetics close to TV melodrama, Argentine cinema in the wake and aftermath of the millennium has been a form of historical consciousness by making the image conscious of itself.

Consciousness, for Rancière, arises from the state of non-identity inscribed at the heart of cinema's at once historical and diegetic ('fictional') image – the distinction between the two becoming less straightforward the more the image is actively implicated in the construction of narrative. In new Argentine cinema, this constant and uncertain oscillation between materiality and simulation, between the real and the staged, also proved an extremely powerful mode of representing the social crisis ensuing from the bust of an at once real and imaginary, credit-based consumption spree, prompted by a barrage of political slogans and advertising messages during the 1990s promising to lift the country 'into the First World'. In this chapter, I conclude my survey of Argentine cinema over the last two decades by looking at several films which, I argue, incorporate in their own composition, as a question of narrative temporality, the crisis of historical experience that is also their subject. I start by discussing Lucrecia Martel's trilogy of family dramas based in the provincial middle class of Salta – *La ciénaga* (*The Swamp*, 2001), *La niña santa* (*The Holy Girl*, 2004) and *La mujer sin cabeza* (*The Headless Woman*, 2007) – before comparing their intricate constructions of temporality with Enrique Bellande's remarkable documentary *Ciudad de María* (*Mary's City*, 2001). I end with a brief outlook on new Argentine cinema's achievements over the last two decades in its engagement with the present and past of society in a period of crisis and recomposition, and the challenges and pitfalls resulting from its in many ways unprecedented success.

States of grace

In *La niña santa*, there is a brilliant – and crucial – moment when Amalia, the adolescent protagonist (María Alché) is confronted for the second time with the sexual advances of the middle-aged Dr Jano (Carlos Belloso). One of the speakers attending the medical congress that is taking place at the hotel run by Helena, Amalia's mother (Mercedes Morán), Dr Jano has already taken advantage once before of the crowd gathering in front of the music store across the street, watching a theremin performance, to approach Amalia from behind and press his genitals against her buttocks. The theremin, also known as etherophone or thereminvox, is an electronic instrument invented by a Soviet physician in the 1920s, which is played without physical contact from the player, who controls pitch and volume through movements of his hands that are sensed and transformed into audio signals by two metal antennas. The crowd's gazes, then, are captivated by something that cannot be seen – the invisible origin of a sound without any physical anchorage. At the same time, this spectacle of the invisible also provides Dr Jano with the condition of anonymity he exploits to impose himself on Amalia, confident that the young girl will not dare to leave her position of spectator to challenge him and reveal herself the victim of sexual aggression. What Jano is looking for – as becomes clear in the course of his stay at the hotel, where he nervously confronts Helena's seductive advances – is not merely the gratification of physical contact but, moreover, the assertion of (male) power over an objectified body that does not dare to return his gaze. Yet this is precisely what happens in the second scene in front of the music store – the theremin player performing, of all things, the 'Habanera' aria from Bizet's *Carmen* – when Amalia first moves her body actively into Jano's reach, forcing him to select her from the girls in the crowd, then touches his hand and, almost simultaneously, turns her head to look him right in the face, forcing him into a hurried and undignified escape.

From a feminist critique of the male gaze as a voyeuristic assault on, and objectification of, the female body, this sequence could be read as an act of female empowerment: the victim of aggression asserting her subjectivity by returning the gaze not just to the intradiegetic aggressor but the spectator as well, thereby also exposing the complicity of cinema in the commodification

Figure 24 Amalia (María Alché) facing Dr Jano (Carlos Belloso) in Lucrecia Martel's La niña santa (*The Holy Girl, 2004*) – *the gaze returned challenges the assertion of male power over an unseeing, objectified female body, forcing Dr Jano and us to engage with its own, more complex desires.*

and passivisation of women as sexual objects. Yet while all this is certainly going on in *La niña santa* – right from his first approach Dr Jano, unaware of Amalia's identity as a permanent hotel-resident, is himself turned into an object of visual scrutiny, often seen from behind in a reversal of the first theremin sequence, as Amalia spies on him during his sojourn at the hotel – the challenge of her returned look is also more complex. In fact, following a discussion in her catechism class about the nature and form of divine calling, Amalia has decided that God himself has entrusted her with a mission to redeem Dr Jano. The 'discovery' of her sexuality, as she was listening to the ethereal music of the theremin, she resolves, must be God's gift, setting her on course to relieve the sinner of his burden – indeed, the film's elliptic ending presages a cataclysmic, more likely catastrophic than cathartic, exposure of Jano's as well as Helena's sentimental problems.

The two scenes in front of the music store are crucial, of course, not only for the way in which they unleash and precipitate diegetic action to its dramatic, and potentially traumatic, climax – exposing Dr Jano's paedophile leanings to his family and to Helena, with whom he has almost inadvertently become embroiled in a passionate relationship. They also compress in a single sequence the problem of sensorial disjuncture between sight, hearing and touch which in all of Martel's cinema provides a kind of basic grammar of composition. While making the shot uncertain and ambiguous for the spectator, this sensorial disjuncture at the same time forges an enigmatic interpellation of the intradiegetic subject, which is never fully in perceptual control of the situation in which she finds herself involved. Accidents are thus often the consequence of an insufficient awareness of, and control over, the out-of-field, which intrudes into and shatters the internal coherence of the screen as a self-contained audio-visual and narrative space. In *La ciénaga*, the invisible storm Mecha hears growling in the *monte* compels her to start collecting the glasses from her party guests languishing around the pool and eventually provokes her drink-fuelled accident – all of which is in turn invisible to Momi and Isabel drowsing away in one of the bedrooms, who only perceive the goings-on outside as flurries of sound carried over by the wind that rattles the curtains. Later on, Luciano's death – which itself occurs off camera and out of sight from his family – is provoked by the barking of a dog on the other side of the patio wall. In *La mujer sin cabeza*, Vero's accident is perceived by her and the audience only as the noise of something hitting her car and as the impact of the collision, making her hit her head against the steering wheel. But the visible evidence she is both looking for and actively looking away from never materialises – or rather, what does materialise (the body of a dog glimpsed through the rear mirror, much later the corpse of a child fished from the roadside canal, which may or may not have been involved in the accident) is never enough to charge or exonerate her from the crime that burdens her conscience. Yet, at the same time, this sense of guilt also puts her in a state of trance and clairvoyance towards her own social world and that of the 'others' relegated almost by reflex to the margins of vision: the poor who live on the outskirts of town yet who also regularly show up on Vero's doorstep to offer their services or simply to collect some household leftovers.

Martel's shots are often not so much elliptic – withholding pieces of visual or aural information both for the characters and the audience – as overcrowded with numerous little acts taking place on various planes of the image and in varying degrees of focus. As already pointed out in chapter 3 with regard to *La ciénaga*, Martel has a particular preference for using the cinemascope format with relatively short focus lengths, to the effect that actors move quickly in and out of focus whilst staying in the image, sometimes with an aural presence that drowns out the 'main action' taking place in the area highlighted by the camera. The somewhat tumultuous gathering of mums and kids saying their goodbyes and getting into their cars at the start of *La mujer sin cabeza* or the conversations Vero's niece Candela (Inés Efrón) keeps with her working-class friends outside her front door while her mother and aunt chat in the living room, the poolside games of the children and adolescents in *La ciénaga* or indeed the group sequences around the hotel swimming pool in *La niña santa*, are only some examples of shots which overwhelm and distract our attention much in the same way as it does the characters' own. The extended family and, within it, the children and adolescents, have such a prominent place in Martel's cinema because the experiences of ambiguous, enigmatic interpellation and of sensorial incoherence and the ensuing lack of mastery and control over the world outside the subject is also proper to intrafamilial relations, and in particular to the perceptions of a growing body struggling with its own unrelenting transformation and immersed in a fluid, uncertain and somewhat incestuous affective universe. Crucially, however, this infantile or adolescent sensorial experience in Martel's films permeates the world of the adults as well, either because these have regressed (as Mecha and Gregorio in *La ciénaga*) to a state of immobility and autism due to the effects of alcohol, accidents and physical decay, or because (as Vero in *La mujer sin cabeza*) their traumatised state has kicked their perceptual routines out of joint.

More widely speaking, sensorial uncertainty *as a mode of narrative organisation*, keeping the characters and viewers in a constant state of imminence where sudden intrusions are always liable to occur but seldom do, also functions in Martel's cinema as a form of social and affective chronicle. The ordinary day-to-day life of the provincial middle class, narrated from an intrinsic point of view, stages a mode of historical experience in which time manifests itself as stagnation and repetition, and change only comes about in the form of 'accidents' and 'miracles'. It is, I would argue, the very temporality proper to the neo-liberal 'end of history' – triumphantly proclaimed by US political

Figure 25 The use of shallow focus lengths in Lucrecia Martel's La mujer sin cabeza *(The Headless Woman, 2007) singles out Vero (María Onetto) from the space surrounding her, introducing into the shot itself the perceptual disorientation and uncertainty experienced by the character.*

philosopher Francis Fukuyama after the fall of the Berlin Wall – encountered here on the level of an everyday experience located in some unspecified time between the military dictatorship and the present (even temporal markers such as clothing, hairstyles, intradiegetic music and car models are carefully chosen in all three of Martel's films in order to avoid any clear, unequivocal dating of the action – which in itself points to a disturbing continuity between everyday routines then and now).

In *La ciénaga*, as David Oubiña has observed: 'the series of little accidents and situations of danger never changes the characters' behaviour; yet this alternation between danger and passivity [...] produces an accumulation of conflicts and, consequently, an incrementation of dramatic tension that can only be resolved through a catastrophe.'[245] Meanwhile, in *La mujer sin cabeza*, change appears to come about as a result of Vero's accident, putting her into a state of fragility and confusion that seems to incubate a new self-awareness. But in the end, settling back into the stifling routines of her dental surgery, housework and gardening, intercalated with regular journeys accompanying her sister and niece to the out-of-town workshop from which they have ordered some large flower pots (a trip that is at the same time a kind of memory ritual, forcing her to return to the site of the accident), Vero is more than happy to accept and connive in the little cover-ups and precautions taken by her family to ensure there will be no consequences. The only change that does eventually occur in *La mujer sin cabeza*, definitely sealing off the possibility of a less epidemic transformation, is that of Vero's hair colour.

In *La niña santa*, by contrast, radical change is about to happen but it is kept out of the film through narrative ellipsis – or rather, the decision to focus attention on the two girls, Amalia and Josefina (Julieta Zylberberg), bathing in the empty swimming pool while the emotional storm they have let loose unfolds around them. Here, the scandal is unleashed by Amalia's 'misreading' as a divine calling – a miracle, singling her out from the other girls – of what Josefina discovers rather more profanely in her sexual encounters with her cousin. Amalia insists on exploring this sexual awakening on her own terms, inverting the order of masculine, ocularcentric desire and instead transforming Jano into the object of aural, haptic and olfactory inquisitiveness: invading his room to smell his clothes and towels, or teasing him with little metallic noises, clicking her fingernails against the railings, whilst remaining out of sight to him as he tries to relax in the pool. As Gonzalo Aguilar suggests, Amalia produces a rip, a confusion in the symbolic order through her embrace of sexuality and simultaneous refusal to resign the multisensory world of child-play, insisting on being 'a desiring subject and not a desired object produced by the gaze of others. Amalia triumphs: she is a girl and she is holy, she is beyond representation in a world where representation frustrates all possibility of desire.'[246]

The miracle, like the accident, is a form of temporal change which simultaneously perpetuates sameness: it keeps things in place by introducing among them a moment of radical discontinuity. In *La ciénaga*, a 'miracle' of a rather more conventional kind is represented by a local girl's sightings of the Virgin Mary reported on television, news of which is being watched by all members of Mecha's household incessantly. The televised miracle thus provides a kind of horizon, a point of flight, which rejoins the gazes of all the characters dispersed through the mansion's labyrinthine interior. But not just theirs, the gazes of the both despised and feared lower-class, mestizo inhabitants of the town and the *finca*'s own surroundings, with whom the family only interacts through orders and occasional outbursts of violence, are likewise in thrall to the small screen, as we can infer from the appearance, shortly after the first transmission, of 'pilgrims' gathering outside the visionary's family home, their modest clothing and popular accents contrasting sharply with those of the reporter interviewing them. It is also while watching news of the miracle on TV, crashed out on the bed during the time of the siesta, that the moments of greatest intimacy between Momi and the maid Isabel (Andrea López) take place, the only ones who seem capable at times of breaking through the familial circle of compulsory repetitions, reproducing a deeply racist, patriarchal and class-prejudiced system of affects. The miracle on TV, then, provides a kind of external centre, which organises and connects from the virtuality of the small screen, the multiplicity of gazes and locations converging on it. As such, it also functions as an intradiegetic double or mirror-image of our own external gaze, narrating the relationship Martel's film constructs with the audience by frustrating the desire for imaginary suture through its fragmented composition and editing of shots. Incidentally, the miracle sequences are themselves discontinuous, every item of news footage being interrupted 'acousmatically' from another external centre of the action: a telephone call from Mercedes' (Sylvia Baylé) apartment in Buenos Aires, the real financial centre on which the declining family business depends, and to which it renders sexual tribute in the form of subsequent generations of male lovers.

Let us analyse the sequence in more detail. On the first occasion we hear of the apparition, a television screen occupying the entire space of the image shows a middle-aged housewife addressing the camera: "Now that I'm looking, frankly I can't see anything..." From off screen, other voices interrupt her: "But look, there's the lady who lives here!" – "But there you see it!" – "Frankly I can't see anything", the woman continues, "I've been here for two hours now". A shot of Momi and Isabel on the bed is cut against the footage, illuminated by the blue rays from the television set, eating peanuts. The sequence has a vaguely erotic quality to it, the first shot showing the seated Isabel feeding the nuts to Momi who is lying next to her, followed by a close-up of Momi's face, with an expression of intense pleasure as she accepts the beloved one's gift. Meanwhile, the TV footage continues on the soundtrack, the reporter's voice asking: "Is your daughter there?" A woman answers: "Shall I call her?" "Yes, please." The TV once more covers the screen, as a young woman emerges from inside the house: "You've seen the Virgin." – "Yes, yes." – "How did you see her?" – "I was hanging the clothes out to dry, when I saw a light on the water tank and, well, I had a closer look and there I saw the Virgin." The TV camera, as if to confirm her words, hectically pans over the roof until it finds the water tank, before cutting to close-ups of the faces of bystanders looking on, while on the soundtrack the reporter insists: "Have you seen her before? Is this the first time? From up close or far away?" Cut onto the young woman's face: "Well, more or less, I was down there in my patio and I saw her up on the water tank..." A telephone rings; Martel cuts back to Isabel's room, while a man's voice from the TV continues to be heard – "...she told me she'd seen her..." Finally, Isabel picks up the phone and the sequence ends with a cut onto José (Juan Cruz Bordeu) at the other end, talking from Mercedes' fancy apartment in Buenos Aires.

In this first instalment of the series of news coverage recurring throughout the film, all the main elements are already in place that will repeat themselves, with only minimal variations, in the subsequent ones (such as the diegetic point of view, which oscillates between Isabel's and Mecha's bedrooms): the reporter's and bystanders' insistence for the young woman to reproduce, 'in her own words', the unspeakable truth of her vision, reinforced through a blatantly intrusive camera, in sharp contrast with the rest of the film's visual composition. Instead of the curious yet uncertain framing of actions, as if ignoring their origin or destination (a type of perspective 'identified with a child's vision',[247] which predominates throughout), here the camera claims an omniscient point of view, a position of authority and control over time and space manifest in the rapid zoom-ins that find faces and objects always at their disposal. Together, these unsubtle and tautological articulations between the verbal and the visual, in a relation of mutual confirmation, aim at nothing less than at forcing the miracle to reproduce itself onscreen. Obviously, this imminent re-apparition has to be postponed time and again until after the next publicity break, making the temporalities of faith and the commodity coincide and reinforce one another.

In the final instalments, television's machinery of the spectacle consequently swallows up and takes control over the 'miracle', despite the original witness's failure to cooperate. Again, the TV set takes over the screen, the voice of the mother being heard over a medium-length shot of the young woman: "My daughter doesn't want to speak, she's very tired. She really doesn't want to speak to anyone." A zoom-in on the girl's face ensues, the camera penetrating into the dimly lit room, evading the mother's protective body. The reporter asks: "Miriam? The Virgin hasn't appeared again?" The young woman shakes her head, an expression of sorrow and exhaustion on her face. "Well, alright." The mother closes the door; off screen, a telephone rings. To a shot of the street outside Miriam's house, the reporter's voice-over resumes: "On this intersection at Barrio San Francisco, something is going on that hasn't stopped puzzling everyone…" Cut to Mecha in her bed, answering the phone: "Hello, Mercedes? No, it's these *indios* who just can't answer the phone… what?" José enters to get the phone; from the TV, prayers can be heard, the voice of the reporter insisting: "The apparition has taken place right there on the water tank."

What the sequence of news items chronicles, then, is not the 'miracle' as such but its dislocation from the epiphanic – or psychotic – intimacy of the neighbourhood visionary into the melodramatic public space of TV spectacle, where it finally and truly *takes place*. That is, the apparition only 'has taken place' fully once it has assumed the logic of the spectacle, once the spectacle and the apparition have become one and the same as if by miracle. Therefore, Momi's attempt at the end of *La ciénaga* to restore lost happiness – the time before Luciano's death and Isabel's departure – by visiting the sacred site results in failure: "I went to where the Virgin appeared", she tells her sister, "I didn't see anything". *There*, indeed, nothing remains to be seen once television has engulfed vision, turning it into spectacle: but between one and the other, between religious epiphany and the televisual exhaustion of the invisible, cinema intervenes as a different, critical temporalisation of the image. That is to say, the diegetic time of *La ciénaga* (a time caught in-between two accidents) is also chronometrised by the way it is set against the time between the Virgin's apparition and disappearance, between miracle and spectacle, as a time which critically interrupts the continuity between these two. As in *La niña santa*, the figure of the miracle is also subtly associated here with a state of grace or bliss –

Momi's passionate, unrequited love for Isabel, brusquely cut short by the latter's discovery of her pregnancy and subsequent departure from the *finca* (incidentally, the first words we hear in the film are those of Momi praying to God and thanking him for the gift of Isabel).

In its association with a lost time of happiness – of 'love' – I would argue the miracle cannot so easily be reduced to a mere state of ideological false consciousness; 'the false and artificial [...], the brute manipulation'[248] of televised faith, as Oubiña suggests, which Momi has finally learned to see through. Rather, in a way not unlike Amalia's sense of divine calling in *La niña santa*, it also remains connected for Momi to the more intimate and intense experience of a 'miraculous' love transgressing classist and patriarchal conventions, a state of bliss that is suddenly perforated by the 'accident' of Isabel's pregnancy. Hence, Momi's 'pilgrimage' is perhaps not so much a moment of consciousness-awakening disenchantment, as Oubiña claims, as it is a private ritual of mourning her lost love (perhaps, even, of mourning the end of her childhood). For miraculous, accidental and other enigmatic occurrences are still 'true' forms of experience in the fluid, transformative world of children and young adolescents such as Momi and Amalia.[249] It is only in the world of the adults that they become forms of a disenfranchised mode of historical experience, marked by an incapacity to be actively involved with one's own life and those of others. They are, to return to my argument anticipated earlier in this chapter, 'posthistoric' experiences of time: as a change that befalls the subject from an enigmatic, opaque exterior, without any active intervention on his or her own part. Accidents and miracles are in fact 'weak' narrative substitutes for the logics of tragedy and comedy – the master genres, as Hayden White has claimed, of the historical narratives of nation-foundation in the nineteenth and early twentieth century.[250] It is no mere coincidence that their demise, or weakening, coincides with that of the nation-state itself in the face of global economic actors and forces. The tragic hero is the one who struggles for self-determination and against the impositions of fate (in Greek classic drama) or social convention (in bourgeois *Trauerspiel*); even as destiny takes its course, the hero's ultimate triumph lies in assuming it as an act of will. The comic plot, meanwhile, follows the making of the couple despite all mishaps and obstacles, through the lovers' successful mastering of a series of tests. None of these narrative logics, and their ethical and political implications for an idea of the subject, hold sway in a world of accidents and miracles – a world that has relapsed into a state of absolute determination. This strange, superstitious and fatalistic universe at the end of history – a world not unlike that of a re-emergent mythical consciousness Horkheimer and Adorno foresaw as the perverse outcome of illuminism – is the one Martel's characters inhabit, and against which the teenage girls' rebellion is directed, even if only in trying to appropriate its internal forms to make sense of their own experiences and

Miracles of postdictatorship

affects. But their ingenuous, credulous saintliness all the more cruelly exposes a world that appears to have advanced beyond redemption.

Martel's cinematic fables, to return to Rancière's expression, thwart the continuity from the children's enchanted world to the infantilised adults' one of historical disempowerment, intervening as a critical force of observation and analysis of different points of view and experience where the TV image attempts to collapse these into one. Her films, I would argue, are also a form of historiography, precisely because of the way they resort to religious, mythical and fairy-tale forms of representation. To fully understand this political dimension of the narrative form, I shall turn now to Enrique Bellande's *Ciudad de María*, a documentary on the transformation of San Nicolás, a former steel town in the province of Buenos Aires, into the sanctuary of a new, postindustrial religiosity. As in Martel, the critical force of the narrative stems from the incorporation, as a formal principle of shot composition and editing, of the 'innocent', 'ingenuous' point of view solicited by faith and the spectacle (and by the spectacle of faith). This point of view turns into a form of critical exposure precisely as it becomes part of a visual *narrative*, forcing it into a logic different from its own. Being submitted to the cinematographic process of montage and editing, the image's ingenuousness is thwarted by something it has sought to suppress in its pretended sensory immediacy. Contrariness, in other words, stems from a difference between the mode of historical experience represented by the image and that of the cinematic narrative into which it is inserted; modes of experience which, in Argentina, are intimately related – as *Ciudad de María* makes clear – with, on the one hand, the cycle of Peronism between 1945 and 1974 and, on the other hand, with post-Peronism or *menemismo* as the culmination of a postdictatorial mindset forged and fuelled by mass-medial spectacle.

The story of *Ciudad de María* advances in two strands, recreating in film form itself the double spatio-temporal movement proper to Virgin worship. On the one hand, Bellande accompanies the pilgrims on their journey to the sacred site; on the other, he delves into the history of her miraculous apparition, one that is being retold year after year, as we learn on accompanying a local journalist during his routine of interviewing local authorities, shopkeepers and housewives – something he has been doing, he explains to camera, ever since he first 'revealed' the Virgin's visits to Gladys Motta, an old lady living in the town. Both strands, the journey in space and the one in time (to the 'origin' and back to the present) finally come back together in the ecstatic ritual of the procession, held every year on the anniversary of the Virgin's first apparition.

This final sequence, in which the film's rhythm appears to coincide entirely with that of its object, has been criticised by some as an expression of surrender, the film-maker 'putting down his weapons – in Aguilar's words – as if recognizing the impossibility of resisting the seduction of the spectacle'.[251] Yet the sequence, as Aguilar himself is quick to add, admits the opposite reading as well, since its position at the end not just of the ritual itinerary but also of the two strands of cinematographic narrative into which it has been incorporated, has already saturated this sequence with narrative, with historicity. The multitudinous expression of faith, intervened by cinema, cannot but become an expression of history. And thus the sequence in which the spectacle of the miracle celebrates its triumph is actually the triumph of the work of cinema over this very spectacle, on which it has imposed the narrative rigour of its thwarted fable.

This triumph is simultaneously marked and disavowed by the two panning shots opening and closing the film. In the first one, the camera takes in, in a long, sweeping pan across the city from left to right, the riverbank with its steel factories and cranes, the office towers and apartment blocks in the centre, and finally the giant basilica under construction. In the final shot, the

Figure 26 The closing shot of Enrique Bellande's Ciudad de María (Mary's City, 2001) *shows the city of San Nicolás in a zoom-out from the basilica, cancelling out the narrative, historical movement of the opening panning shot from the riverside factories across the centre to the monuments of post-industrial religiosity.*

frame gradually opens up from the temple to a panoramic view of the city under a kitschy pink sunset. Now, neither the river nor the factories are anywhere in sight. The narrative movement of the first pan has been replaced by the radial movement of the miraculous event, which eradicates the historicity of the former just as it does its own. Its triumph, however, comes too late: the film has already shown us the history of this image, the history of how it came to displace the initial shot. *Ciudad de María*, in fact, is the story of the passage from one kind of vision to another. Yet in this way, the radial shot of the sanctuary-city is also forced to reveal its own historicity, to become a vision of history, figuring the historical moment it has sought to cast in the time of eschatology.

All of Bellande's film can be read, in fact, as unfolding this tension between two images belonging to entirely different regimes of vision. The struggle between them is actively inscribed in the film text from the very first sequence following the opening panning shot: a female reporter from a private TV channel prepares herself for an on-site news feature in front of Gladys Motta's home, surrounded by a multitude of pilgrims (rather than on the TV monitor, we see her through Bellande's camera, countering television's effect of immediacy by showing us the *work* of news production). She goes on air, saying: "This is the house of Gladys Motta. According to tradition, the Virgin appeared to her for the first time on September 25th, 1983..." Cut to a mobile camera immersing itself into the multitude, interspersed with the title credits, listening in on the interviews the reporter makes with several women pilgrims: "She never comes out on days like this..." – "She won't come out!" – "But of course, she always greets the pilgrims!" – "Yes, they've seen her, they've seen her!" By the end of the credits, as if it had used them for cover, the camera has somehow got to the front porch, where an elderly man is picking up bucketloads of letters. As he becomes aware of the camera, his expression changes and he almost throws himself at the cinematographer: "Hey, asshole, what do you think you're doing, filming me here!" The camera draws back, but now the pilgrims join the attack: "Go away!" – "How can you do that!" – "With the cameras present, it's impossible..." An emaciated, worn-out looking woman becomes a kind of improvised spokesperson: "For a question of the lady's privacy. It's the only thing we ask for. Could you please remove the cameras from the sector. It's for the good of everyone."

Time and again, throughout the film, the crew loses the battle against the faithful who, on one occasion, even improvise a spontaneous street demo (to shouts of "¡Que se vayan! ¡Que se vayan!" – "Away with them! Away with them!") in order to prevent Bellande from filming the camera-shy visionary, thus driving her out of their sight as well. This violent hostility against the attempts to record Gladys on film, as if visual capture could irrevocably damage or obstruct their own, personal vision of the visionary, contrasts with the baroque proliferation of images of Mary generated by the Virgin cult: from the statues, medallions and handkerchiefs of every size and value sold everywhere in the city, including various actresses performing as 'living statues', having their photographs taken alongside babies, elderly and disabled pilgrims, to the non-stop media and TV coverage of the ritual in progress. Between secrecy and exhibitionism, Bellande reveals a twofold regime of visibility pointing towards a duplicity within the cult of the Virgin itself, a double *mise-en-scène* of miraculousness. On the one hand, there is the basilica under construction, a 'sanctuary' of truly Babelian dimensions, where the Virgin's image is being adored in a variety of rituals, from kissing its glass casket to filling plastic bottles with blessed water, directly from the on-site pipework. On the other, there is Gladys Motta's humble bungalow, where the pilgrims leave letters with their pleas to the visionary. Thus, Gladys – the modest housewife who has returned to her domestic enclosure in order to leave the protagonism to God and the Virgin, in the words of Father Pérez, the parish priest now transformed into 'Rector of the Basilica of Our Lady of the Rosary' – becomes just as her celestial visitor, a woman spoken by others, by a variety of ecclesiastical as well as televisual interlocutors.[252] The film shows how 'the miracle' only takes place, as event and as spectacle, from the moment the Virgin's appearance to the visionary medium has been covered by the mass media. At the same time, the miracle's spectacular power – its capacity to attract tens of thousands of pilgrims each year and refloat the local economy – crucially depends on this ongoing, mute and near-invisible, presence of the seer alongside (on the margins of) the mass ritual.

The miracle's twofold regime of visibility, then, is also based on two spatiotemporal logics: on the one hand, the *virtuality* of the spectacle, whose rituals take place, just as in *La ciénaga*, in and for the audio-visual and digital mass media; on the other hand, there are the pilgrims' intimate, personal exchanges, through the medium of writing, with the visionary who has to remain off camera in order to safeguard a material, *localised*, form of mediation, which the logic of the spectacle can only refer to as a 'tradition' or founding myth. It is interesting that writing, and the epistolary genre in particular, should make its appearance at this level, pointing as it does to a form of personal narrative and memory that is still mediated by history as a sequence of causes and effects: a mode of experience the film identifies with the national welfare state; that is, with the dream of a national miracle of universal well-being that shipwrecked around the time of Mary's first coming to San Nicolás. Prompted to delve into the audio-visual archives of modernity in search of the origins of 'tradition', Bellande finds himself faced with the tradition of cinema itself as the medium of modernity's dreamwork. Marked as a piece of cinematographic evidence by the numbers announcing the start of a film spool, Bellande splices into his narrative an advert by the Somisa steel company, introducing an image radically different in content and texture from the ones preceding it (Bellande's own footage was shot in digital video). The clip lays out a kind of industrial Golden Age, starting with shots of the river at dawn, to orchestral music on the soundtrack, workers in the factory, a newborn baby at the factory-owned model clinic, followed by a close-up of the mother's joyful face, 'a city identified with the company', 'preparing itself for the future', enjoying 'an ever improving quality of life'. Image and sound eventually build up towards their climax and conclusion: 'Acero es vida', steel is life. Here, however, Bellande interrupts the clip by cutting to a video shot of today's urban centre. On the soundtrack, a newsreader's voice remembers: "The century-old San Nicolás de los Arroyos was a city awash with industries and workers, inhabited by people of great religious faith…"

Against this soothing narrative in praise of a stealthy faith that passed the test even of the steel factory's closure, Bellande edits a sequence of TV news footage telling a very different story: one of lay-offs, of struggle and defeat ensuing after the sell-out of the state-owned steelworks in 1991. Skimming through the newsflashes from a still recent past, the film locates the exact moment when unionist struggles and political demands for workplaces gave way to religious pleas, the moment when a combative workers' movement was crushed and dispersed. It is only then that we see banners with the Virgin's figure making their appearance among the laid-off steelworkers gathering outside the factory doors: "I have five children, and I'm left without a job in San Nicolás", one worker screams into the TV cameras, "I've got five kids!" In despair, he raises a placard of the Virgin, shouting: "I'm a Catholic just like you! God bless you, Maria, full of grace! Let's go!" They all begin to pray, a reporter's voice-over explaining: "The workers raise banners with the Virgin of the Rosary, recently enthroned at San Nicolás following the visions of a local woman…" Bellande cuts back to video footage of the present, a street vendor walking up and down the road to the basilica: "Two pesos the chocolates!"

Only after the defeat of 1991, then, did the Virgin's apparition to Gladys Motta in 1983 become a public event, having previously been confined to a small and obscure group of faithful whose exact links with the dictatorship, which ended that same year, the film leaves unexplored. (One witness, a 'psychiatrist' to whom Father Pérez had entrusted a clinical study of Motta's mental health, asserts: "I believed from the very beginning that it was true, because of what had just happened to us.") Rather than a shortcoming, however, this lack of emphasis on the links between the Church and state terror in order to maintain a documentary attitude of mute, external observation is perhaps what allows Bellande's film to reveal a more important form of continuity, identifying the decade of the 1990s as the full constitution of a 'postdictatorial' time, in which the dictatorship's principal consequence – the neo-liberal remaking of Argentine society – was reaching its cusp.[253]

For it is this proposition which, on my reading, Bellande puts forward in editing the final part of *Ciudad de María* in a parallel montage between the reconstruction of history and the spatial journey of the pilgrims towards the sacred site. Just as the former, the latter is narrated in a series of news flashes, this time from the Catholic channel Telefé ('Faith TV'), covering the journey from Buenos Aires to San Nicolás of blind cyclist Cristian Reboa (travelling on a tandem bike together with a cousin) to bring the Virgin the pleas of child patients hospitalised at the Casa Cuna clinic. Using a whole barrage of affective techniques, from sentimental background music to recurrent slow-motion close-ups of the children Cristian had visited in the first instalment of the series, the clips constantly call on their audience's emotional identification, relying not least on the pilgrim-hero's considerable thespian talents: "We're not gonna stop until San Nicolás ... and we ask all the Argentine people to pray with us. And as you know: follow me, all together, on Telefé!" – "I'm doing this for all of you, don't forget to pray for me! Ciao!" Cristian's message is drummed home by Milva, the blonde anchorwoman in the studio ("And of course the Virgin will listen to him! The Virgin is expecting Cristian! And you know why? Because he's on his way for the weak, for the children ... he's going for life, and that's all it needs!"), by an army of reporters covering the story on-location and by the subtitles offering further variations on the same mantra: "With the eyes of the heart: visually impaired Cristian Reboa left for San Nicolás" – "Cristian for the children. We join him on his journey to San Nicolás" – "Crusade for the children. The emotion of Cristian Reboa" – and so forth. An over-abundance of images and sounds, of sentences spoken and written that repeat over and over again the same combinations of words, with the 'visually impaired' Cristian providing an ideal object for everyone's gaze to converge on, the series also enters into dialogue, as a kind of perverse mirror-image, with Bellande and his crew's aborted attempts at filming the elusive visionary's home. Where Gladys the seer remains mysterious and invisible, the blind pilgrim's crusade unleashes a relentless bombardment of images incessantly referring back to itself.

As pure spectacle, therefore, the blind cyclist's pilgrimage can only culminate at Father Pérez's basilica rather than in front of Gladys' home. Alternating TV footage with video shots taken by Bellande's own crew, the sequence is choreographed in a kind of ecstatic *crescendo*, where mystical exaltation becomes indivisible from the reality show's ferocious exhibitionism. An impeccably dressed reporter receives the exhausted hero together with a frenetic multitude – subtitle: 'Cristian for the children. Emotional arrival at San Nicolás' – acting as mediator between the pilgrim-hero, the audience on site and at home, and Jorge and Milva, the anchors in the studio: "You've arrived, Cristian, you've arrived! Look who's here! There's daddy Mario, there's mummy Rosa!" They join in a tearful embrace, the anchorman's voice in the studio commenting: "That's Cristian's mum, exactly. The mother is visually impaired, too, the father as well." Milva adds: "And there's Mirta, Cristian's wife, who accompanies him on all his initiatives, for life, for the kids, for Telefé!" The on-site reporter takes over once more, drawing Cristian towards the microphone: "What an emotional reception! Cristian, Jorge and Milva in the studio are listening to you now!" Cristian, pressing the headphones to his ear together with a rosary, his voice cracking: "Hello... I can't hear, I can't hear..." Now Father Pérez enters the frame, kissing and embracing Cristian, while he leads the cyclist into the basilica's interior (the reporter brings his microphone closer so we can follow their conversation). Cristian turns back to the reporter: "It's a happy moment, but I can't go on anymore, my leg is hurting a lot, the people were mobbing me, Jorge..." He starts crying, his legs giving way, the reporter sustaining him with his free hand: "We're entering the sanctuary now, Jorge, he's having a hard time, his leg is hurting a lot!" And so, among tears, applause and screams of support, they arrive at last at the Virgin's glass casket ("Make an effort, Cristian ... your last effort!"), the reporter counting the steps separating the almost fainting Cristian from the shrine he eventually manages to reach and kiss with the reporter' and Father Pérez's help. They all begin to pray, only Cristian occasionally interrupting himself for tremors of pain: "I can't go on anymore... man, I can't go on... Holy Mary, Mother of God..."

Faced with the same impossibility of filming Gladys Motta, the woman who saw the Virgin, television does the opposite of cinema: it invents its own miracle, vaguely modelled on the passion of Christ, thus creating a time-space of pure self-referentiality, an effect of immediacy based on the absolute elimination of the out-of-field. The rosary meeting the headphones in the blind cyclist's hand, to facilitate the mystical union, at one and the same time, with Mary in the heavens and with Mirta in the TV studio, is the very emblem of this faith in the spectacle. In its hysterical baroque, the language of the spectacle must overburden every instant until it bursts into the next, an excess of stimuli that must be relentlessly kept up in order to maintain a constant state of excitation before the next publicity break. As it is lifted onto the big screen of cinema, however, this audio-visual language suffers an intervention, which exposes its intrinsically grotesque nature. Stripped of its small-screen immediacy, Cristian's imitation of the suffering Christ suddenly appears as merely an awkward, obscene form of overacting.

If cinema, as I suggested at the beginning of this chapter drawing on Jacques Rancière's work, was the medial form separating the theatrical stage from the television screen, Bellande's documentary incorporation of the TV image stages nothing less than the radical farce of a false theatricality returning to the big screen. For this, it turns out, has been Bellande's intervention throughout *Ciudad de María*, reminding us of Walter Benjamin's likening of the film-maker to the surgeon, cutting and intruding into the deep tissue of events, and replacing the faith-healer's visual detachment by analytical dissection:[254] cinema, in *Ciudad de María*, interposes itself, as the discontinuity proper to audio-visual modernity, between an archaic, visionary seeing and the specularisation and commodification of faith. Cinema *inter*-venes, it exposes and takes its place in, the distance between Gladys Motta's house and the temple (including the latter's ramifications through TV and the internet). *Inter*-vention, because cinema unmakes the effect of simultaneity, with its attendant negation of history generated by collapsing miracle and spectacle into one. Of course, this triumph of cinema cannot but be a bitter one. At the end of *Ciudad de María* – and of *La ciénaga* – the miracle has become history once more, but only to reveal that history, reinstated through the critical work of cinematic editing, has today become a mode of experience confronting subjects from the radical exteriority of miracles and accidents, rather than as a work of their own making.

Ordinary stories?

In the previous sections of this chapter I have focused on the ways in which fiction and documentary cinema, in *La ciénaga* and *Ciudad de María*, approach the subject of popular religiosity as a mode of historical experience, a 'sign of the times'. Rather than doing so directly, both films choose instead to critically dissect the way in which another medium – television – forges a sense of immediacy and proximity which as these films discover is not altogether unlike the ghostly, or celestial, visitations experienced by the visionary women of popular, small-town neighbourhoods. Thus, Martel and Bellande's films can show how miracle worship provides both a way of making sense of a present characterised by the comprehensive specularisation of life *and* a way of resisting the latter by drawing on, or inventing, a more archaic form of devotion. Thus, by forcing out the complexities of social experience by way of the thwarted incorporation of the mass-medial archives of the present, cinema acquires a uniquely analytical, critical dimension. Therefore, rather than refraining from formal experimentation in order to embark on an observation of real worlds in their singularity and strangeness, as some of the critics of new Argentine cinema have claimed, in this book I have been arguing instead that film has been, over the last two decades, a mode of social enquiry *thanks to* novel forms of experimentation, refraction and self-reflexivity.

That is, in order to observe the real, cinema had to become more, not less, complex. In previous chapters I have proposed and tested a number of categories and corpuses in order to understand this *at once* observational and analytical attitude of film towards the real: from the re-explorations of urban and rural locations and their narrative and symbolic implications, to the relations between 'experience' and 'performance' in modes of screen acting and of documentary construction of events, to the tension between allegory and realism in genre narrative. By thus concentrating my attention on film as a mode of cognitive mapping, in Fredric Jameson's terminology – of 'screening' the social and political present through the way a medium such as film thinks and refers to its own position and role in it – I have deliberately bypassed issues of state and corporate funding, which often dominate debates about film in Argentina. Often these can remain on a rather sterile level, pinning a virtuous, 'independent' new or young Argentine cinema against the rapacious and corrupting film industry, or defending the superiority of film entertainment over the self-indulgent experimentalism of arthouse cinema on grounds of their respective box-office success or failure. Lately, this discussion has once again flared up as a result of the much-applauded release of Mariano Llinás' remarkable, four-and-a-half-hour low-budget epos *Historias extraordinarias* (Extraordinary Stories, 2008) and the award, shortly thereafter, of an Oscar for best foreign-language film to Juan José Campanella's *El secreto de sus ojos* (*The Secret in Their Eyes*, 2009). While a discussion of these very recent films remains outside the scope of this book, they are nonetheless worth mentioning for the way in which their success has been taken, for completely opposite reasons, as one more occasion to proclaim 'the death of New Argentine Cinema'. Hailed as 'a deeply rewarding throwback to the unself-conscious days when cinema still strove to be magical',[255] Campanella's film was praised by some as the vigorous, high-grossing yet aesthetically satisfying example to follow instead of an anaemic experimentalism. Llinás' monumental work, meanwhile, has been greeted as 'a multiple challenge to the status quo of cinema',[256] reminding everyone what true independent cinema should be about: working on a shoestring budget (*Historias* was reportedly made with just 30,000 dollars) in exchange for total creative and imaginative freedom, in particular from the constraints of local colour and social realism.

But even without getting into a discussion about the merits of Campanella's latest film and the relation it constructs between the present and the dictatorial past, it is probably safe to assume that *Los rubios* or *Garage Olimpo* have had a more lasting, and intellectually stimulating, impact on historical and aesthetic debates in Argentina than *El secreto de sus ojos*, regardless of their respective box-office earnings. At the same time, other recent releases such as Trapero's *Carancho* (Hawk, 2010) or Caetano's *Francia* (France, 2010) are attracting considerable audiences without either director having compromised on their previous standards of self-consciousness. Rather than a return of the once-youthful rebels into the arms of the film industry, what we are witnessing is, I think, merely a greater variety of production models and budgets made possible precisely by these directors' early successes a decade or so ago. On the other hand, while Llinás' labyrinthine, formally adventurous spider's web of stories and digressions (multiplied almost beyond our grasp by the internal split between onscreen action and narratorial voice-over) has vastly expanded the modes and formal possibilities of film-making in Argentina and beyond, the count is still open on claims that it has also ushered in a 'new school' of directors blissfully unconcerned with social realities and immersed in refining a cool formalism – Alejo Moguillansky's recent BAFICI-winner *Castro* (2009), produced by Llinás, is substantially more convincing in that regard than Matías Piñeiro's *Todos mienten* (*They All Lie*, 2009).

Whatever the final score may be on those counts, however, from a different angle both the 'return of the film industry' and the arrival of a 'new experimentalism' probably indicate a period of re-approximation between cinema and other cultural forms, thus marking the end of an era in which cinema had to wrest its autonomy back from the literary and televisual models of narrative and actorship in which it remained caught during the 1980s. Cinema's very success in establishing itself as perhaps the most influential cultural language in present-day Argentina has also made it possible for it to re-engage with neighbouring ones such as television – in *El secreto de sus ojos* but also, in a more visceral and exciting way, in Caetano's and Trapero's recent work (both of whom, like Campanella, have successfully directed TV serials in the past). On the other edge of the cinematic field, theatre and literature have once more become important sources of inspiration. (Llinás' film, for instance, nods towards the narrative of Adolfo Bioy Casares and the poetry of Vicente Barbieri and Juan L. Ortiz; Moguillansky's is an adaptation of Beckett's novel *Murphy*.) As long as film can maintain its 'thwarted fable' (Rancière) – its analytical, dissective relationship towards the cultural forms it swallows or teams up with, rather than attempting to imitate or recreate their mannerisms – such an opening towards other fields of cultural endeavour can only enhance the possibilities of contemporary film-making. The last 15 to 20 years have considerably raised the benchmark for innovative film-making in Argentina – however, many of the directors, actors, cinematographers and editors discussed in this book are still only in their 30s and 40s, with new ones fast emerging. This, then, cannot but be a provisional balance – for now, it only feels safe to say that we haven't seen the end of new Argentine cinema just yet.

Endnotes

1 English translations of film titles will be displayed in italics whenever these correspond to commercial or festival releases. For films that have not been released internationally I shall use my own translations of titles, which will be displayed without italics.
2 Quintín, 'De una generación a otra: ¿hay una línea divisoria?', in Horacio Bernardes, Diego Lerer and Sergio Wolf (eds), *El nuevo cine argentino. Temas, autores y estilos de una renovación* (Buenos Aires: Fipresci, 2002), p.114.
3 Page, Joanna, *Crisis and Capitalism in Contemporary Argentine Cinema* (Durham, NC: Duke University Press, 2009), p.2.
4 Aguilar, Gonzalo, *Otros mundos. Un ensayo sobre el nuevo cine argentino* (Buenos Aires: Santiago Arcos, 2006), pp.8, 176.
5 Cozarinsky, Edgardo, 'Letter from Buenos Aires', *New Left Review* 26 (March 2004), p.106.
6 Amado, Ana, 'Cine argentino: cuando todo es margen', *Pensamiento de los confines* 11 (2002), p.8795.
7 For a discussion of the film's reception by Martel herself, see Matheou, Demetrios, 'Latin American iconoclast: Lucrecia Martel', in *The Faber Book of New South American Cinema* (London: Faber & Faber, 2010), pp.302–22.
8 For an overview of market patterns in world cinema, see Moretti, Franco, 'Planet Hollywood', *New Left Review* 9 (May–June 2001), pp.90–101.
9 Nagib, Lúcia, 'Towards a Positive Definition of World Cinema', in *Remapping World Cinema: Identity, Culture and Politics in Film*, ed. Stephanie Dennison and Song Hwee Lim (London: Wallflower Press, 2006), pp.31, 34.
10 Jameson, Fredric, 'Cognitive Mapping', in *Marxism and the Interpretation of Culture*, ed. Cary Nelson and Lawrence Grossberg (Bloomington, IN: University of Illinois Press, 1990), pp.352.
11 MacCabe, Colin, 'Preface', in Jameson, Fredric, *The Geopolitical Aesthetic. Cinema and Space in the World System* (Bloomington, IN: Indiana University Press, 1992), p.xv.
12 See Jameson, *The Geopolitical Aesthetic*: pp.25, 49.
13 Andrew, Dudley, 'An Atlas of World Cinema', in Dennison and Lim, *Remapping World Cinema*: pp.24–25.
14 Dissanayake, Wimal, 'Issues in World Cinema', in *The Oxford Guide to Film Studies*, ed. John Hill and Pamela Church Gibson (Oxford, New York: Oxford University Press, 1998), pp.528.

15 Burton-Carbajal, Julianne, 'South American Cinema', in *World Cinema: Critical Approaches*, ed. John Hill and Pamela Church Gibson (Oxford, New York: Oxford University Press, 2000), p.198.
16 Stock, Ann Marie, 'Through Other Worlds and Other Times: Critical Praxis and Latin American Cinema', in *Framing Latin American Cinema: Contemporary Critical Perspectives* (Minneapolis: University of Minnesota Press, 1997), p.xxx.
17 Page, *Crisis and Capitalism*: pp.9–17.
18 Willemen, Paul, *Looks and Frictions: Essays in Cultural Studies and Film Theory* (London: British Film Institute, 1994), p.211.
19 Bentes, Ivana, 'The *Sertão* and the *Favela* in Contemporary Brazilian Film', in *The New Brazilian Cinema*, ed. Lúcia Nagib (London: I.B.Tauris, 2003), p.125.
20 Willemen, *Looks and Frictions*: p.212.
21 Getino, Octavio, *Cine argentino: entre lo posible y lo deseable* (Buenos Aires: INCAA/Ciccus, 2005), p.177.
22 Falicov, Tamara, *The Cinematic Tango: Contemporary Argentine Film* (London: Wallflower Press, 2007), p.84.
23 Aprea, Gustavo, *Cine y políticas en Argentina. Continuidades y discontinuidades en 25 años* (Buenos Aires / Los Polvorines: Biblioteca Nacional / Universidad Nacional General Sarmiento, 2008), pp.20–1.
24 Minghetti, Claudio D., 'Todo el cine argentino que se verá en 2007', *La Nación* (Buenos Aires, 10 January 2007. Sección Espectáculos), p.8.
25 Getino, *Cine argentino*: 313, n. 11. On the politics of film subsidies and distribution in Argentina, see also Page, *Crisis and Capitalism*: pp.9–16.
26 Aufderheide, Patricia, 'Awake Argentina!', *Film Comment* 22, 2 (1986), p.54.
27 Antín quoted in Falicov, *The Cinematic Tango*: p.48.
28 Rich, B. Ruby, 'An/Other view of New Latin American Cinema', in *New Latin American Cinema*, vol. 1, 'Theory, Practices, and Transcontinental Articulations', ed. Michael T. Martin (Detroit, MI: Wayne State University Press, 1997), p.282.
29 Jameson, Fredric, *The Geopolitical Aesthetic. Cinema and Space in the World-System* (London: BFI, 1992), pp.37–8.
30 Aprea, *Cine y políticas*: p.55.
31 Falicov, *The Cinematic Tango*: p.53; see also César Maranghello, *Breve historia del cine argentino* (Barcelona: Laertes, 2004), pp.221–40.
32 Di Núbila, Domingo, 'Argentine pix heat up at home', *Variety*, 23–29 March 1998, p.48.
33 Aguilar, *Otros mundos*: pp.195–7.
34 Getino, *Cine argentino*: pp.328, 336–7; Máximo Eseverri and Ezequiel Luka, 'Introducción', in *Generaciones 60/90: cine argentino independiente*, ed. Fernando Martín Peña (Buenos Aires: Fundación Eduardo F. Constantini, 2003), p.13.
35 Falicov, *The Cinematic Tango*: pp.55–6; Aguilar, *Otros mundos*: pp.15–17.
36 See, on the tendencies of 1960s political documentary, Emilio Bernini, 'Politics and the documentary film in Argentina during the 1960s', *Journal of Latin American Cultural Studies* 13, 2 (2004), pp.155–70.
37 Zadoff, Magalí, 'El cine de las escuelas de cine', in Peña, *Generaciones 60/90*: pp.268–75; also Aguilar, *Otros mundos*: pp.213–15; Falicov, *The Cinematic Tango*: pp.117–18. On the changes of film culture between film-club cinephilia and

academic professionalisation in Argentina, see also Emilio Bernini, 'Noventa-Sesenta: Dos generaciones en el cine argentino', *Punto de Vista* 87 (2007), pp.30–3.
38 Aguilar, *Otros mundos*: p.15.
39 Aprea, *Cine y políticas*: p.94.
40 Beceyro, Raúl, Rafael Filipelli, David Oubiña, Alan Pauls, 'Estética del cine, nuevos realismos, representación (debate sobre el nuevo cine argentino)', en *Punto de Vista* 67 (2000), p.3.
41 For an ambitious, complex reading of *Hoteles* based on the tension between disavowal and re-inscription of locality versus globality, see Page, *Crisis and Capitalism*: pp.136–43.
42 Aguilar, *Otros mundos*: pp.36–7; also Sílvia Schwarzböck, 'Los no realistas', *El Amante de Cine* 115 (October 2001), accessed online March 2010 (http://www.elamante.com).
43 Peirce, Charles Sanders, *Philosophical Writings*, ed. Justus Buchler (New York: Dover Press, 1955), p.109.
44 UNCIPAR continues its activities, holding an annual, well-attended international festival of short films at Villa Gesell, Provincia de Buenos Aires. For more information, see the organisation's website, http://www.solocortos.com/uncipar/, accessed March 2010.
45 Listorti, Leandro, Leandro Godón and Octavio Fabiano, 'Entrevista con Raúl Perrone', in Peña, *Generaciones 60/90*: p.141.
46 Perrone, Raúl, 'Labios de churrasco', at http://www.raulperrone.com/filmografia/filmografiafr.htm, accessed March 2010.
47 Perrone, Raúl, 'Algunos puntos que tengo en cuenta a la hora de filmar', at http://www.raulperrone.com/decalogo/decalogo.htm, accessed March 2010.
48 Bermúdez, Nicolás, 'Raúl Perrone: una cámara de video pedorra,' in *La Fuga*, primavera de 2009, http://lafuga.cl/raul-perrone-una-camara-de-video-pedorra/270, accessed online March 2010.
49 Listorti, Godón and Fabiano, 'Entrevista con Raúl Perrone': p.141.
50 Aguilar, *Otros mundos*: p.202.
51 Jameson, *The Geopolitical Aesthetic*: p.5.
52 Page, *Crisis and Capitalism*: p.108.
53 Bermúdez, 'Raúl Perrone', op. cit.
54 Quintín, 'Martín Rejtman: un cine contemporáneo', *El Amante de Cine*, julio de 1996, accessed online April 2010, http://elamante.com.ar/nota/0/0690.shtml.
55 Bernini, Emilio, *Estudio crítico de* Sílvia Prieto. *Un film sin atributos* (Buenos Aires: Picnic, 2008), p.20.
56 Jameson, Fredric, 'The existence of Italy,' in *Signatures of the Visible* (London: Routledge, 1992), pp.158–60.
57 Hartley's version of the *bonmot* is 'what we're creating is a flat surface with an image on it'. Quoted in Donald Lyons, *Independent Visions. A Critical Introduction to Recent Independent American Film* (New York: Ballantine Books, 1994), p.44.
58 Suárez, Pablo, 'Martín Rejtman: la superficie de las cosas', in *Nuevo cine argentino: temas, autores y estilos de una renovación*, ed. Horacio Bernardes, Diego Lerer and Sergio Wolf (Buenos Aires: Fipresci, 2002), p.47.
59 Bernini, *Estudio crítico de* Sílvia Prieto: p.64.

60 Quintín, 'Martín Rejtman: un cine contemporáneo', op. cit.
61 Page, *Crisis and Capitalism*: p.78.
62 Quintín, 'Martín Rejtman: un cine contemporáneo,' op. cit.
63 Rejtman's literary oeuvre comprises (just as his filmography) three volumes of fictions: *Rapado* (1992, re-edited 2007); *Velcro y yo* (1996); and *Literatura y otros cuentos* (2005).
64 Sarlo, Beatriz, 'Shot, repetition: on living in the New City', *Journal of Latin American Cultural Studies* 14, 3 (2005), pp.303–4.
65 Indeed, one of the most chilling examples of this blending into one of image and action was the killing, a week later, of three young men who were watching – and loudly cheering – news footage of another *cacerolazo* march by a street corner kiosk in the Floresta neighbourhood and were shot on the spot by an incensed ex-policeman. See Indymedia Argentina, http://argentina.indymedia.org/news/2002/12/71922.php, accessed November 2009.
66 See Indymedia Argentina, http://argentina.indymedia.org/news/2002/12/71922.php, accessed November 2009.
67 Kracauer, Siegfried, *Theory of Film: The Redemption of Physical Reality* (New York: Oxford University Press, 1960), p.98.
68 Film professionals had also already taken to the streets a month earlier, along with thousands of cultural workers, in protest against the de la Rua government's extension of IVA taxation to cultural products, while at the same time withholding legally guaranteed subsidies under 'economic emergency' legislation. See, on the impact of the financial crisis before and after 2001 on state cultural policies and especially the INCAA, Getino, *Cine Argentino*: pp.306–10.
69 Bruno, Giuliana, 'Motion and emotion: film and the urban fabric', in *Cities in Transition: The Moving Image and the Modern Metropolis*, ed. Andrew Webber and Emma Wilson (London: Wallflower Press, 2008), pp.21–2.
70 Virilio specifically refers this new regime to so-called world cities: 'The real city, locally situated, and which even gave its name to the politics of nations, concedes its primacy to the virtual city, that "deterritorialized" megacity, which thus becomes the host of a metropolitics, the totalitarian – or rather, globalitarian – character of which nobody ignores' (Paul Virilio, 'Un monde surexposé. Fin de l' histoire ou fin de la géographie?', *Le Monde Diplomatique*, Août 2007: 17; online version, http://www.monde-diplomatique.fr/1997/08/VIRILIO/8948.html, accessed November 2009. My translation, JA). See also Christian Gundermann, 'La libertad entre los escombros de la globalización', *Ciberletras* 13 (2005), http://www.lehman.cuny.edu/faculty/guinazu/ciberletras/v13/gundermann.htm, accessed November 2009.
71 Page, *Crisis and Capitalism*: pp.37–8.
72 On the contemporary megacity's 'architecture of fear' – high-speed motorways, gated communities – see Mike Davis, *Planet of Slums* (London: Verso, 2006), pp.114–20; also Maristella Svampa, *Los que ganaron: la vida en los countries y barrios privados* (2nd ed., Buenos Aires: Biblos, 2010).
73 Amado, Ana, *La imagen justa. Cine argentino y política (1980–2007)* (Buenos Aires: Colihue, 2009), pp.217–21. See also, by the same author, 'Caetano: imágenes de la revuelta', *Portal del cine y el audiovisual latinoamericano y caribeño*, http://www.cinelatinoamericano.org/texto.aspx?cod=91, accessed November 2009.

74 On urban youths and their experiences as a critical perspective in contemporary Latin American cinema, on social decline after neo-liberal adjustment, see Laura Podalsky, 'Out of depth: the politics of disaffected youth and contemporary Latin American cinema', in *Youth Culture in Global Cinema*, ed. Timothy Shary and Alexandra Seibel (Austin, TX: University of Texas Press, 2006), pp.109–30.
75 La Boca is also the site of Ricardo Longhini's workshop, who in *Espejo…* is filmed several times walking along the shores of the Riachuelo – bridges in background – to collect scrap metal from derelict ships, at roughly the same spot where Sandra and El Cordobés go for a stroll and dream of a different future for themselves and their unborn child. Curiously, then, La Boca figures in both films, for all their differences, as a place of relative autonomy that still holds the (however fleeting) promise of a different historical becoming.
76 Page, Crisis and Capitalism: p.48.
77 Quoted in Jorge Ruffinelli, 'De los otros al nosotros: familia fracturada, visión política y documental personal', in *Imágenes de lo real. La representación de lo político en el documental argentino*, ed. Josefina Sartora and Silvina Rival (Buenos Aires: Libraria, 2007), p.145.
78 Aprea, *Cine y políticas*: p.73.
79 Aguilar, *Otros mundos*: pp.43–7.
80 At least, it is no longer available if we shed the romanticising overtones of 'nomadism' and relate it, as I suggest, to the historical experience of social precarisation. In this sense, the denial of affective identification in films such as *Pizza, birra, faso* has a political dimension, as it draws attention to the incommensurability between the characters' and the film viewers' experience: between *inhabiting* and (imaginarily) *travelling* to the social margins. Zygmunt Bauman's opposition between *vagabonds* and *tourists* captures this incommensurability quite well: 'The tourists move because they find the world within their (global) reach irresistibly *attractive* – the vagabonds move because they find the world within their (local) reach unbearably *inhospitable*. The tourists travel because *they want to*; the vagabonds because *they have no other bearable choice*.' Zygmunt Bauman, *Globalization: The Human Consequences* (New York: Columbia University Press, 1998), pp.92–3.
81 Williams, Raymond, *Marxism and Literature* (Oxford: Oxford University Press, 1977), pp.132–4.
82 See Getino, *Cine argentino*: pp.321, 334.
83 For an introduction to the concept of suture, see Daniel Dayan, 'The tutor-code of classical cinema', in *Film Theory and Criticism: Introductory Readings*, ed. Leo Braudy and Marshall Cohen (New York, Oxford: Oxford University Press, 1999), pp.118–29.
84 Lefebvre, Martin, 'Between setting and landscape in the cinema', in *Landscape and Film* ed. Martin Lefebvre (London: Routledge, 2006), pp.22, 40.
85 Russell, Catherine, *Experimental Ethnography. The Work of Film in the Age of Video* (Durham, NC: Duke University Press, 1999), p.120.
86 Massey, Doreen, *For Space* (London: Sage, 2005), p.141.
87 Nichols, Bill, *Representing Reality: Issues and Concept in Documentary* (Bloomington, IN: Indiana University Press, 1991), pp.32–75.

88 Lerer, Diego, 'Crónicas de inmigrantes', *Clarín*, 22 September 2005, accessed online March 2010.
89 Fatimah Tobing Rony calls attention to this inheritance of nineteenth-century scientific exoticism in the way early ethnographic cinema sought to 'salvage' an authentic yet vanishing otherness, distinguishing between a 'scientific', a 'taxidermic' and a 'commercial' mode of deploying the exotic on film. See her *The Third Eye: Race, Cinema and Ethnographic Spectacle* (Durham, NC: Duke University Press, 1996), p.91.
90 Balász, Béla, 'The close-up', in Braudy & Cohen, pp.304–5; Deleuze, Gilles, *L'image-mouvement. Cinéma I* (Paris: Minuit, 1983), p.126.
91 Gundermann, Christian, 'The stark gaze of the New Argentine Cinema: restoring strangeness to the object in the perverse age of commodity fetishism', *Journal of Latin American Cultural Studies* 14, 3 (2005), pp.244, 260.
92 Page, *Crisis and Capitalism*: pp.60–1. Gonzalo Aguilar emphasises the territoriality of these spaces of work whose lyrical qualities Page foregrounds: conflict ensues whenever Freddy leaves the space next to the barbecue to which his work confines him, and crosses over into the territory of the bar customers. His death, moreover, occurs on the boundary between the bar and the city, literally on the doorstep, as if punished for having crossed this double threshold. See Aguilar, *Otros mundos*: 171.
93 Lefebvre, 'Between setting and the landscape': pp.21–2.
94 Ibid. p.38.
95 See, on the privatisation of state companies under the government of Carlos S. Menem, María Seoane, *El saqueo de la Argentina* (Buenos Aires: Sudamericana, 2003); and on the emergence of the *piquetero* movements in Neuquén, Jujuy and Salta, Maristella Svampa and Sebastián Pereyra, *Entre la ruta y el barrio. La experiencia de las organizaciones piqueteras* (Buenos Aires: Biblos, 2003). The struggle against Catamarca's feudal lords, the Saadi family, fuelled by the kidnapping, rape and killing of a local girl during an upper-class orgy, was made into a film by Héctor Olivera, *El caso María Soledad* (2003), starring Valentina Bassi and Juan Palomino. On the Santiago del Estero uprising of 1993, during which the provincial government palace went up in flames, see Raúl Dargoltz, *El santiagueñazo. Gestación y crónica de una pueblada argentina* (Buenos Aires: El Despertador, 1994).
96 Aguilar, *Otros mundos*: p.42.
97 Maranghello, *Breve historia del cine argentino*: pp.27–8, 41, 75.
98 On *El último malón*, see Jorge Miguel Couselo, 'El aporte de Alcides Greca al cine argentino', *Todo es Historia* 49 (1971), pp.74–9.
99 For a comprehensive study of the place and function of the rural interior in Argentine cinema, see Eduardo Romano, *Literatura/cine argentinos sobre la(s) frontera(s)* (Buenos Aires: Catálogos, 1991).
100 See, on Latin American literary romanticism's allegorical founding of the nation through the encounter of lovers marked by racial or political difference, Doris Sommer, *Foundational Fictions. The National Romances of Latin America* (Berkeley, CA: University of California Press, 1991).
101 Aguilar, *Otros mundos*: pp.160–1.
102 Yako, Dani and Martín Caparrós, *Extinción: últimas imágenes del trabajo en la Argentina* (Buenos Aires: Norma, 2001).

103 Bernardes, Horacio, 'Cuando la pesadilla no tiene horizontes', *Página 12*, Thursday 26 October 2006, http://www.pagina12.com.ar/diario/suplementos/espectaculos/5-4260-2006-10-26.html, accessed May 2010.
104 Heath, Stephen, 'Narrative space', in *Questions of Cinema* (Bloomington: Indiana University Press, 1981), pp.41–2.
105 Schwarzböck, Sílvia, 'La imposibilidad contemporánea de no retornar de lo real. El misterio en cinco películas argentinas recientes', paper presented at the symposium *Reality Effects: Poetics of Locality, Memory and the Body in Contemporary Argentine and Brazilian Cinema*, Birkbeck College, London, 26–28 November 2009.
106 On the literary construction of a 'national landscape', in Argentina and its relation to the travel-narrative form see Adolfo Prieto, *Los viajeros ingleses en la emergencia de la literatura argentina* (Buenos Aires: Sudamericana, 1996); also my own *Mapas de poder: una arqueología literaria del espacio argentino* (Rosario: Beatriz Viterbo, 2000).
107 Holland, Jonathan, 'Opus' (film review), *Variety*, 3 May 2005, accessed online May 2010, http://www.variety.com/review/VE1117926952.html?categoryid=31&cs=1&p=0
108 Bernini, Emilio, 'Un estado (contemporáneo) del documental. Sobre algunos films argentinos recientes', *Kilómetro 111* 5 (2004), pp.41–57; see especially pp. 42–3.
109 Russell, *Experimental Ethnography*: p.16.
110 Jameson, *The Geopolitical Aesthetic*: pp.4–5.
111 Benjamin, Walter, 'The storyteller: reflections on the work of Nikolai Leskow', in *Illuminations*, transl. Harry Zohn, ed. Hannah Arendt (New York: Schocken, 1968).
112 Aguilar, *Otros mundos*: p.41.
113 Jones, Owain, 'Idylls and othernesses: childhood and rurality in film', in *Cinematic Countrysides*, ed. Robert Fish (Manchester, New York: Manchester University Press, 2007), p.179.
114 Deleuze, Gilles, *Cinema 2. The Time-Image*, transl. Hugh Tomlinson and Robert Galeta (London: Athlone Press, 1989), pp.3 20.
115 Leyshon, Michael and Catherine Brace, 'Deviant Sexualities and Dark Ruralities in *The War Zone*', in Fish (ed.), *Cinematic Countrysides*: p.207.
116 Previously, Martel had already made a number of shorts, among them the feminist western *Rey Muerto* (Dead King, 1995), included in the Universidad del Cine's first compilation of *Historias breves*, as well as the TV feature *Las dependencias* (Dependencies, 1999).
117 Bernini, Emilio and Domin Choi, '*La ciénaga* o el arte de la infancia', *Kilómetro 111* 2 (2001), p.151.
118 My translation, http://www.litastantic.com.ar, accessed May 2010.
119 Oubiña, David, *Estudio crítico sobre* La ciénaga (Buenos Aires: Picnic, 2007), p.51.
120 Amado, Ana, 'Velocidades, generaciones y utopías: a propósito de *La ciénaga*, de Lucrecia Martel', *ALCEU* 6, 12 (2006): p.50. See also, by the same author, 'Imagen-síntoma y temporalidad en Lucrecia Martel', in *La imagen justa. Cine argentino y política (1980–2007)* (Buenos Aires: Colihue, 2009), pp.227–36.
121 Amado, 'Velocidades': p.53.
122 See Norman Bryson, *Vision and Painting: The Logic of the Gaze* (Basingstoke: Palgrave, 1983), p.122.

123 Oubiña, *Estudio crítico*: pp.15–16.
124 Tuan, Yi-Fu, *Space and Place: The Perspective of Experience* (Minneapolis, London: University of Minnesota Press, 2003 [1977]), pp.19–33.
125 See Michel Chion, 'The acousmêtre', in *The Voice in Cinema*, transl. Claudia Gorbman (New York: Columbia University Press, 1999), pp.17–29.
126 Doane, Mary Ann, 'Ideology and the practice of sound editing and mixing', in *Film Sound: Theory and Practice*, ed. Elisabeth Weis and John Belton (New York: Columbia University Press, 1985), pp.54–62.
127 Constantini, Gustavo, 'La banda sonora en el nuevo cine argentino', *Cuadernos hispanoamericanos* 679 (2007) pp.7–17.
128 Oubiña, David, 'El cine como intención amorosa. Entrevista a Lucrecia Martel', in *Estudio crítico*: p.60.
129 Williams, Raymond, *The Country and the City* (Oxford, New York: Oxford University Press, 1973), pp.289–306.
130 Deleuze, Gilles, *Cinema 1. The Movement-Image*, transl. Hugh Tomlinson and Barbara Habberjam (London: Athlone, 1986), p.124.
131 Pinto, Iván, 'Entrevista a Albertina Carri. A propósito de *La rabia*,' in *La Fuga. Revista de Cine*, otoño de 2009, http://lafuga.cl/entevista-a-albertina-carri/5, accessed May 2010. See also John Berger, *Pig Earth* (London: Chatto & Windus, 1992).
132 Aguilar, Enrique, 'Lo que no se ve', *Contrapicado.net* 31, marzo/abril 2009, http://www.contrapicado.net/alternativa.php?id=27, accessed May 2010.
133 Delgado, Maria, 'A Trilogy of Closely Observed Characters', *Sight & Sound*, November 2008: http://www.bfi.org.uk/sightandsound/feature/49486, accessed May 2010.
134 Tomlinson and Habberjam translate Deleuze's term 'image-pulsion' as 'impulse-image'. I have chosen to retain the original expression here, as it remains closer to the ideas of pulse or pulsation – a bassline or throbbing presence beneath the surface – whereas 'impulse' takes it towards an idea of action and motoric release (and thus, towards the action-image, of which it is indeed a boundary). See Deleuze, *Cinema 1*, esp. chapter 8.
135 Aguilar, *Otros mundos*: p.67.
136 Gundermann, Christian, '*La libertad*, entre los escombros de la globalización', *Ciberletras: Revista de Crítica Literaria y de Cultura* 13 (2005): http://www.lehman.cuny.edu/ciberletras/v13/gundermann.htm, accessed December 2009.
137 Nichols, Bill, *Representing Reality* (Bloomington: Indiana University Press, 1991), p.77.
138 Rival, Silvina and Domin Choi, 'Última tendencia del cine argentino', in *Kilómetro 111* 2 (2001), pp.154–9.
139 On the concept of 'bare life', see Giorgio Agamben, *Homo Sacer. Sovereign Power and Bare Life*, transl. Daniel Heller-Roazen (Stanford, CA: Stanford University Press, 1998). I have discussed its implications for Alonso's work more extensively in 'La imagen limítrofe: naturaleza, economía y política en dos filmes de Lisandro Alonso', *Estudios* 15, 30 (julio/diciembre de 2007), pp.279–304.
140 In a short produced for the 2009 BAFICI festival, Alonso returned to this association of the camera with a non-human gaze: the one-minute long film featured a

bird – a small raptor – in close-up, looking straight at the camera and breathing heavily.
141 The film is also an open homage to Tsai Ming-Liang's eulogy to the seedy art deco cinemas of old, *Bu San* (Goodbye Dragon Inn, 2003). For a detailed analysis of Alonso's film, see my 'Luminosa repercusión: el cine como fantasma', *Grumo* 6, 1 (noviembre de 2007), pp.38–42.
142 Chanan, Michael, *The Politics of Documentary* (London: BFI, 2007), pp.3, 15.
143 'Datos del circuito de producción y consumo', *Cine.ar*: Industria, online database, http://www.cine.ar/contenidos/72-Industria/, accessed January 2011.
144 Aprea, *Cine y políticas*: p.78.
145 Bruzzi, Stella, *New Documentary: A Critical Introduction* (London: Routledge, 2006 [2000]), p.186.
146 Guarini, Carmen, 'De lo real a la realidad: el documental de creación en América Latina', in *Hacer cine. Producción audiovisual en América Latina*, ed. Eduardo A. Russo (Buenos Aires: Paidós, 2008), p.355.
147 Bernini, Emilio, 'Un estado (contemporáneo) del documental. Sobre algunos films argentinos recientes', *Kilómetro 111* 5 (2004), pp.41–3.
148 Chanan, *The Politics of Documentary*: p.241.
149 Renov, Michael, *The Subject of Documentary* (Minneapolis: University of Minnesota Press, 2004), p.176.
150 On activist and documentary practices in the visual arts during and after the 2001 crisis, see Andrea Giunta, 'Crisis y colectivización del arte', in *Poscrisis. Arte argentino después de 2001* (Buenos Aires: Siglo Veintinuo, 2009), p.54–64.
151 Cine Insurgente, 'Retomar las experiencias interrumpidas en el 76', in Gabriela Bustos, *Audiovisuales de combate. Acerca del videoactivismo contemporáneo* (Buenos Aires: CCEBA / La Crujía, 2006), p.115.
152 On independent video and film activism, see Bustos, *Audiovisuales de combate*; also Kathryn Lehman, 'Choreographing people's power in Argentina: documentaries of the crisis and the new wave in Latin American cinema', *Journal of Iberian and Latin American Studies* 10, 1 (2004), pp.113–30. On Adoc Argentina, see Jairo Straccia, 'Cine desde abajo en Argentina: luz y cámara para la acción', *Segundo Enfoque*, Mayo 2003, http://www.segundoenfoque.com.ar/camara_accion.htm, accessed November 2009.
153 Aprea, *Cine y políticas*: p.87. On the relations between documentary and autonomous workers' and *piquetero* movements, see also Claudio Remedi, 'Cine documental y trabajadores: ensayo sobre una experiencia', *DOCA (Documentalistas Argentinos)*, sección artículos, 2008, http://www.docacine.com.ar/articulos/remedi03.html, accessed June 2010. On video activism as counterinformation, see Kathryn Lehman, 'Las crisis argentina y los medios de comunicación: estrategias para hacer del espectador un testigo', in *El cine argentino de hoy: entre el arte y la política*, ed. Viviana Rangil (Buenos Aires: Biblos, 2007), pp.23–40.
154 Nichols, *Representing Reality*: pp.32–75.
155 Bruzzi, *New Documentary*: pp.1, 218.
156 Bernini, 'Un estado (contemporáneo) del documental': p.44.
157 Fragments of *Memoria del saqueo* can be found on a YouTube channel called, with scant subtlety, 'Pino Presidente'. For a more sympathetic reading of Solanas' politics

and cinematographic output, see Amado, *La imagen justa*: pp.65–88; Jessica Stites Mor, 'Imágenes de un sur desplazado: Fernando Solanas y el imaginario de la transición', in *El pasado que miramos. Memoria e imagen ante la historia reciente*, ed. Claudia Feld and Jessica Stites Mor (Buenos Aires: Paidós, 2009), pp.221–54.
158 Aguilar, *Otros mundos*: p.150.
159 Quoted in Renov, *The Subject of Documentary*: p.178.
160 Bruzzi, *New Documentary*: pp.185–7.
161 Jameson, Fredric, 'The Existence of Italy', in *Signatures of the Visible* (London: Routledge, 1992), p.158.
162 Ranzani, Oscar, 'Julio es como un embajador de la villa. Los directores Federico León y Marcos Martínez, junto con Julio Arrieta, hablan de *Estrellas*', *Página 12*, Thursday 13 December 2007, http://www.pagina12.com.ar/diario/suplementos/espectaculos/5-8621-2007-12-13.html, accessed June 2010.
163 Bruzzi, *New Documentary*: pp.185–6.
164 See Luis Camnitzer, *Didáctica de la liberación. Arte conceptualista latinoamericano* (Montevideo: HUM, 2008), p.228.
165 On Rouch's idea of 'shared anthropology', see Russell, *Experimental Ethnography*: pp.77–8; also Michael Taussig, *Mimesis and Alterity. A Particular History of the Senses* (London: Routledge, 1993), pp.240–43.
166 See Ana Longoni and Gustavo Bruzzone, *El siluetazo* (Buenos Aires: Adriana Hidalgo, 2008); also Diana Taylor, *Disappearing Acts: Spectacles of Gender and Nationalism in Argentina's 'Dirty War'* (Durham, NC: Duke University Press, 1997).
167 Aguilar, *Otros mundos*: p.37; Aprea, *Cine y políticas*: p.69; Sergio Wolf, 'The Aesthetics of New Argentine Cinema', *FIPRESCI* dossier 'Cinemas of the South' (2006), http://www.fipresci.org/world_cinema/south/south_english_argentinean_cinema_new_wave.htm, accessed June 2010.
168 Quoted in Laia Quílez Esteve, 'Autobiografía y ficción en el documental contemporáneo argentino. *Los rubios* de Albertina Carri: un caso paradigmático', in *El cine argentino de hoy. Entre el arte y la política*, ed. Viviana Rangil (Buenos Aires: Biblos, 2007), p.76.
169 Hirsch, Marianne, *Family Frames: Photography, Narrative and Postmemory* (Cambridge, MA: Harvard University Press, 1997), p.22. See also 'Surviving images: Holocaust photographs and the work of postmemory', *The Yale Journal of Criticism* 14, 1 (2001), pp.5–37.
170 Amado, *La imagen justa*: p.165.
171 Bruzzi, *New Documentary*: pp.83, 85.
172 Aguilar, Gonzalo, 'Maravillosa melancolía: *Cazadores de utopías*, una lectura desde el presente', in *Cines al margen. Nuevos modos de representación en el cine argentino contemporáneo*, ed. María José Moore and Paula Wolkowicz (Buenos Aires: Libraria, 2007), pp.19–20.
173 Altamirano, Carlos, 'Montoneros', *Punto de Vista* 55 (1996), p.1.
174 Vezzetti, Hugo, *Pasado y presente. Guerra, dictadura y sociedad en la Argentina* (Buenos Aires: Siglo Veintiuno, 2002), p.207.
175 Bernini, Emilio, 'El documental político argentino. Una lectura', in *Imágenes de lo real. La representación de lo político en el documental argentino*, ed. Josefina Sartora and Silvina Rival (Buenos Aires: Libraria, 2007), p.31.

176 Aguilar, 'Maravillosa melancolía', pp.22–6. An early English-language account of the history of Montoneros is Richard Gillespie's *Soldiers of Perón: Argentina's Montoneros* (Oxford: Clarendon, 1982).
177 Gundermann, Christian, *Actos melancólicos. Formas de resistencia en la posdictadura argentina* (Rosario: Beatriz Viterbo, 2007), p.19.
178 Apart from the films commented here, other documentaries dealing with – and mostly made by – the children of the disappeared include Rodrigo Vázquez's *Hasta la memoria siempre* (Forever Until Memory, 1997), Laura Bondarevsky's *Panzas* (Wombs, 2001), Marcelo Cespedes and Carmen Guarini's *H.I.J.O.S., el alma en dos* (H.I.J.O.S., the Divided Soul, 2002), Lucía Cedrón's *En ausencia* (In Absence, 2002), and Natalia Bruschtein's *Encontrando a Víctor* (Finding Victor, 2005).
179 On the Argentine concentration camps' logic of intimidation through the strategic use of obscurity, silence and immobility imposed on the prisoners (a methodology initially devised by French counterinsurgency specialists in the Algerian independence war and subsequently imposed throughout Latin America in the 1970s through the United States' 'School of the Americas' training facility at Panama – still operating today at Fort Benning, Georgia, under the euphemism 'Western Hemisphere Institute for Security Cooperation'), see Pilar Calveiro, *Poder y desaparición. Los campos de concentración en Argentina* (Buenos Aires: Colihue, 2006).
180 Esteve, Quilez, 'Autobiografía y ficción': p.75.
181 Nouzeilles, Gabriela, 'Postmemory cinema and the future of the past in Albertina Carri's *Los rubios*', *Journal of Latin American Cultural Studies* 14, 3 (2005), p.269.
182 Aguilar, Gonzalo, 'Con el cuerpo en el laberinto: Sobre M de Nicolás Prividera,' in Sartora and Rival (eds), *Imágenes de lo real*: pp.173–4.
183 Nichols, *Representing Reality*: p.109.
184 Moreno, María, 'Esa rubia debilidad', *Página 12*, suplemento 'Radar', Sunday, 19 October 2003: http://www.pagina12.com.ar/diario/suplementos/radar/9-1001-2003-10-22.html, accessed June 2010.
185 Kohan, Martín, 'La apariencia celebrada', *Punto de Vista* 78 (2004), p.29.
186 Noriega, Gustavo, *Estudio crítico sobre los rubios* (Buenos Aires: Picnic, 2009), pp.35–6.
187 Sarlo, Beatriz, *Tiempo pasado. Cultura de la memoria y giro subjetivo: una discusión* (Buenos Aires: Siglo Veintiuno, 2005), p.146. In her attempt to reinstate the 'historical truth' to which Carri supposedly remains indifferent, Sarlo even goes so far as speculating that her parents, for reasons of cover while living underground, might actually have dyed their own and their daughter's hair blonde.
188 Charly García, 'Influencia', from album *Influencia* (EMI Argentina, 2002).
189 On the spatial organisation of *Los rubios*, see Joanna Page's insightful analysis, 'Memory and mediation in *Los rubios*: a contemporary perspective of the Argentine dictatorship', *New Cinemas* 3, 1 (2005), p.31.
190 Sarlo, *Tiempo pasado*: pp.155–6.
191 Prividera, Nicolás, 'Restos', *El Ojo Mocho* 20 (2006), p.44.
192 We could also include here the literary biographies *Cortázar* (Tristán Bauer, 1994), *Macedonio Fernández* (Andrés Di Tella, 1995), *Retrato de Juan José Saer* (Rafael Filipelli, 1996) and *Paco Urondo, la palabra justa* (Daniel Desaloms, 2004).

193 Di Tella, Andrés, *Cine documental y archivo personal. Conversación en Princeton*, ed. Paul Firbas and Pedro Meira Monteiro (Buenos Aires: Siglo Veintiuno, 2006), p.44.
194 Chanan, *The Politics of Documentary*: p.247. On the concept of double voicing, see Mikhail Bakhtin, 'Discourse in the Novel', in *The Dialogic Imagination: Four Essays by M. M. Bakhtin*, transl. Caryl Emerson and Michael Holquist (Austin: University of Texas Press, 1985).
195 Di Tella, *Cine documental y archivo personal*: p.28.
196 Santoro, Daniel, 'Proyecto Pulqui. OVJ Objeto volador justicialista', in *Mundo Peronista. Pinturas, dibujos, libros de artista, objetos e instalaciones* (Buenos Aires: La Marca, 2006), p.212.
197 Amado, *La imagen justa*: p.93.
198 Mulvey, Laura, *Death 24x Second: Stillness and the Moving Image* (London: Reaktion, 2006), p.18.
199 Bernini, 'Un estado (contemporáneo) del documental': p.50.
200 Bernini, 'Noventa-setenta': p.31; Zadoff, 'El cine de las escuelas de cine': pp.268–70.
201 Aguilar, *Otros mundos*: p.223.
202 Aguilar, *Otros mundos*: p.221.
203 Page, *Crisis and Capitalism*: p.49.
204 Aguilar, Gonzalo, 'Entrevista a Pablo Trapero', in *Estudio crítico sobre El bonaerense* (Buenos Aires: Picnic, 2008), p.70.
205 On the idea of stardom as an effect of consumer identification and projection, see the discussion in Richard Dyer, *Stars* (London: BFI, 1979), pp.19–22; also Edgar Morin, 'La star et nous', in *Les stars* (Paris: Éditions du Seuil, 1972), pp.121–34.
206 Kuschevatzky, Axel, 'Sus ojos hablan', in *.dom. La revista de Tiempo Argentino*, Sunday 16 May 2010, p.25.
207 For a discussion of Darín's impact on Trapero's cinema in *Carancho*, see Leonardo M. D'Esposito, 'Una temporada en el infierno', *El Amante* 216, (May 2010), pp.2–4.
208 Aprea, *Cine y políticas*: pp.41–2.
209 Deleuze, *Cinema 2*: p.20.
210 Klevan, Andrew, *Film Performance: From Achievement to Appreciation* (London: Wallflower Press, 2005), p.13.
211 Klevan, *Film Performance*: p.13.
212 Deleuze, *Cinema 2*: pp.68–97.
213 Gundermann, Christian, 'The stark gaze of the New Argentine Cinema: restoring strangeness to the object in the perverse age of commodity fetishism,' *Journal of Latin American Cultural Studies* 14, 3 (2005), p.255.
214 Gundermann, 'The stark gaze': p.258.
215 Deleuze, *Cinema 2*: p.23.
216 Jameson, *The Geopolitical Aesthetic*: pp.37–8.
217 Deleuze, *Cinema 2*: p.20.
218 Ravaschino, Guillermo, 'El asadito,' film review at *Cineismo.com*, http://www.cineismo.com/criticas/asadito-el.htm, accessed online, July 2010.
219 Altman, Rick, *Film/Genre* (London: BFI Publishing, 1999), p.15.

220 Caetano, Israel Adrián, 'Agustín Tosco propaganda', in *El Amante de Cine* 4, 41 (July 1995), p.50.
221 Schwarzböck, Sílvia, *Estudio crítico de* Un oso rojo (Buenos Aires: Picnic, 2009), pp.15–16.
222 Schwarzböck, *Estudio crítico*: pp.17–18.
223 Oubiña, David, 'El espectáculo y sus márgenes. Sobre Adrián Caetano y el nuevo cine argentino', *Punto de Vista* 76 (2003), p.30.
224 Wright, Will, *Sixguns and Society. A Structural Study of the Western* (Berkeley: University of California Press, 1975), p.69.
225 Schwarzböck, *Estudio crítico*: p.10.
226 Page, *Crisis and Capitalism*: pp.98, 100.
227 Scorer, James, 'Once upon a time in Buenos Aires: vengeance, community and the urban western', *Journal of Latin American Cultural Studies* 19, 2 (2010), p.150.
228 Oubiña, 'El espectáculo y sus márgenes': p.32.
229 Bernini, Emilio, 'Un proyecto inconcluso. Aspectos del cine contemporáneo argentino', *Kilómetro 111* 4 (2003): p.105.
230 Aguilar, *Otros mundos*: p.125.
231 Ravaschino, Guillermo, 'El bonaerense', *Cineismo.com*, http://www.cineismo.com/criticas/bonaerense-el.htm, accessed online, July 2010.
232 Aguilar, 'Entrevista a Pablo Trapero': p.66.
233 Aguilar, *Estudio crítico*: p.36.
234 González, Horacio, 'Sobre El bonaerense y el nuevo cine argentino', *El Ojo Mocho* 17 (2003), p.158.
235 Copertari, Gabriela, '*Nine Queens*: a dark day of simulation and justice', *Journal of Latin American Cultural Studies* 14, 3 (2005), p.279.
236 Page, *Crisis and Capitalism*: p.85.
237 Sabat, Cynthia, 'El ilusionista del millón', *Holacine*, September 2004, http://www.holacine.com.ar/interview/Interview.asp?Pagina=1&interview=2, accessed July 2010.
238 Lerer, Diego, 'Perros de la calle,' *Clarín*, Thursday 31 August 2000, http://old.clarin.com/diario/2000/08/31/c-00905.htm, accessed online, July 2010.
239 Beceyro, Raúl, '*Nueve reinas*: la última estafa,' *El Amante de Cine* 103 (2000): p.3.
240 Page, *Crisis and Capitalism*: p.93.
241 Copertari, '*Nine Queens*': p.280.
242 Copertari, '*Nine Queens*': p.287.
243 Rancière, Jacques, *La fable cinématographique* (Paris: Seuil, 2001), 29. English edition *Film Fables* (Oxford: Berg, 2006).
244 Rancière, *La fable cinématographique*: p.27.
245 Oubiña, *Estudio crítico de* La ciénaga: p.27.
246 Aguilar, *Otros mundos*: p.105.
247 Oubiña, *Estudio crítico de* La ciénaga: p.16.
248 Oubiña, *Estudio crítico de* La ciénaga: p.44.
249 Relations between childhood and emergent forms of self-narrative, before they begin to cohere into chronological autobiography with the advent of adulthood, have been the subject of a rapidly increasing bibliography in literary, feminist and psychoanalytical studies. For an initial orientation, see Charlotte

Linde, *Life Stories: The Creation of Coherence* (New York: Oxford University Press, 1993).
250 White, Hayden, 'The question of narrative in contemporary historical theory,' in *The Content of the Form. Narrative Discourse and Historical Representation* (Baltimore: Johns Hopkins University Press, 1987), pp.26–57.
251 Aguilar, *Otros mundos*: p.159.
252 On the vast literary, architectonic and entrepreneurial oeuvre of Father Pérez, author, among others, of the improbably titled book *Soy tu madre* (I'm Your Mother), see the San Nicolás sanctuary's official website – including a virtual pilgrimage, forms for submitting pleas to the Virgin by email, as well as a sign-up campaign for canonic recognition of the San Nicolás miracle, http://www.virgen-de-san-nicolas.org/default.asp, accessed July 2010.
253 I use the concept of 'postdictatorship' here in the sense proposed by Idelber Avelar and others, who have argued that, against the idea of a 'transition to democracy' in the mould of the end of the Franco regime in Spain, the right-wing dictatorships in Latin America between the 1960s and the early 1990s were themselves a form of violent 'transition' from the national-popular welfare state to the neo-liberal societies of the turn of the millennium. See Idelber Avelar, *The Untimely Present: Postdictatorial Latin American Fiction and the Work of Mourning* (Durham, NC: Duke University Press, 1999).
254 Benjamin, Walter, 'Das Kunstwerk im Zeitalter seiner technischen Reproduzierbarkeit' (Dritte Fassung), in *Gesammelte Schriften*, Bd. I, 2 (Frankfurt am Main: Suhrkamp, 1991), p.496. English edition: *The Work of Art in the Age of Mechanical Reproduction*, transl. J. Underwood (Harmondsworth: Penguin, 2008).
255 Holland, Jonathan, 'Review of *The Secret in their Eyes*,' *Variety*, 12 September 2009, http://www.variety.com/review/VE1117941041.html?categoryid=2863&cs=1, accessed July 2010.
256 Quintín, 'Día de fiesta. Sobre *Historias extraordinarias* de Mariano Llinás,' *La lectora provisoria*, 19 April 2008, http://www.lalectoraprovisoria.com.ar/?p=2194, accessed July 2010.

Filmography

English titles indicated only where these were translated for international release.

180 grados. 2008. Director and Script: Raúl Perrone; Editing: Zaida de Pedro; Cinematography: Fabián Blanco, Bernardo Demonte and Raúl Perrone; cast Ezequiel Sabella, Mariana Fernández, Gastón Cambiasso.
5 pa'l peso. 1998. Director: Raúl Perrone; Script: Raúl Perrone and Roberto Barandalla; Editing: Benjamín Ávila; Cinematography: Serpe Sayas; Sound: Juan Pablo Di Bitonto; cast Martín Campilongo, Mauro Altchuler, Valentina Bassi.
76-89-03. 1999. D. and Sc. Cristian Bernard and Flavio Nardini; E. Eliane Katz; C. Daniel Sotelo; S. Sergio Iglesias; cast Sergio Baldini, Gerardo Chendo, Diego Mackenzie.
Agua [Water]. 2006. D. and Sc. Verónica Chen; E. Luis César D'Angiolillo and Jacopo Quadri; C. Sabine Lanoelin; S. Martín Grignaschi and Federico Billordo; cast Rafael Ferro, Nicolás Mateo, Gloria Carrá.
Ana y los otros [Ana and the Others]. 2003. D. and Sc. Celina Murga; E. Martín Mainoli; C. Marcelo Lavintman and José María Gómez; S. Federico Billordo; cast Camila Toker, Ignacio Uslenghi, Natacha Massera.
Ángeles. 1992. D. Raúl Perrone; Sc. Raúl Perrone and Roberto Barandalla; cast Carlos Briolotti, Horacio Graniero, Raúl Perrone.
Argentina latente. 2006. D. and Sc. Fernando E. Solanas; E. Mauricio Minotti, Alberto Ponce and Fernando E. Solanas; C. Alejandro Fernández Mouján, Rino Pravatto and Fernando E. Solanas; S. Marcos Dickinson, Abelardo Kuschmir and José Luis Díaz.
Banderas de humo. 1989. D, Sc., E. and C. Alejandro Fernández Mouján.
Bar 'El Chino'. 2003. D. Daniel Burak; Sc. Daniel Burak, Mario Lion and Beatriz Pustilnik; E. Andrés Tambornino; C. Germán Constantino; S. Pedro Marra; cast Boy Olmi, Jimena Latorre, Ernesto Larrese.
Bolivia. 2001. D. and Sc. Israel Adrián Caetano; E. Lucas Scavino and Santiago Ricci; C. Julián Azpeteguia; S. Diego Arancibia; cast Freddy Flores, Rosa Sánchez, Oscar Bertea, Enrique Liporace.
Bonanza (En vías de extinción). 2001. D. and Sc. Ulises Rosell; E. Nicolás Goldbart; C. Guillermo Nieto; S. Federico Esquerro.
Brukman confecciones (El segundo desalojo). 2002. D., S., E. and C. Grupo Alavío.

Buenos Aires 100 kilómetros. 2004. D. and Sc. Pablo José Meza; E. Andrés Tambornino; C. Carla Stella; S. Federico Esquerro; cast Juan Ignacio Pérez Roca, Emniliano Fernández, Alan Ardel.

Caballos salvajes [Wild Horses]. 1995. D. Marcelo Piñeyro; Sc. Aída Bortnik and Marcelo Piñeyro; E. Juan Carlos Macias; C. Alfredo F. Mayo; S. Aníbal Libenson; cast Héctor Alterio, Leonardo Sbaraglia, Cecilia Dopazo.

Caja negra [Black Box]. 2001. D., Sc. and C. Luis Ortega; E. César Custodio; S. Martín Porta; cast Dolores Fonzi, Eduardo Couget, Eugenia Bassi.

Cama adentro [Live-in Maid]. 2004. D. and Sc. Jorge Gaggero; E. Guillermo Represas; C. Javier Julia; S. José Caldararo; cast Norma Aleandro, Norma Argentina, Marcos Mundstock.

Camila. 1984. D. and Sc. María Luisa Bemberg; E. Luis César D'Angiolillo; C. Fernando Arribas; S. Jorge Stavropoulos; cast Susú Pecoraro, Héctor Alterio, Imanol Arias.

Canadá. 2006. D. and Sc. Raúl Perrone; E. Lorna Santiago; C. Ángel Arozamena; S. Gaspar Scheuer; cast Heber Huang, Jacqueline Cordero.

Cándido López – los campos de batalla. 2005. D. and Sc. José Luis García; E. Marie-José Nenert, Fernando Cricenti, Miguel Colombo, Miguel Schwerdfinger and José Luis García; C. Marcelo Iaccarino; S. Carlos Olmedo.

Carancho. 2010. D. Pablo Trapero; Sc. Alejandro Fadel, Martín Mauregui, Santiago Mitre and Pablo Trapero; E. Ezequiel Borovinsky and Pablo Trapero; C. Julián Apezteguia; S. Federico Esquerro; cast Ricardo Darín, Martina Gusman, Carlos Weber.

Castro. 2009. D. and Sc. Alejo Moguillansky; E. Mariano Llinás and Alejo Moguillansky; C. Gustavo Biazzi; cast Edgardo Castro, Julia Martínez Rubio, Alberto Suárez.

Cazadores de utopías [Hunters of Utopia]. 1995. D. David Blaustein; Sc. Eduardo Jauretche; E. Juan Carlos Macías; C. Alejandro Fernández Mouján.

Cenizas del paraíso [Paradise Ashes]. 1997. D. Marcelo Piñeyro; Sc. Marcelo Piñeyro and Aída Bortnik; E. Juan Carlos Macias; C. Alfredo F. Mayo; S. Fabián Ayala; cast Héctor Alterio, Cecilia Roth, Leonardo Sbaraglia.

Ciudad de María [Mary's City]. 2001. D. and Sc. Enrique Bellande; E. Alejandro Brodersohn; C. Florencia Blanco and Guillermo NIeto; S. Martín Grignaschi and Federico Esquerro.

Comodines. 1997. D. Jorge Nisco; Sc. Gustavo Belatti, Ricardoi Piglia and Mario Segade; E. Alejandro Alem; C. Ricardo de Angelis (h.); cast Carlos Calvo, Adrián Suar, Rodolfo Ranni.

Copacabana. 2006. D. and Sc. Martín Rejtman; E. Martín Mainoli; C. Diego Poleri; S. Javier Farina and Jésica Suárez.

Corazón de fábrica [Heart of the Factory]. 2008. D., Sc., E., C. and S. Ernesto Ardito and Vilma Molina.

Cordero de Dios [Lamb of God]. 2008. D. Lucía Cedrón; Sc. Lucía Cedrón, Santiago Giralt and Thomas Philippon; E. Rosario Suárez; C. Guillermo Nieto; S. Víctor Tendler and Guido Beremblum; cast Mercedes Morán, Juan Minujín, Leonora Balcarce.

Crónica de una fuga [Buenos Aires] 1977. D. Israel Adrián Caetano; Sc. Israel Adrián Caetano, Esteban Student and Julián Loyola; E. Alberto Ponce; C. Julián

Azpeteguia; S. Fernando Soldevila; cast Rodrigo de la Serna, Pablo Echarri, Nazareno Casero.

Darse cuenta. 1984. D. Alejandro Doria; Sc. Jacobo Langsner and Alejandro Doria; E. Sílvia Ripoll; C. Miguel Rodríguez; cast Luis Brandoni, Dora Baret, Luisina Brando.

Días de mayo [Days of May]. 2009. D. and Sc. Gustavo Postiglione; E. Lucio García; C. Héctor Molina; S. Carlos Rossano; cast Agustina Guirado, Santiago de Jesús Díaz, Caren Hulten.

Dibu, la película. 1997. D. Carlos Olivieri and Alejandro Stoessel; Sc. Daniel Kuzniecka and Ricardo Rodríguez; E. Norberto Rapado; C. Ricardo Rodríguez; So. Maximiliano Gorriti; cast Germán Krauss, Stella Maris Closas, Alberto Anchart (voices).

El abrazo partido [Lost Embrace]. 2003. D. Daniel Burman; Sc. Daniel Burman and Marcelo Birmajer; E. Alejandro Brodersohn; C. Ramiro Civita; S. Martín Grignaschi; cast Daniel Hendler, Adriana Aizemberg, Jorge D' Elia.

El amor es una mujer gorda [Love is a Fat Woman]. 1987. D. and Sc. Alejandro Agresti; E. René Wiegmans; C. Néstor Sanz; cast Elio Marchi, Sergio Poves Campos, Carlos Roffe.

El asadito. 2000. D., Sc. and E. Gustavo Postiglione; C. Fernando Zago; S. Carlos Rossano; cast Tito Gómez, Gerardo Dalub, Raúl Calandra.

El bonaerense. 2002. D. and Sc. Pablo Trapero; E. Nicolás Goldbart; C. Guillermo Nieto; S. Catriel Vildosola; cast Jorge Román, Mimí Ardu, Darío Levy.

El camino de San Diego [The Road to San Diego]. 2006. D. and Sc. Carlos Sorín; E. Leonardo Camporeale; C. Hugo Colace; S. Carlos Abbate; cast Ignacio Benítez, Carlos Wagner La Bella, Paola Rotela.

El caso María Soledad. 1993. D. Héctor Olivera; Sc. Héctor Olivera and Graciela Maglie; E. Eduardo López; C. Juan Carlos Lenardi; cast Carolina Fal, Valentina Bassi, Belén Blanco.

El cielito [Little Sky]. 2003. D. María Victoria Menis; Sc. María Victoria Menis and Alejandro Fernández Murray; E. Alejandro Brodersohn; C. Marcelo Iaccarino; S. Adriano Salgado; cast Leonardo Ramírez, Darío Levy, Mónica Lairana.

El cumple. 2002. D. and Sc. Gustavo Postiglione; E. Lucio García; C. Fernando Zago; S. Carlos Rossano; cast Raúl Calandra, Bárbara Peters, Carlos Resta.

El custodio. 2005. D. and Sc. Rodrigo Moreno; E. Nicolás Goldbart; C. Bárbara Álvarez; S. Catriel Vildasola; cast Julio Chávez, Omar Núñez, Marcelo D'Andrea.

El exilio de Gardel (Tangos) [Tangos, the Exile of Gardel]. 1985. D. and Sc. Fernando E. Solanas; E. Luis César D'Angiolillo and Jacques Gaillard; C. Félix Monti; cast Marie Laforet, Miguel Ángel Solá, Philippe Léotard.

El hijo de la novia [Son of the Bride]. 2001. D. Juan José Campanella; Sc. Juan José Campanella and Fernando Castets; E. Camilo Antolini; C. Daniel Shulman; S. Carlos Abbate and José Luis Díaz; cast Ricardo Darín, Héctor Alterio, Norma Aleandro.

El lado oscuro del corazón [The Dark Side of the Heart]. 1992. D. and Sc. Eliseo Subiela; E. Marcela Sáenz; C. Hugo Colace; S. Carlos Abbate and José Luis Díaz; cast Darío Grandinetti, Sandra Ballesteros, Nacha Guevara.

El nexo. 2007. D. Sebastián Antico; Sc. Sebastián Antico and Diego Rosso; E. Sebastián Antico and Juanma Ibáñez; C. José María Gómez; S. Lucas Sobral; cast Julio Arrieta, Ester Oviedo, Ramón Piedrabuena.

El perro [Bombón: El Perro]. D. Carlos Sorín; Sc. Carlos Sorín, Salvador Roselli and Santiago Calori; E. Mohamed Rajid; C. Hugo Colace; S. Carlos Abbate; cast Juan Villegas, Walter Donado, Rosa Valsecchi.

El secreto de sus ojos [The Secret in Their Eyes]. 2009. D. and E. Juan José Campanella; Sc. Juan José Campanella and Eduardo Sacheri; C. Félix Monti; S. José Luis Díaz; cast Ricardo Darín, Soledad Villamil, Guillermo Francella.

El ratón Pérez [The Hairy Tooth Fairy]. 2006. D. Juan Pablo Buscarini; Sc. Enrique Cortés; E. César Custodio; C. Miguel Abal; S. Lucas Meyer; cast Ana María Orozco, Fabián Mazzei, Delfina Varni.

El resultado del amor [The Effect of Love]. 2007. D. and Sc. Eliseo Subiela; E. Marcela Sáenz; C. Marc Cuxart; S. Fabián Ayala; cast Sofia Castiglione, Guillermo Pfening, Romina Ricci.

El tiempo y la sangre. 2004. D., Sc., E. and C. Alejandra Almirón; S. Luciano Bertone.

El último malón [The Last Indian Attack]. 1917. D. and Sc. Alcides Greca; cast Alcides Greca, Jesús Salvador, Rosa Paiquí.

El verso. 1995. D. and Sc. Santiago Carlos Oves; E. Jorge Valencia; C. Jorge Ruiz; cast Luis Brandoni, Virginia Lago, Hugo Arana.

El viaje [The Voyage]. 1990. D. and Sc. Fernando E. Solanas; E. Alberto Borello and Jacques Gaillard; C. Félix Monti; S. Daniel Fainzilber; cast Walter Quiroz, Dominique Sanda, Fito Páez.

En ausencia [In Absentia]. 2002. D. and Sc. Lucía Cedrón; E. Miguel Pérez and Gonzalo Santiso; C. Marcelo Lavintman; S. Juan Carlos Di Bitonto; cast Ana Celentano, Pablo Cedrón, Juana Lanzi.

Encontrando a Víctor. 2005. D., Sc. and E. Natalia Bruschtein; C. Alejandro Ester and Everardo González; S. Matías Barberis.

Errepé. 2004. D. and Sc. Gabriel Corvi and Gustavo de Jesús; E. Bruno Robotti and Pablo De Feo; C. Gustavo de Jesús and Alberto de Fazio.

Esas cuatro notas. 2004. D. Rafael Filipelli; Sc. David Oubiña, Hernán Hevia, Santiago Palavecino and Rafael Filipelli; E. Alejo Moguillansky; C. Carlos Essmann, Paola Rizzi and Martín Mohadeb; S. Hernán Hevia and Federico Esquerro.

Espejo para cuando me pruebe el smoking. 2005. D., Sc., E. and C. Alejandro Fernández Mouján; S. Gaspar Scheuer.

Estrellas. 2007. D. and Sc. Federico León and Marcos Martínez; E. Catalina Rincón; C. Julián Azpeteguia and Guillermo Nieto; S. Rufino Basavilbaso and Jésica Suárez.

Extraño [Strange]. 2003. D. and Sc. Santiago Loza; E. Ana Poliak' C. Willy Behnisch; S. Perfecto de San José; cast Julio Chávez, Valeria Bertuccelli, Chunchuna Villafañe.

Familia rodante [Rolling Family]. 2004. D. and Sc. Pablo Trapero; E. Nicolás Goldbart; C. Guillermo Nieto; S. Martín Grignaschi; cast Graciana Chironi, Liliana Capuro, Bernardo Forteza.

Fantasma. 2006. D. and Sc. Lisandro Alonso; E. Lisandro Alonso and Delfina Castagnino; C. Lucio Bonelli, S. Catriel Vildasola; cast Argentino Vargas, Misael Saavedra, Rosa Martínez Rivero.

Fasinpat – fábrica sin patrón. 2004. D., Sc. and C. Daniele Incalaterra; E. Fausta Quattrini; S. Gaspar Scheuer.

Flores de septiembre. 2003. D. Pablo Osores, Roberto Testa and Nicolás Wainszelbaum; Sc. Roberto Testa; E. Lucas Blanco; C. Sebastián Sperling.

Fotografías. 2007. D. and Sc. Andrés Di Tella; E. Alejandra Almirón; C. Víctor González; S. Lena Esquenazi.

Francia [France]. 2009. D. and Sc. Israel Adrián Caetano; E. Omar Ester; C. Julián Azpeteguia; S. Manuel Pinto; cast Natalia Oreiro, Milagros Caetano, Mónica Ayos.

Garage Olimpo. 1999. D. Marco Bechis; Sc. Lara Fremder and Marco Bechis; E. Jacopo Quadri; C. Ramiro Aisenson; cast Antonella Costa, Carlos Echevarría, Enrique Piñeyro.

Géminis [Gemini]. 2005. D. Albertina Carri; Sc. Albertina Carri and Santiago Giralt; E. Rosario Suárez; C. Guillermo Nieto; S. Jésica Suárez; cast Cristian Banegas, Daniel Fanego, María Abadi.

Gerónima. 1986. D. Raúl Tosso; Sc. Raúl Tosso and Carlos Paola; E. Fernando Gueriniello and Sílvia Ripoll; C. Carlos Torlaschi; cast Luisa Calcumil, Patricio Contreras, Mario Luciani.

Graciadió. 1997. D. Raúl Perrone; Sc. Raúl Perrone and Roberto Barandalla; E. Benjamín Ávila; C. Serpe Sayas; S. Gustavo Triviño; cast Gustavo Prone, Violeta Naón, Mauro Altchuler.

Habitación disponible. 2004. D. and Sc. Eva Poncet, Marcelo Burd and Diego Gachassin; E. Eva Poncet; C. Diego Gachassin; S. Fernando Vega.

Hasta la memoria siempre. 1997. D. and Sc. Rodrigo Vásquez; E. Pierre Haberer; C. Abel Peñalba; S. Billy Quinn.

Hay unos tipos abajo [There's Some Guys Downstairs]. 1985. D. and Sc. Emilio Alfaro and Rafael Filipelli; E. Oscar Esparza; C. Yito Blanc; S. Ernesto Sansalvador Viales; cast Luis Brandoni, Luisina Brando, Soledad Silveyra.

Hermanas [Sisters]. 2004. D. and Sc. Julia Solomonoff; E. Rosario Suárez; C. Ramiro Aisenson; S. Gaspar Scheuer; cast Valeria Bertuccelli, Ingrid Rubio, Adrián Navarro.

H.I.J.O.S., el alma en dos. 2002. D., C. and E. Carmen Guarini and Marcelo Cespedes; Sc. Carmen Guarini; S. Alejandro Alonso and Cote Álvarez.

Historias breves I. 1995. D. Daniel Burman, Israel Adrián Caetano, Jorge Gaggero, Tristán Gicovate, Sandra Gugliotta, Lucrecia Martel, Pablo Ramos, Ulises Rosell, Bruno Stagnaro and Andrés Tambornino.

(h)istorias cotidianas. 2000. D. Andrés Habegger; Sc. Lucía Puenzo and Andrés Habegger; E. Laura Mattarollo; C. Mariano Cúneo; S. Sebastián Coll and Fernando Vega.

Historias extraordinarias [Extraordinary Stories]. 2008. D. and Sc. Mariano Llinás; E. Alejo Moguillansky and Agustín Rolandelli; C. Agustín Mendilaharzu; S. Rodrigo Sánchez Mariño and Nicolás Torchinsky; cast Walter Jakob, Agustín Mendilaharzu, Mariano Llinás.

Historias mínimas [Minimal Stories]. 2002. D. Carlos Sorín; Sc. Carlos Solarz; E. Mohamed Rajid; C. Hugo Colace; cast Javier Lombardo, Antonio Benedictis, Javiera Bravo.

Hombres de barro. 1988. D. Miguel Mirra; Sc. Miguel Mirra and Eulogio Frites; E. Mabel Leonetti; C. Gerardo Silvatici; cast Eulogio Frites, Máximo Frites, Mercedes Tolay.

Hoteles. 2003. D. and Sc. Aldo Paparella; E. Julio Di Risio; C. Airel Vilches and Mariano Molinari; S. Sergio Iglesias; cast Noemí Amaya, Fernando Carballo, Jorge Richter.
Hotel Gondolín. 2005. D., Sc., E. and C. Fernando López Escriva.
Hoy y mañana [Today and Tomorrow]. 2003. D. and Sc. Alejandro Chomsky; E. Alex Zito; C. Guillermo Nieto; S. Abel Tortorelli; cast Antonella Costa, Romina Ricci, Ricardo Merkin.
Jimidin. 1995. D. Raúl Perrone; Sc. Raúl Perrone and Roberto Barandalla; cast Román Motura, Violeta Naón, Félix Tornquist, Gustavo Prone.
Juan, como si nada hubiera sucedido. 1987. D. and Sc. Carlos Echeverría; E. Fritz Baumann; C. Horacio Herman and Carlos Echeverría; S. Juan Vera, Dorothee Schön and Ingrid Thorhauer; cast Esteban Buch.
Juan Moreira. 1973. D. Leonardo Favio; Sc. Jorge Zuhair Jury and Leonardo Favio; E. Antonio Ripoll; C. Juan Carlos Desanzo; S. Miguel Babuini; cast Rodolfo Bebén, Elcira Olivera Garcés, Edgardo Suárez.
La amiga [The Girlfriend]. 1988. D. Jeanine Meerapfel; Sc. Jeanine Meerapfel and Alcides Chiesa; E. Juliane Lorenz; C. Axel Block; S. Dante Amoroso; cast Liv Ullman, Cipe Lincovsky, Federico Luppi.
Labios de churrasco. 1994. D. and Sc. Raúl Perrone; E. Luis Barros; C. Carlos Briolotti; cast Fabián Vena, Violeta Naón, Gustavo Prone.
La ciénaga [The Swamp]. 2001. D. and Sc. Lucrecia Martel; E. Santiago Ricci; C. Hugo Colace; S. Hervé Guyader and Emannuel Croset; cast Graciela Borges, Mercedes Morán, Martín Adjemián.
La cruz del sur [The Southern Cross]. 2002. D. and Sc. Pablo Reyero; E. Fabio Pallero; C. Marcelo Iaccarino and María Ibáñez Lago; S. Abel Tortorelli; cast Leticia Lestido, Luciano Suardi, Humberto Tortolese.
La deuda interna [The Debt]. 1988. D. and Sc. Miguel Pereira; E. and C. Gerry Feeny; S. Gustavo Araya; cast Juan José Camero, Gonzalo Morales, René Olaguivel.
La dignidad de los nadies [The Dignity of the Nobodies]. 2005. D., Sc. and C. Fernando E. Solanas; E. Juan Carlos Macías and Martín Subirá; S. Marcos Dickinson and Abelardo Kuschmir.
La fe del volcán [The Faith of the Volcano]. 2001. D. and E. Ana Poliak; Sc. Ana Poliak and Willi Behnisch; C. Wili Behnisch; S. Luis Corazza; cast Mónica Donay, Jorge Prado.
La fuga [The Escape]. 2001. D. Eduardo Mignogna; Sc. Graciela Maglie, Jorge Goldemberg and Eduardo Mignogna; E. Juan Carlos Macías; C. Marcelo Camorino; S. Daniel Goldstein and Ricardo Steinberg; cast Miguel Ángel Solá, Ricardo Darín, Gerardo Romano.
La furia [The Fury]. 1997. D. and Sc. Juan Bautista Stagnaro; E. Miguel Pérez; C. Carlos Torlaschi; S. Alexis Stavropoulos; cast Luis Brandoni, Diego Torres, Laura Novoa.
La gaucha. 1921. D. José Agustín Ferreyra; Sc. José Agustín Ferreyra and Leopoldo Torres Ríos; C. Carlos Torres Ríos; cast Lidia Liss, Elena Guido, Elsa Rey.
La historia oficial [The Official Story]. 1985. D. Luis Puenzo; Sc. Aída Bortnik and Luis Puenzo; E. Juan Carlos Macías; C. Félix Monti; S. Abelardo Kuschnir; cast Héctor Alterio, Norma Aleandro, Chunchuna Villafañe.

La hora de los hornos – Notas y testimonios sobre el neocolonialismo, la violencia y la liberación [The Hour of the Furnaces]. 1968. D. and Sc. Fernando E. Solanas and Octavio Getino; E. Juan Carlos Macías, Antonio Ripoll and Norma Torrado; C. Juan Carlos Desanzo and Fernando E. Solanas; S. Octavio Getino, Abelardo Kuschmir and Aníbal Libenson.

La León. 2006. D. and Sc. Santiago Otheguy; E. Sebastián Sepúlveda and Valeria Otheguy; C. Paula Grandío; S. Abel Tortorelli; cast Jorge Román, Daniel Valenzuela, José Muñoz (II).

La libertad [Freedom]. 2001. D. and Sc. Lisandro Alonso; E. Lisandro Alonso and Martín Mainoli; C. Cobi Migliora; S. Catriel Vildasola; cast Misael Saavedra, Humberto Estrada, Rafael Estrada.

La mecha. 2003. D. and Sc. Raúl Perrone; E. Benjamín Ávila; C. Ángel Arozamena; S. Alejandro Alonso; cast Nicéforo Galván, Daniel Pelinacci, Juan Ramón Sánchez.

La mujer sin cabeza [The Headless Woman]. 2007. D. and Sc. Lucrecia Martel; E. Miguel Schverdfinger; C. Bárbara Álvarez; S. Guido Berenblun; cast María Onetto, Claudia Cantero, César Bordón.

La niña santa [The Holy Girl]. 2004. D. and Sc. Lucrecia Martel; E. Santiago Ricci; C. Félix Monti; S. Guido Beremblun and Víctor Tendler; cast Mercedes Morán, María Alché, Carlos Belloso.

La noche eterna. 1991. D. and Sc. Marcelo Céspedes and Carmen Guarini; E. José María del Peón; C. Andrés Silvart; S. Lívio Pensavalle and Edgardo Rudnitzky.

La Patagonia rebelde [Rebellion in Patagonia]. 1974. D. Héctor Olivera; Sc. Osvaldo Bayer, Fernando Ayala and Héctor Olivera; E. Oscar Montauti; C. Víctor Hugo Caula; S. Norberto Castronuovo; cast Héctor Alterio, Luis Brandoni, Federico Luppi.

La peli. 2006. D. and Sc. Gustavo Postiglione; E. Lucio García; C. Héctor Molina; S. Carlos Rossano; cast Darío Grandinetti, Norman Briski, Carlos Resta.

La película del rey [A King and His Movie]. 1986. D. Carlos Sorín; Sc. Carlos Sorín and Jorge Goldemberg; E. Alberto Yaccelini; C. Esteban Pablo Courtalón; S. Javier Salinas; cast Ulises Dumont, Julio Chávez, Villanueva Cosse.

La película del taller. 1998. D. and Sc. Raúl Perrone; C. Raúl Perrone and Roli Rauwolf.

La próxima estación. 2008. D. and Sc. Fernando E. Solanas; E. Alberto Ponce, Mauricio Minotti and Fernando E. Solanas; C. Rino Pravatti, Mauricio Minotti, Alejandro Fernández Mouján and Fernando E. Solanas; S. Lena Esquenazi.

La rabia [Anger]. 2008. D. and Sc. Albertina Carri; E. Alejo Moguillansky; C. Sol Lopatin; S. Rufino Basavilbaso; cast Nazarena Duarte, Gonzalo Pérez, Víctor Hugo Carrizo.

Las aguas bajan turbias [River of Blood]. 1952. D. Hugo del Carril; Sc. Eduardo Borrás; E. Gerardo Rinaldi; C. José María Beltrán; cast Hugo del Carril, Adriana Benetti, Raúl del Valle.

Las Palmas, Chaco. 2002. D. and Sc. Alejandro Fernández Mouján; E. Sebastián Mignogna; C. Alejandro Fernández Mouján and Sebastián Mignogna; S. Gaspar Scheuer.

Las vidas posibles [Possible Lives]. 2007. D. and Sc. Sandra Gugliotta; E. Juan Pablo Di Bitonto and Víctor Cruz; C. Lucio Bonelli; S. Leandro de Loredo; cast Ana Celentano, Germán Palacios, Natalia Oreiro.

La televisión y yo (notas en una libreta). 2002. D., Sc. and E. Andrés Di Tella; C. Estebam Sapir; S. Gaspar Scheuer.

La vida según Muriel [Life According to Muriel]. 1997. D. Eduardo Milewicz; Sc. Eduardo Milewicz and Susana Silvestre; E. Marcela Sáenz; C. Esteban Sapir; S. Guido Beremblum; cast Soledad Villamil, Inés Estevez, Jorge Perugorría.

Lesbianas de Buenos Aires [Lesbians of Buenos Aires]. 2002. D. and Sc. Santiago García; E. Julia Soto and Santiago García; C. Diana Quiroga; S. Federico Billordo.

Liverpool. 2008. D. Lisandro Alonso; Sc. Lisandro Alonso and Salvador Roselli; E. Lisandro Alonso, Fernando Epstein and Martín Mainoli; C. Lucio Bonelli; S. Catriel Vildasola; cast Juan Fernández, Nieves Cabrera, Giselle Irrazabal.

Los dueños del silencio. 1987. D. and Sc. Carlos Lemos; E. Luis Mutti; C. Juan Carlos Lenardi; cast Thomas Hellberg, Bibi Andersson, Arturo Bonín.

Los fusiladitos [The Executed]. 2003. D. and Sc. Cecilia Miljiker; C. Diego Echave; S. Julian Catz; cast Florencia Argento, Carlos Portaluppi, Malena Solda.

Los guantes mágicos [The Magic Gloves]. 2003. D. and Sc. Martín Rejtman; E. Rosario Suárez; C. José Luis García; S. Guido Berenblum; cast Gabriel Fernández Capello, Valeria Bertuccelli, Fabián Arenillas.

Los hijos de Fierro. 1975. D. and Sc. Fernando E. Solanas; E. Luis César D'Angiolillo; C. Juan Carlos Desanzo; S. Abelardo Kuschmir; cast Julio Troxler, Martiniano Martínez, José Almejeiras.

Los inundados [Flooded Out]. 1961. D. and Sc. Fernando Birri; E. Antonio Ripoll; C. Adelqui Camuso; S. Jorge Castronuovo; cast Pirucho Gómez, Lola Palombo, María Vera.

Los muertos [The Dead]. 2004. D. and Sc. Lisandro Alonso; E. Lisandro Alonso, Delfina Castagnino and Ezequiel Borovinsky; C. Cobi Migliora; S. Catriel Vildasola; cast Argentino Vargas, Francisco Dornez, Yolanda Galarza.

Los paranoicos [The Paranoids]. 2008. D. and Sc. Gabriel Medina; E. Nicolás Goldbart; C. Lucio Bonelli; S. Fernando Soldevila; cast Daniel Hendler, Jazmín Stuart, Walter Jakob.

Los rubios [The Blondes]. 2003. D. and Sc. Albertina Carri; E. Alejandra Almirón; C. Carmen Torres and Albertina Carri; S. Jésica Suárez; cast Analía Couceyro.

Lugares comunes [Common Ground]. 2002. D. Adolfo Aristarain; Sc. Adolfo Aristarain and Kathy Saavedra; E. Fernando Pardo; C. Porfirio Enríquez; S. Juan Ferro; cast Federico Luppi, Mercedes Sampietro, Arturo Puig.

Luna de Avellaneda [Moon of Avellaneda]. 2004. D. Juan José Campanella; Sc. Juan José Campanella, Fernando Castets and Juan Pablo Domenech; E. Camilo Antolini; C. Daniel Shulman; S. José Luis Díaz Ousande; cast Ricardo Darín, Mercedes Morán, Eduardo Blanco.

M. 2007. D. and Sc. Nicolás Prividera; E. Malu Herdt; C. Carla Stella, Josefina Semilla and Nicolás Prividera; S. Demian Lorenzatti.

Maten a Perón. 2005. D. Fernando Musante; Sc. Leonardo Nápoli and Fernando Musante; E. Cristian Frascino and Juan Francisco Botto; C. Fernando Silva; S. Aldo Marchese.

Mbya, tierra en rojo. 2004. D., Sc. and C. Philip Cox and Valeria Mapelman; E. Ben Stark.

Memoria del saqueo [Social Genocide]. 2003. D. and Sc. Fernando E. Solanas; E. Juan Carlos Macías and Fernando E. Solanas; C. Alejandro Fernàndez Mouján and Fernando E. Solanas; S. Abelardo Kuschmir, Marcos Dickinson and Eric Vaucher.

Monobloc. 2004. D. Luis Ortega; Sc. Luis Ortega and Carolina Fal; E. César Custodio; C. Coby Migliora; S. Martín Porta and Catriel Vildasola; cast Graciela Borges, Rita Cortese, Carolina Fal, Evangelina Salazar.

Montoneros, una historia. 1994. D. Andrés Di Tella; Sc. Roberto Barandalla and Andrés Di Tella; C. Fabián Hofman; S. Oscar Bertea.

Mundo grúa [Crane World]. 1999. D. and Sc. Pablo Trapero; E. Nicolás Goldbart; C. Cobi Migliora; S. Catriel Vildasola and Federico Esquerro; cast Luis Margani, Adriana Aizemberg, Daniel Valenzuela.

Nacido y criado [Born and Bred]. 2006. D. Pablo Trapero; Sc. Pablo Trapero and Mario Rulloni; E. Pablo Trapero and Ezequiel Borovinsky; C. Guillermo Nieto; S. Guillermo Pico; cast Guillermo Pfening, Federico Esquerro, Martina Gusman.

Nadar solo [Swimming Alone]. 2003. D. Ezequiel Acuña; Sc. Ezequiel Acuña and Alberto Rojas Apel; E. Sergio Flamminio; C. Octavio Lobisolo; S. Javier Farina; cast Nicolás Mateo, Santiago Pedrero, Antonella Costa.

Nobleza gaucha [Gaucho Nobility]. 1915. D. Humberto Cairo; Sc. José González Castillo; C. Ernesto Gunche and Eduardo Martínez de la Pera; cast Arturo Mario, María Padín, Celestino Petray.

No mueras sin decirme adónde vas [Don't Die Without Telling Me You're Going]. 1995. D. and Sc. Eliseo Subiela; E. Marcela Sáenz; C. Hugo Colace; S. Boris Herrera Allende and Álvaro Felipe Silva Wuth; cast Darío Grandinetti, Mariana Arias, Oscar Martínez.

Nordeste [Northeast]. 2005. D. Juan Solanas; Sc. Juan Solanas and Juan Pablo Domenech; E. Virginie Deroubaix; C. Félix Monti and Juan Solanas; S. Juan Ferro; cast Carole Bouquet, Aymará Rovera, Mercedes Sampietro.

No sos vos, soy yo [It's Not You, It's Me]. D. Juan Taratuto; Sc. Cecilia Dopazo and Juan Taratuto; E. César Custodio; C. Marcelo Iaccarino; S. Guido Beremblum and Víctor Tendler; cast Diego Peretti, Soledad Villamil, Cecilia Dopazo.

Nueve reinas [Nine Queens]. 2000. D. and Sc. Fabián Bielinsky; E. Sergio Zottola; C. Marcelo Camorino; So. Osvaldo Vacca; cast Ricardo Darín, Gastón Pauls, Leticia Brédice.

Obreras sin patrón [Workers Without Bosses]. 2003. D., Sc., E., C. and S. Kino – Nuestra Lucho, Grupo Boedo Films.

Ocho años después. 2005. D. and Sc. Raúl Perrone; E. Luis Barros; C. Clodo Luque; S. Pablo Demarco and Gaspar Scheuer; cast Violeta Naón, Gustavo Prone.

Operación Algeciras. 2003. D. Jesús Mora; Sc. Antonio Llorens, Iván Aleda and Jesús Mora; E. Iván Aledo; C. Federico Ribes; S. José María Bloch.

Opus. 2005. D., Sc., E. and S. Mariano Donoso; C. Agustín Mendilaharzu and Ignacio Masllorens.

Otra vuelta. 2004. D. and Sc. Santiago Palavecino; E. Alejo Moguiillansky; C. Fernando Lockett; S. Hernán Hevia; cast José Ignacio Marsiletti, Valentina Bassi, Roberto Carnaghi.

Paco Urondo, la palabra justa. 2004. D. and Sc. Daniel Desaloms; E. Miguel Pérez; C. Victoria Panero; S. Esteban Golubicki and Fernando Vega.

Panzas. 1999. D. and Sc. Laura Bondarevsky; E. Ramiro Abrevaya; C. Lucas Brunetto.
Papá Iván. 2000. D. and Sc. María Inés Roqué; E. Fernando Pardo; C. Hugo Rodríguezx and Carlos Arango; S. Lena Esquenazi.
Perón, sinfonía del sentimiento. 1999. D. and Sc. Leonardo Favio; E. Paola Amor and Alberto Ponce; S. Marcelo Garderes.
Pizza, birra, faso [Pizza, Beer and Cigarettes]. 1997. D. and Sc. Bruno Stagnaro and Israel Adrián Caetano; E. Andrés Tambornino; C. Marcelo Lavintman; S. Martín Grignaschi; cast Héctor Anglada, Jorge Sesán, Pamela Jordán.
Plata quemada [Burning Money]. 2000. D. Marcelo Piñeyro; Sc. Marcelo Piñeyro and Marcelo Figueras; E. Juan Carlos Macias; C. Alfredo F. Mayo; S. Carlos Abbate and José Luis Díaz; cast Leonardo Sbaraglia, Pablo Echarri, Leticia Brédice.
Por sus propios ojos [Proper Eyes]. 2008. D. and Sc. Liliana Paolinelli; E. Lorena Moriconi; C. Martín Mohadeb; S. Santiago Douton; cast Ana Carabajal, Luisa Núñez, Maximiliano Gallo.
Por la vuelta. 2002. D. and Sc. Cristian Pauls; E. Alejandra Almirón and Carmen Guarini; C. Carlos Essmann and Carmen Guarini; S. Sergio Iglesias.
Por un nuevo cine un nuevo país. 2001. D., Sc. and E. Myriam Angueira and Fernando Krichmar.
Prisioneros de la tierra [Prisoners of the Land]. 1939. D. Mario Soffici; Sc. Ulises Petit de Murat and Darío Quiroga; E. José de Nico and Gerardo Rinaldi; C. Pablo Tabernero; cast Francisco Petrone, Ángel Magaña, Roberto Fugazot.
Puente Alsina. 1935. D. José Agustín Ferreyra; Sc. Marcos Bronenberg; E. Daniel Spósito; C. Gumer Barreiros; S. Alfredo Murúa; cast José Gola, Delia Durruty, Miguel Gómez Bao.
Pulqui, un instante en la patria de la felicidad. 2007. D., Sc., E. and C. Alejandro Fernández Mouján; S. Jésica Suárez.
Rapado. 1991. D. and Sc. Martín Rejtman; E. Gerry Lane; C. José Luis García; S. Gabriel Coll Barberis; cast Ezequiel Cavia, Damián Dreizik, Mirta Busnelli.
Raymundo. 2002. D., Sc., E. and S. Ernesto Ardito and Vilma Molina; C. Ernesto Ardito, Sebastián Díaz and Vilma Molina.
Riachuelo [Brook]. 1934. D. Luis Moglia Barth; Sc. José Bustamante y Ballivián and Luis Moglia Barth; C. Francis Boeniger; cast Luis Sandrini, Maruja Pibernat, Margarita Sola.
Río arriba. 2004. D. Ulises de la Orden; Sc. Paz Encine, Germán Cantore, Miguel Pérez and Ulises de la Orden; E. Germán Cantore; C. Lucio Bonelli; S. Rufino Basavilbaso.
Rompecabezas [Puzzle]. 2009. D. and Sc. Natalia Smirnoff; E. Natacha Valerga; C. Bárbara Álvarez; S. Fernando Soldevila; cast María Onetto, Gabriel Goity, Arturo Goetz.
Ronda nocturna [Night Watch]. 2005. D. and Sc. Edgardo Cozarinsky; E. Martine Bouquin; C. Javier Miquelez; S. Alejandro Alonso; cast Gonzalo Heredia, Mono Anghileri, Rafael Ferro.
Silvia Prieto. 1999. D. and Sc. Martín Rejtman; E. Gustavo Codella; C. Paula Grandío; S. Néstor Frenkel; cast Rosario Bléfari, Valeria Bertuccelli, Gabriel Fernández Capello.
Sol de noch, La historia de Olga y Luis. 2003. D. Pablo Milstein and Norberto Ludin; Sc. Javier Rubel, Ariel Ludin, Norberto Ludin and Pablo Milstein; E. and S. Droopy; C. Ariel Ludin.

Sólo por hoy [Just For Today]. 2000. D. Ariel Rotter; Sc. Lautaro Núñez de Arco and Ariel Rotter; E. Pablo Giorgelli; C. Guillermo Nieto; S. Martín Grignaschi; cast Sergio Boris, Ailí Chen, Damián Dreizik.

Süden. 2008. D. and Sc. Gastón Solnicki; E. Andrea Kleinmann; C. Diego Poleri and Gatón Solnicki; S. Jason Candler.

Sur [The South]. 1987. D. and Sc. Fernando E. Solanas; E. Juan Carlos Macias and Pablo Mari; C. Félix Monti; S. Aníbal Libenson; cast Miguel Ángel Solá, Susú Pecoraro, Philippe Léotard.

Tan de repente [Suddenly]. 2002. D. Diego Lerman; Sc. Diego Lerman and María Meira; E. Benjamín Ávila and Alberto Ponce; C. Orilo Blandini; S. Leandro de Loredo; cast Carla Crespo, Verónica Hassan, Tatiana Saphir.

Todos mienten [They All Lie]. 2009. D. and Sc. Matías Piñeiro; E. Delfina Castagnino; C. Fernando Lockett; S. Emilio Iglesias; cast Romina Paula, María Villar, Julia Martínez Rubio.

Tosco, grito de piedra. 1998. D. Adrián Jaima and Daniel Ribetti; Sc. Adrián Jaime; E. Claudio Rosa; C. Daniela Acacia.

Trelew. 2003. D. and Sc. Mariana Arruti; E. Mariana Arruti and Miguel Schverdfinger; C. Pablo Pupato and Leonardo Aguinaga; S. Marcelo Baraj.

Últimas imágenes del naufragio [Last Images of the Shipwreck]. 1989. D. and Sc. Eliseo Subiela; E. Marcela Sáenz; C. Alberto Basail; S. Carlos Abbate; cast Lorenzo Quinteros, Noemí Frenkel, Hugo Soto.

Un año sin amor [A Year Without Love]. 2004. D. Anahí Berneri; Sc. Anahí Berneri and Pablo Pérez; E. Alex Zito; C. Lucio Bonelli; S. Javier Farina; cast Juan Minujín, Mimí Ardu, Carlos Echevarría.

Un lugar en el mundo [A Place in the World]. 1991. D. and Sc. Adolfo Aristarain; E. Eduardo López; C. Ricardo de Angelis (h.); S. José Luis Díaz; cast José Sacristán, Federico Luppi, Cecilia Roth.

Un oso rojo [Red Bear]. 2002. D. and Sc. Israel Adrián Caetano; E. Santiago Ricci; C. Willy Behnisch; S. Marcos de Aguirre and Jésica Suárez; cast Julio Chávez, Soledad Villamil, Luis Machín.

Vagón fumador [Smokers Only]. 2000. D., Sc. and E. Verónica Chen; C. Nicolás Theodossiou; S. Juan Pablo Di Bitonto; cast Cecilia Bengolea, Leonardo Brzezicki, Adrián Fondari.

Viento Norte [North Wind]. 1937. D. Mario Soffici; Sc. Mario Soffici and Alberto Vacarezza; E. Nicolás Proserpio; C. Antonio Merayo; cast Camila Quiroga, Enrique Muiño, Elías Alippi.

XXY. 2007. D. and Sc. Lucía Puenzo; E. Alex Zito and Hugo Primero; C. Natasha Braier; S. Fernando Soldevila; cast Inés Efrón, Ricardo Darín, Valeria Bertuccelli.

Yo no sé qué me han hecho tus ojos [I Don't Know What Your Eyes Have Done to Me]. 2003. D. and Sc. Sergio Wolf and Lorena Muñoz; E. Alejandra Almirón; C. Segundo Cerato, Federico Ransenberg and Marcelo Lavintman; S. Alejandro Alonso, Cote Álvarez, Gaspar Scheuer and Diego Bernaud.

Zapada, una comedia beat. 2002. D. Raúl Perrone; Sc. Raúl Perrone and Sergio Wolf; E. Roli Rauwolf; C. Julián Apezteguia; S. Gaspar Scheuer; cast Diego Capusotto, Martín Campilongo, Santiago Ríos.

Index

180 grados 16
5 pal' peso 11, 14–16
76-89-03 46

action cinema 77, 87, 134, 145
actoral performances, in new Argentine cinema 130–42
actor-medium 130, 133–4, 137, 139–41, 140, 156
actorship, mode of 130, 133, 139
Adoc (organisation) 96
Adoquín Video 96
Agresti, Alejandro 6
Agua 129
Aguilar, Gonzalo 66, 86, 101, 109, 111, 115, 133, 148, 150, 161, 166
    filmic language 15–16
    film production 9
    politics of actors 131
    views on Argentine cinema xi
        misery and rebellion 62
        nomadism and sedentarism 39
        realism and experimentation 11
        'sedentary' mode 75
Alavío 96
Alfaro, Emilio 4
Alfonsín, Raúl 3
alienation effect 36
    see also defamiliarisation
Almirón, Alejandra xiv, 106–7, 126
Alonso, Lisandro xiv, xvi, 7, 63, 85–92, 94, 129, 131–2
Altman, Robert 142
Amado, Ana 34, 79–80, 107, 125

Ana y los otros 76, 141
Ángeles 11
Angueira, Myriam 96
Antín, Manuel 3, 7
Aprea, Gustavo 4, 9, 38, 106, 133
Argentina Arde 96
Argentina, Indymedia 29
Argentina latente 100
Argentina Sono Film (film production company) 4
Aries (film production company) 4
Aristarain, Adolfo 6, 63
Arruti, Mariana 109
Astrada, Carlos 61
audio-visual
    education institutions 96
    language 171
    professionalisation 7
Auyero, Javier xv

Bad Lieutenant 13
bailanta 31, 35, 58
Bakhtin, Mikhail 123
Banderas de humo 7
Barbieri, Vicente 174
Bar 'El Chino' 39, 43–5, 94
Battle of Algiers 112
Bauer, Tristán 93
BD Cine 9
Bechis, Marco 9, 106
Bellande, Enrique xvii, 7, 9, 129, 156, 165–72
Bemberg, María Luisa 3
Benjamin, Walter 30, 50, 75, 171

Bentes, Ivana xx
Bermúdez, Nicolás 16
Bernard, Cristian 45
Berneri, Anahí 9, 46, 49–51
Bernini, Emilio 18–19, 73, 78, 80, 94, 99–100, 111, 126, 148
Beware of a Holy Whore 142
Bielinsky, Fabián xi, xvii, 40, 132, 143, 150–3
Biodramas 132
Birri, Fernando 62
Blaustein, David 107, 109–13, 122
Boedo Films 96
Bolivia 52–3, 57–8, 60, 104, 131, 145
Bonanza 100–5
Bondarevski, Laura 106
Bonelli, Lucio xiv, 71
Bony, Oscar 104
Borges, Graciela 131, 139–40
Boulevards du crépuscule 126
Brukman confecciones 96
Bruno, Giuliana 30–1
Bruzzi, Stella 94, 102–3, 108
Buch, Esteban 108–9
Buenos Aires 77, 107
Buenos Aires Independent Film Festival (BAFICI) xi, 8, 174
Burak, Daniel 39, 43–5, 58, 94
Burd, Marcelo 52
Burman, Daniel 8–9, 42–3, 45, 58, 132, 141

Caballos salvajes 153
Cabezas, José Luis 150
cable TV 46
Caché 72
Caetano, Adrián xvii, 8, 31, 34, 36, 52, 57–9, 103–5, 107, 129–33, 143–7, 153, 173–4
Cairo, Humberto 62
Caja negra 36–7, 131
Cama adentro xv, 39
Cambaceres, Eugenio 83
camera-in-transit device 30
Camila 3, 76

Campanella, Juan José 40–5, 58, 132–3, 173–4
Canadá 11
Cándido López, los campos de batalla 97
Cannes Film Festival xii
Capra, Frank 40
Carancho 133, 173
Carri, Albertina xvi, 7, 9, 82, 84, 107, 114–20, 122, 131
cartoons 14–15, 19, 83
Casares, Adolfo Bioy 174
casting, politics of 132
Castro 129, 174
Cazadores de utopías 107, 109–10
Cedrón, Lucía 107
Cenizas del paraíso 5
Centre for Research and Experimentation in Film and Video (CIEVYC) 8, 17
Chanan, Michael 93–4, 97, 123
Chávez, Julio xvii, 134–40, 145
Chen, Verónica 46–7, 49, 129
Chironi, Graciana 64, 66
Chomski, Alejandro 46
Cine de la Base 95
Cine Grupo de la Base 7
cine-guerrilla 95
Cine Insurgente 95
Cineismo 8
Cine Liberación 7, 95
cinema career 129
Cinemark 5
Cinematographic Classification Authority 3
cinematography 14, 48, 68, 71, 84
cinéma-vérité protocols 51, 94
Cine Ojo 7
Citynema 8
Ciudad de María xvii, 9, 156, 165–7, 171–2
Clarín 152
Clark, Larry 13
cognitive mapping, of cinema xviii–xix, 114
Coll-Saragusti 6

community, reconstruction of 38–45
Comodines 5
Constantini, Gustavo 82
Contraimagen 96
Copacabana 52–3, 55–7, 60
Copertari, Gabriela 150, 153–4
Coppola, Ford 146
Coppola, Horacio 35
Corazón de fábrica 96
Cordero de Dios 107–8
Couceyro, Analía 115, 118–19
Cozarinsky, Edgardo xii, 46, 47, 126
creative documentary 54, 94
crisis of speculative economy 45–51
Crónica de una fuga 107, 108
Crónica TV 34
cultural imperialism 144
cumbia 31, 101

dark ruralities xvi, 77
Darse cuenta 4, 141
Davis, Mike 33
defamiliarisation, effect of 59–60
de la Orden, Ulises 71, 97–8
de la Rua, Fernando 27–8, 44
del Carril, Hugo 62, 66
Deleuze, Gilles 58, 77, 82, 85–6, 133, 140
  characterisation of actor-medium 134
Días de mayo xv, 141
Dibu, la película 2
dictatorship
  amateur film-makers, impact on 11
  cinematographic experiences 95
  contemporary cinema's attitudes towards 107
  ESMA (Naval Mechanics School at Buenos Aires) 108–9, 111, 113
  and miracles of postdictatorship 165–72
  neo-liberal remaking of Argentine society 169
digitalisation, techniques of 126
Direct Cinema 94, 96, 101–2
Dissanayake, Wimal xix

Di Tella, Andrés 111–13, 121–4, 126, 131
DIY ethic of film-making 13
DocBsAs 93
docu-essays
  autobiographical 107
  autofictional 107
documentary
  cinema 28
  creative 54, 94
  documentarists and poverty issues 98–106
  ethnographic 102
  film-making, modes of 52
  and intermedial counterpoints 121–7
  Latin American 93
  as mode of social chronicle 95
  performative 94, 102
  proliferation of 106
  resurgence and refashioning of 95
  share in national production 93
  testimonial 107
Donoso, Mariano 71, 72–4, 94, 123
Don Segundo Sombra 123
Doria, Alejandro 4, 6
Down by Law 17
Dubcovsky, Daniel 9
Duhalde, Eduardo 150
Dutch Hubert Bals Fund 8, 17
Dutil, Carlos 150

Echeverría, Carlos 108, 114–15
'economic convertibility' legislation, for film production 1
El abrazo partido 38, 42–3, 141
El amante de cine 8, 144, 152
El amor es una mujer gorda 6
El asadito 131, 141–2
El bonaerense xvii, 10, 132, 141, 143, 148, 149–50
  shootout scene in 151
El camino de San Diego 63
El caso María Soledad 180
El cielito 71, 103
El cumple 141–2

El custodio 134, 136–8
El estallido 28
El exilio de Gardel 3
El hijo de la novia 39–41, 57, 132
El Kadri, Envar 110
El lado oscuro del corazón 6
El nexo 103
El Ojo Mocho 120, 150
El País group 2
El perro 63
El ratón Pérez 143
El resultado del amor 103
El secreto de sus ojos 132–3, 173, 174
El tiempo y la sangre 107
El tren blanco 95
El último malón 62
El verso 34
El viaje 63
En ausencia 185
Encontrando a Víctor 185
entertainment cinema xiii, 4–5
Errepé 109, 119
Esas cuatro notas 121
ESMA (Naval Mechanics School at Buenos Aires) 108–9, 111, 113
Espejo para cuando me pruebe el smoking 29, 124
Estrada, Ezequiel Martínez 61
Estrellas 100, 103–4, 130–1
  construction of a shantytown film set in 105
  self-mocking interview performance 105
Evita 7, 110, 125
An Excursion to the Ranquel Indians 62
Extinction: Last Pictures of Labour in Argentina 68
Extraño 134, 137–40

Fábricas sin patrón 96
Fahrenheit 9/11 100
Falcón, Ada 126–7
Familia obrera 104
Familia rodante 64–5
  editing of 69

interpersonal conflicts and passions 65
sequence connecting landscape and memory 66
family pictures 107, 114
Fantasma 85, 91
  relation to photographic index and to spectatorship 92
  shot-reverse-shot sequence 92
Fasinpat 96
Favio, Leonardo xiii, 54–5, 63, 100
FBI Story 148
Fernández Mouján, Alejandro 7, 29, 54–5, 96, 121–2, 124–6
Ferrara, Abel 13
Ferreyra, José Agustín 'El Negro' 35, 62
fiction films 7, 93–4, 106, 108, 129, 131
Filipelli, Rafael 4, 121
Film 8
film collectives, 'counter-informational' practices of 95
film genres
  exploration of xvii, 69
  global forms and national figurations 142–54
  in the corralito 142–54
filmic languages 16, 20, 69
filmic naturalism, landscape of 82
film journals 10
film literacy 8, 142
  of audiences 148
film production
  and attitude towards dictatorship 107
  collaborative process 129
  'economic convertibility' legislation (1991) 1
  elective affinities 106–21
  protocols and models of 2
  public and private subsidies for 43
  reconstructing community 38–45
  rural regionalism in 82
  socio-cultural effects and preconditions 18
  taxation scheme 1
film-theatre space 39
First Shantytown Film Festival 103

Flaherty, Robert 87
Flores de septiembre 97
Fonds Sud Cinéma 8
Fotografías 122
Francia 173
Franko, Patrice M. xv
Frites, Eulogio 7
Fukuyama, Francis 160
Fundación Universidad del Cine (FUC) 7

Gachassin, Diego 52–3
Gaggero, Jorge xv, xi, xv, 8, 39
Garage Olimpo 9, 106, 108, 173
García, José Luis 97
García, Santiago 46
gay-lesbian cinema, emergence and viability of 46
Géminis 9
Gerónima 7
Getino, Octavio 2, 7, 40, 95, 98, 111
Gleyzer, Raymundo 7, 95, 97
The Godfather 146
Goldbart, Nicolás xiv, 7, 135
González, Horacio 150
Graciadió 11, 13–16, 18
Greca, Alcides 62
Griersonian principles of objectivity, transparency and civic pedagogy 94
Grokenberger, Otto 17
Grupo Clarín 2
Grupokane 8
Guarini, Carmen 7, 94, 119
Gugliotta, Sandra 71
Güiraldes, Ricardo 123
Gundermann, Christian 33, 59, 86, 113, 138–9

Habitación disponible 52–5, 60
Haciendo cine 8
hand-held cameras 30–1, 37, 72, 80, 114
Haneke, Michael 72
Hasta la memoria siempre 185
Hay unos tipos abajo 4, 140–1
Hendler, Daniel 42, 141

Hermanas 106, 108
H.I.J.O.S., el alma en dos 119
HIJOS organisation 106
Hirsch, Marianne 107
Historias breves xi, 8, 144
(h)istorias cotidianas 107, 114
Historias extraordinarias 173
Historias mínimas 63
Hollywood cinema 6, 148
Hombres de barro 7
Hoteles 10
Hotel Gondolín 97
Hôtel Terminus 108
The Hour of the Furnaces 98, 107
Hoyts General 5
Hoy y mañana 46

'industrial' cinema 2, 129
In the Heat of the Night 148

Jameson, Fredric 4, 16, 18, 75, 102, 140, 145, 148, 173
  concept of 'cognitive mapping' xviii
Jarmusch, Jim 13, 17, 67
Jauretche, Ernesto 110–11
Jewinson, Norman 148
Jimidín 11
joint ventures, international 6
Jones, Owain 77
Juan, como si nada hubiera sucedido 108–9
Juan Moreira 63
Jurassic Park 5

Kamin, Bebe 6
Kids 13
Kilómetro 111 8
Klevan, Andrew 134, 137
Kracauer, Siegfried 28, 30
Krichmar, Fernando 96
Kuhn, Rodolfo 22
Kuschevatzky, Axel 133
Kusch, Rodolfo 61

La amiga 4
Labios de churrasco 11–15, 17, 19–20

La ciénaga xvi, 77, 78, 131, 156
   characters' behaviour in 160
   cohesion of image and sound 81
   editing of 80
   locales of action 80
   opening shots of 79
   relation between bodies and
      surrounding space 79
   representation of social history 79
La cruz del sur 143
La deuda interna 4
La dignidad de los nadies 100
La fe del volcán 36–7
La fuga 82, 133
La furia 5
La gaucha, un poema de los campos 62
La historia oficial 3, 138, 140
La hora de los hornos 98–9, 111
La León 82, 141
   figure of the drift 90
   landscape shot 84
La libertad 85–91, 131
La Mecha 11
La mujer sin cabeza xii, 141, 156, 158–9
   use of shallow focus lengths in 160
La niña santa 156–60, 163–4
La noche eterna 7
Lanzmann, Claude 108, 115
La Patagonia rebelde 63
La peli 141
La película del rey 63
La película del taller 11
La próxima estación 100
La rabia xvi, 82–4
Las aguas bajan turbias 62, 66
Las Palmas, Chaco 96
Las vidas posibles 71–2, 141
L'Atalante 84
La televisión y yo 121–3
Latin American Cinema xix
La vida según Muriel 63
Lefebvre, Martin 49, 61, 69
Lejtman, Roman 28
Lemos, Carlos 4
León, Federico 100, 103–5, 130, 141

Lerer, Diego 107, 152
LeRoy, Mervyn 148
Lesbianas de Buenos Aires 46, 97
Liverpool 85, 90
Longhini, Ricardo 29, 54, 124
Los dueños del silencio 4
Los fusiladitos 97
Los guantes mágicos 9, 17, 24, 30, 134
Los hijos de Fierro 63
Los inundados 62
Los muertos 85, 88–91, 131
   screening of 91
Los paranoicos 141
Los rubios 107, 114–20, 129, 173
Loza, Santiago 134, 137–9
Lugares comunes 63
Luna de Avellaneda 38, 40, 41, 43, 132
Luppi, Federico 133
Lynch, Kevin xviii

Madres de la Plaza de Mayo 93, 106
Mansilla, Lucio V. 62
Mar del Plata film festival (1996) 8
Martel, Lucrecia xvi, xii, 8, 77–82, 132,
   139, 141, 156, 158–62, 164–5, 172
Martínez, Marcos 100, 103, 105, 130
Martín Fierro 62–3
Massey, Doreen 51
Matanza Cine 9
Maten a Perón 97
Mbya, tierra en rojo 96
Meerapfel, Jeanine 4
Memento 72
Memoria del saqueo 98–100
Menem, Carlos 1–2, 5, 16, 33, 62, 68,
   99–100, 113, 154
   free-market reforms 6
   privatisation of state television 2
Menis, María Victoria 71, 103
meta-cinematic film 126
Meza, Pablo José 77
Milewicz, Eduardo 63
Miljiker, Cecilia 97
minority issues 46
Mirra, Miguel 7

Moguillansky, Alejo xiv, 7, 83, 129, 174
Monobloc xv, 10, 131
Montoneros, una historia 111, 113
Moore, Michael 100
Mora, Jesús 97
Morán, Mercedes 78, 131, 139, 156
Moreno, Rodrigo 134–6, 138
Mulvey, Laura 126
Mundo grúa 8, 9, 64, 66–9, 130, 131
    landscape in 68
Munich Academy for Film and Television 108
Muñoz, Lorena 121–2, 126–7
Murga, Celina 76–7, 141
Murphy 174
Musante, Fernando 97

Nachträglichkeit 122
Nacido y criado 64, 66, 68
    landscape in 70
    scenic backdrop 69
Nadar solo 35
Nanook of the North 87
Nardini, Flavio 45–6
national cinemas xvii, xix, 1–2, 143, 150
national entertainment industry 126
national film industry xiv, 6, 46
National Film Institute 1, 3, 7, 120
National Institute for Film and the Audiovisual Arts (INCAA) 2, 8
'national-popular' films 144
national studio cinema, Golden Age of 127
national studio system 5, 130
neo-ruralist films 77
niche productions 46
Nichols, Bill 52, 86, 95, 97, 115
Nisco, Jorge 5
Nobleza gaucha 62
non-professional actors, casting of 36
Nordeste 71
No sos vos, soy yo 143
No te mueras sin decirme adiós 144
Nueve reinas xi, xvii, 40, 132, 143, 150–4

Obreras sin patrón 96
Ocho años después 16
Ojo Obrero 29
Ojos de fuego xi
Olivera, Héctor xiii, 63
Operación Algeciras 97
Ophüls, Marcel 108, 115
Opus 71, 72, 73, 94, 123
    director's encounter with the crisis of his home province 98
    social space 75
    visual evidence of city of San Juan 74
oral storytelling 82
Ortega, Luis xv, 10, 36, 51, 131
Ortiz, Juan L. 174
Otheguy, Santiago 82–4, 90, 141
Otra vuelta 76
Otrocampo 8
Oubiña, David 79, 145, 147, 160, 164
Ozon, François 71

Paco Urondo, la palabra justa 97
Page, Joanna xi, xix, 16, 21, 33, 37, 59, 131, 147, 150, 153
Palavecino, Santiago 76–7
Panzas 106
Paolinelli, Liliana 94
Papá Iván 107, 114–15, 117
Paparella, Aldo 8, 10
Pauls, Cristian 121
Pereira, Miguel 4
Pérez, Pablo 50–1
performative documentary 94, 102, 111
Peronist Youth 110, 113
Perón, sinfonía del sentimiento 100
Perrone, Raúl xvi, 3, 10–20, 131, 133
Piñeyro, Marcelo 5, 133, 153
Piquete Puente Pueyrredón 29
Piqueteros carajo! La masacre de Puente Pueyrredón 29
Pitt, Brad 7
Pizza, birra, faso xiii, 8, 31, 104, 131, 133, 145
    archaeology of the present 36
    choice and treatment of locations 35

Pizza, birra, faso (continued)
   innovations on earlier films 34
   introduction of 'real' actor 36
   opening shots 32
   spatio-temporal sound/vision barrier 33
Plata quemada 153
Poliak, Ana 36–8, 37, 51, 94
Poliladrón 5
political cinema 3, 17, 66, 107
political documentary xiii
Pol-Ka 2, 5, 43
Poncet, Eva 52–3
Pontecorvo, Gillo 112
Por la vuelta 121
pornography, in cinema 49
Por sus propios ojos 94
porteño society 34
Por un nuevo cine un nuevo país 96
postdictatorship cinema 107–9
postgeneric cinema 75
Postiglione, Gustavo xv, xvii, 131–2, 141–2
Prisioneros de la tierra 62
Prividera, Nicolás 114–17, 119–20, 122
product placement advertising 5
Puente Alsina 35
Puenzo, Luis 3, 63, 132, 138
Pulqui – un instante en la patria de la felicidad 121, 124–6
pulsation-image 85–92
Punto de Vista 116
The Puzzle of Latin American Economic Development xv

quality cinema 4–5, 133
The Quickening 7
Quiroga, Horacio 62

Ragendorfer, Ricardo 150
Rapado xiii, 17, 19–21
Raymundo 97
Reboa, Cristian 170
Reguerraz, Jean-Pierre 104–5

Rejtman, Martín xiii–xiv, xvi, 3, 11, 17–25, 32, 131, 133, 143
Copacabana 52, 55–7
Los guantes mágicos 9, 17, 30, 134
Rapado xiii, 19–21
Sílvia Prieto 9, 17, 19, 22, 131, 134, 141
Renov, Michael 95, 97, 100
Representing Reality 115
Reyero, Pablo 143
Riachuelo 35
Rich, B. Ruby 4
Río arriba 71
   approach to historical subjects 97
Rizoma Films 9
role-plays 37, 142
Rompecabezas 141
Ronda nocturna 35, 46, 47, 49
Rosell, Ulises 8, 100–2
Rotter, Ariel 30, 32, 38
Rouch, Jean 102
   ideas about the community of laughter 105
Routine Politics and Violence in Argentina: The Gray Zone of State Power xv
Rubin, Jerry 73
Russell, Catherine 49, 74

Sábado 131
SAC (film distribution company) 6
Schwarzböck, Sílvia 72, 145, 147
screen acting, models of 130
screen space 12, 39, 81
Seven Years in Tibet 7
sexual themes 46
Shoah 108
silent movie 62, 65
Sílvia Prieto 9, 17, 19, 22–4, 131, 134, 141
The Simpsons 13–14
Sistema español 17
'socio-realist' film 11
Soffici, Mario 62
Solá, Miguel Angel 133
Solanas, Fernando E. xiii, 3, 7, 63, 95, 98–101, 105, 111, 122

Solanas, Juan 71
Sol de noche, La historia de Olga y Luis 97
Solnicki, Gastón 121
Solomonoff, Julia 8, 106
Sólo por hoy 30, 38
sound film 1, 35, 81
Sous le sable 71
Spanish television 43
spectatorship, modes of 61
Spielberg, Steven 5
Stagnaro, Bruno xiii, 8, 31, 34, 36, 133
Stagnaro, Juan Bautista 5
Stewart, James 133, 148
Stranger than Paradise 17, 67
studio-based star system 126
Subiela, Eliseo 6, 34, 103, 144
subsidies, for film production 43
süden 121
sujet 123
Sundance Institute 8
Sur 3, 63
Syndicate of Film Buffs of Short Breath 11

Tan de repente 35
taxation scheme 1
Telefé (Catholic channel) 170–1
Telefónica de España 2
television channels, privatisation of 2, 4, 43
televisual models, of narratives 174
Tellas, Vivi 132
Tercer Cine 94
testimonial documentaries 107
Todos mienten 174
Tosco, Agustín 97, 144
Tosco, grito de piedra 97
Tosso, Raúl 7
transition phase of Argentine cinema, crisis of 3–10
transnational audio-visual economy 44
Trapero, Pablo xvi–xvii, 7–10, 64–5, 68–70, 76, 129–30, 132–3, 141, 143, 148–51, 173–4

Trelew 109–10
Tres veces Ana 22
Tumberos 103–4, 144
TV talk shows 103

Últimas imágenes del naufragio 34
Un año sin amor 9, 46, 49–50
Unión de Cineistas de Paso Reducido (UNCIPAR) 11
Universidad del Cine 144
Un lugar en el mundo 6
Un oso rojo xvii, 143
    portrayal of acts of justice 147
    post-2001 perception of national politics 147
    shootout sequence in 146
    tutor-code of cinematic modernism 147

Vagón fumador 35, 46, 47, 49
video-activism 28, 96–7, 103
video rentals 1, 93, 141
Viento Norte 62
Vigo, Jean 84
Village (multiplex company) 5
Villegas, Juan 7, 131
violence
    choreography 146
    depiction of 75–85

Walt Disney Productions 2
White Heat 148
Wilder, Billy 126
Williams, Raymond 39, 82
Wiseman, Frederick 101
Wolf, Sergio 8, 121, 126–7

XXY 63

Yo no sé qué me han hecho tus ojos 121, 126–7
    photograph of Ada Falcón in 127

Zapada, una comedia beat 11

www.ingramcontent.com/pod-product-compliance
Ingram Content Group UK Ltd.
Pitfield, Milton Keynes, MK11 3LW, UK
UKHW021907220326
469204UK00008B/237